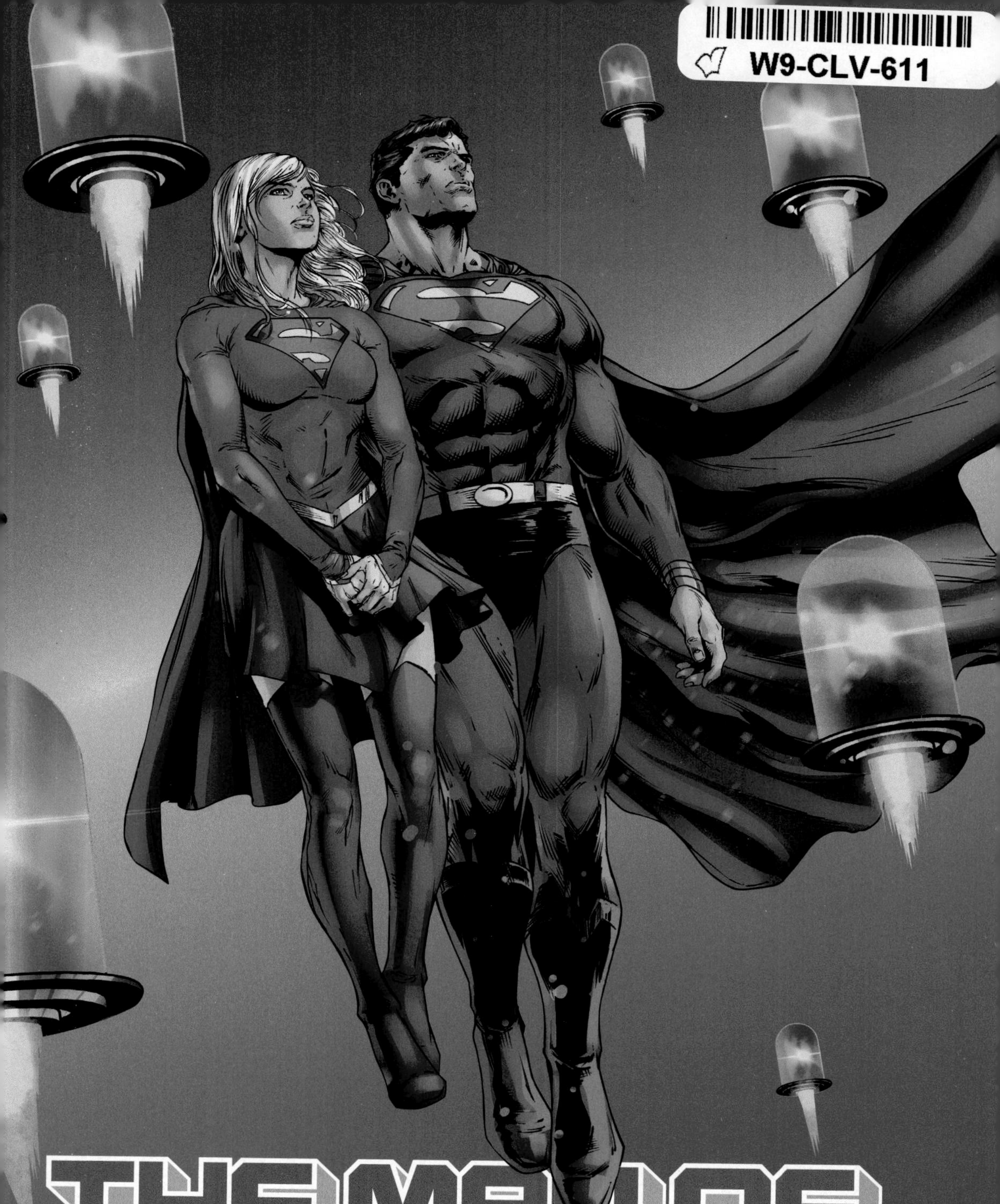

THE MAN OF STEEL

BY BRIAN MICHAEL BENDIS

THE MAN OF STEEL

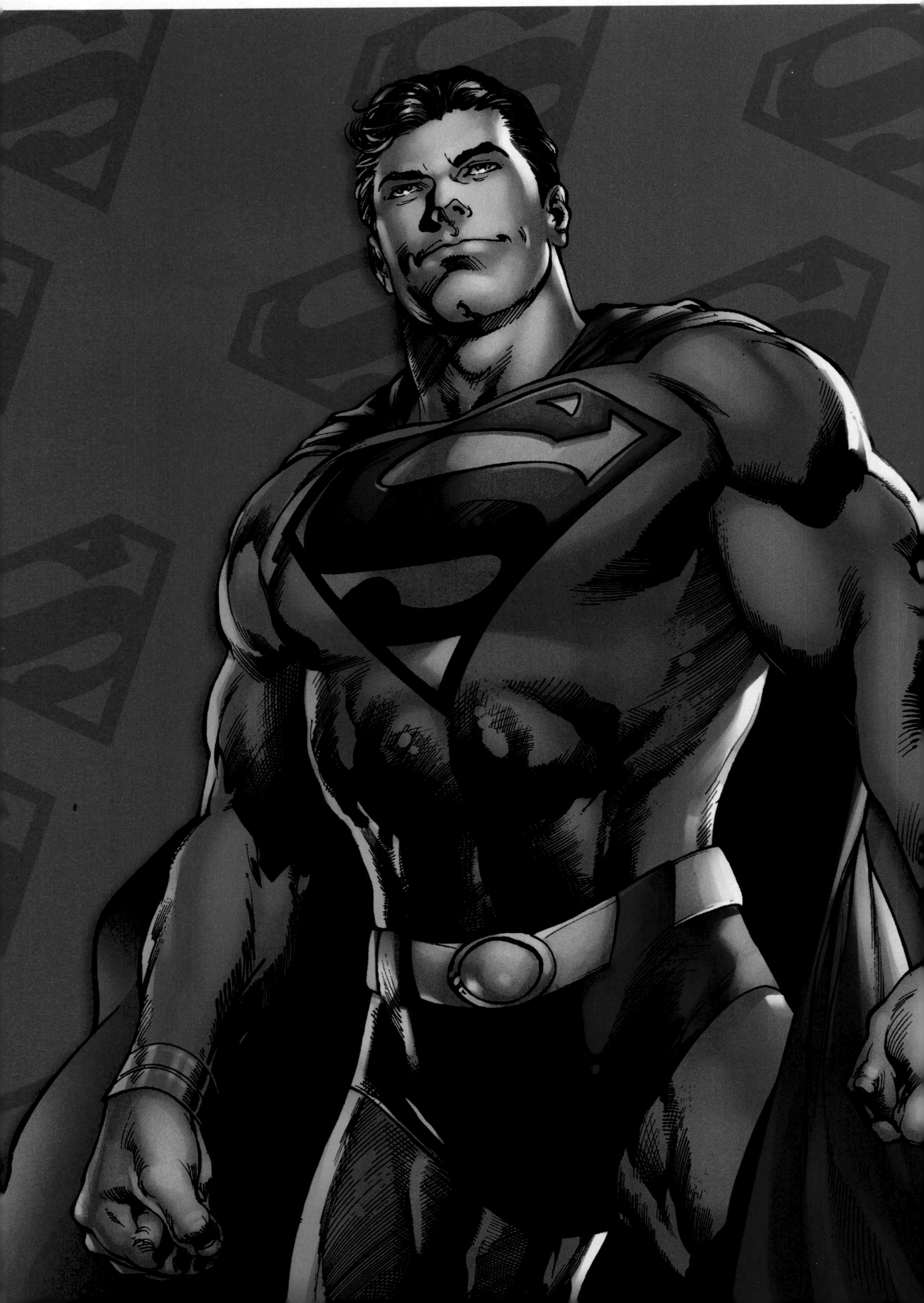

BY BRIAN MICHAEL BENDIS

BRIAN MICHAEL BENDIS
WRITER

JIM LEE
SCOTT WILLIAMS
JOSÉ LUIS GARCÍA-LÓPEZ
DEXTER VINES
IVAN REIS
JOE PRADO
JASON FABOK
EVAN "DOC" SHANER
STEVE RUDE
RYAN SOOK
WADE VON GRAWBADGER
KEVIN MAGUIRE
ADAM HUGHES
ARTISTS

ALEX SINCLAIR
ADAM HUGHES
COLORISTS

JOSH REED
CORY PETIT
LETTERERS

IVAN REIS, JOE PRADO and ALEX SINCLAIR
COLLECTION COVER ART AND ORIGINAL SERIES COVERS

SUPERMAN created by JERRY SIEGEL and JOE SHUSTER
SUPERBOY created by JERRY SIEGEL
SUPERGIRL based on the characters created by JERRY SIEGEL and JOE SHUSTER
by special arrangement with the Jerry Siegel family

MIKE COTTON
Editor – Original Series

JESSICA CHEN
Associate Editor – Original Series

JEB WOODARD
Group Editor – Collected Editions

SCOTT NYBAKKEN
Editor – Collected Edition

STEVE COOK
Design Director – Books

MEGEN BELLERSEN
Publication Design

ADAM RADO
Publication Production

BOB HARRAS
Senior VP – Editor-in-Chief, DC Comics

PAT McCALLUM
Executive Editor, DC Comics

DAN DiDIO
Publisher

JIM LEE
Publisher & Chief Creative Officer

BOBBIE CHASE
VP – New Publishing Initiatives & Talent Development

DON FALLETTI
VP – Manufacturing Operations & Workflow Management

LAWRENCE GANEM
VP – Talent Services

ALISON GILL
Senior VP – Manufacturing & Operations

HANK KANALZ
Senior VP – Publishing Strategy & Support Services

DAN MIRON
VP – Publishing Operations

NICK J. NAPOLITANO
VP – Manufacturing Administration & Design

NANCY SPEARS
VP – Sales

MICHELE R. WELLS
VP & Executive Editor, Young Reader

THE MAN OF STEEL BY BRIAN MICHAEL BENDIS

DC Comics, 2900 West Alameda Ave., Burbank, CA 91505
Printed by LSC Communications, Kendallville, IN, USA. 5/24/19. First Printing.
ISBN: 978-1-4012-9173-0

Library of Congress Cataloging-in-Publication Data is available.

PEFC Certified

Printed on paper from sustainably managed forests and controlled sources

PEFC/29-31-337   www.pefc.org

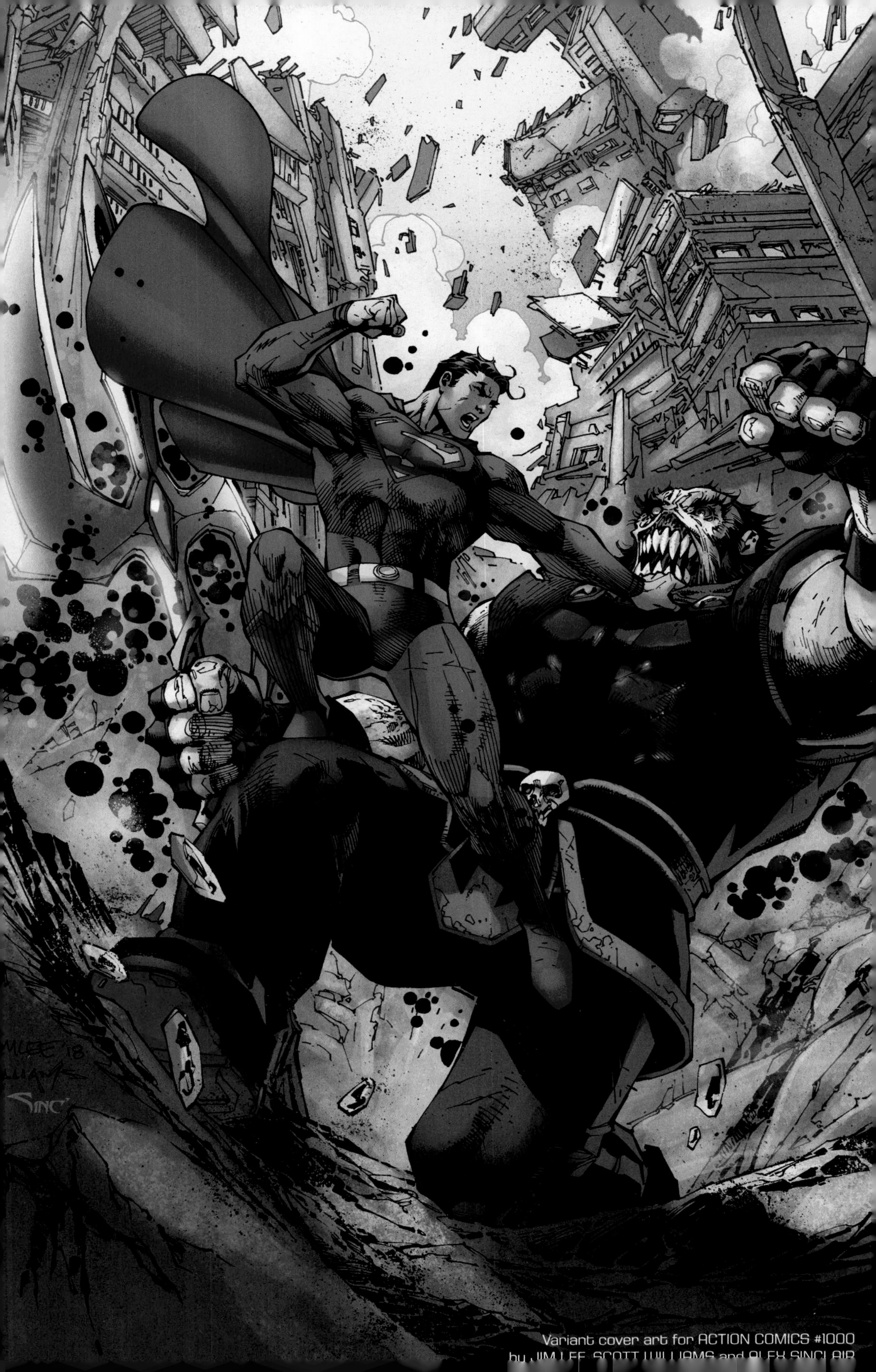

Variant cover art for ACTION COMICS #1000
by JIM LEE, SCOTT WILLIAMS and ALEX SINCLAIR

Variant cover art for ACTION COMICS #10
by Jim Lee, Scott Williams and Alex Sincl

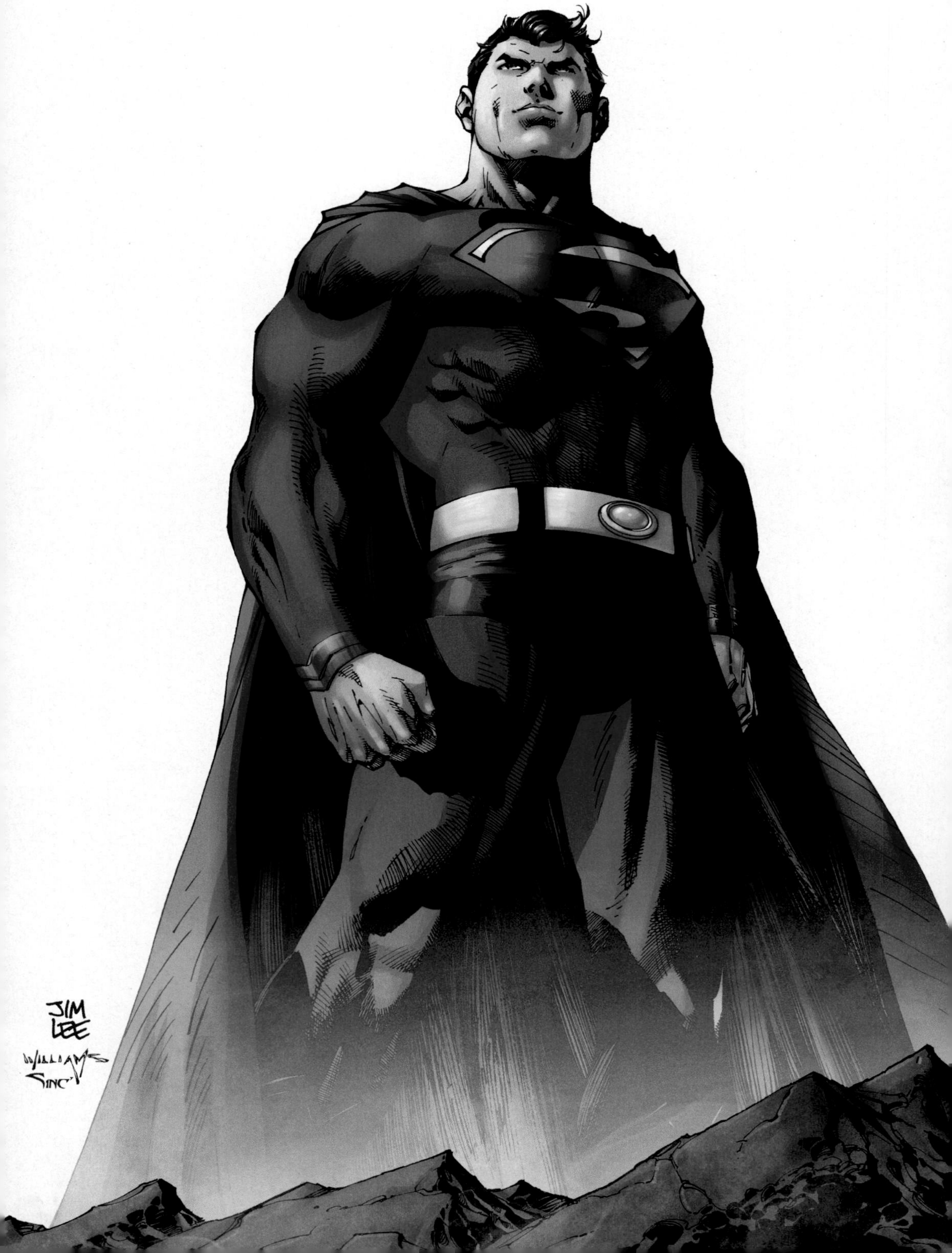
JIM
LEE

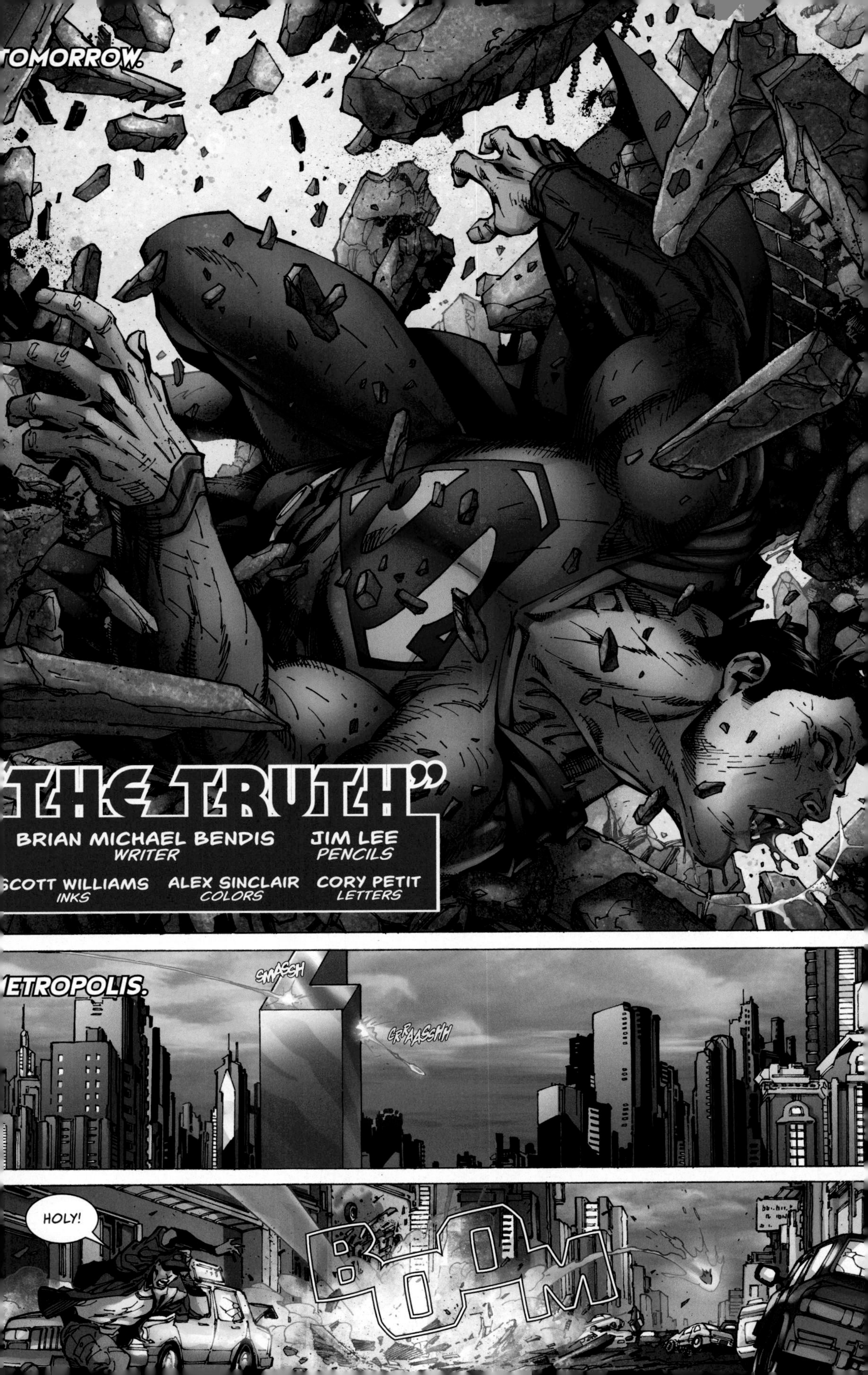
TOMORROW.
THE TRUTH"
BRIAN MICHAEL BENDIS WRITER
JIM LEE PENCILS
SCOTT WILLIAMS INKS
ALEX SINCLAIR COLORS
CORY PETIT LETTERS
ETROPOLIS.
SMASSH
CRRAASSHH
HOLY!
BOOM

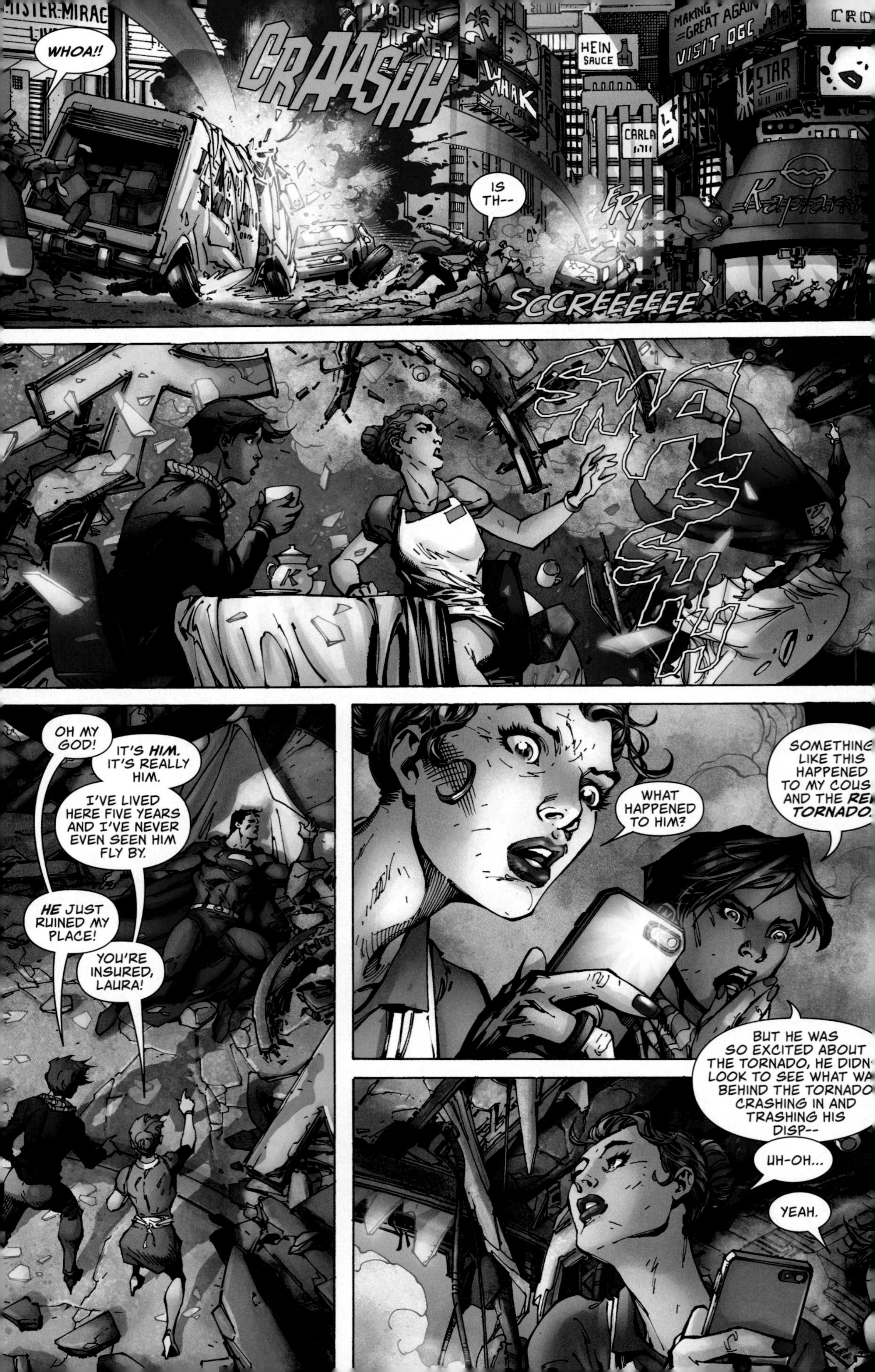
MISTER MIRAC
WHOA!!
CRAASHH
HEIN SAUCE
MAKING GREAT AGAIN VISIT OGC
STAR
CARLA
IS TH--
Kaptan's
SCCREEEEEEE
SMASH
OH MY GOD!
IT'S HIM. IT'S REALLY HIM.
I'VE LIVED HERE FIVE YEARS AND I'VE NEVER EVEN SEEN HIM FLY BY.
HE JUST RUINED MY PLACE!
YOU'RE INSURED, LAURA!
WHAT HAPPENED TO HIM?
SOMETHING LIKE THIS HAPPENED TO MY COUS AND THE RE TORNADO.
BUT HE WAS SO EXCITED ABOUT THE TORNADO, HE DIDN LOOK TO SEE WHAT WA BEHIND THE TORNADO CRASHING IN AND TRASHING HIS DISP--
UH-OH...
YEAH.

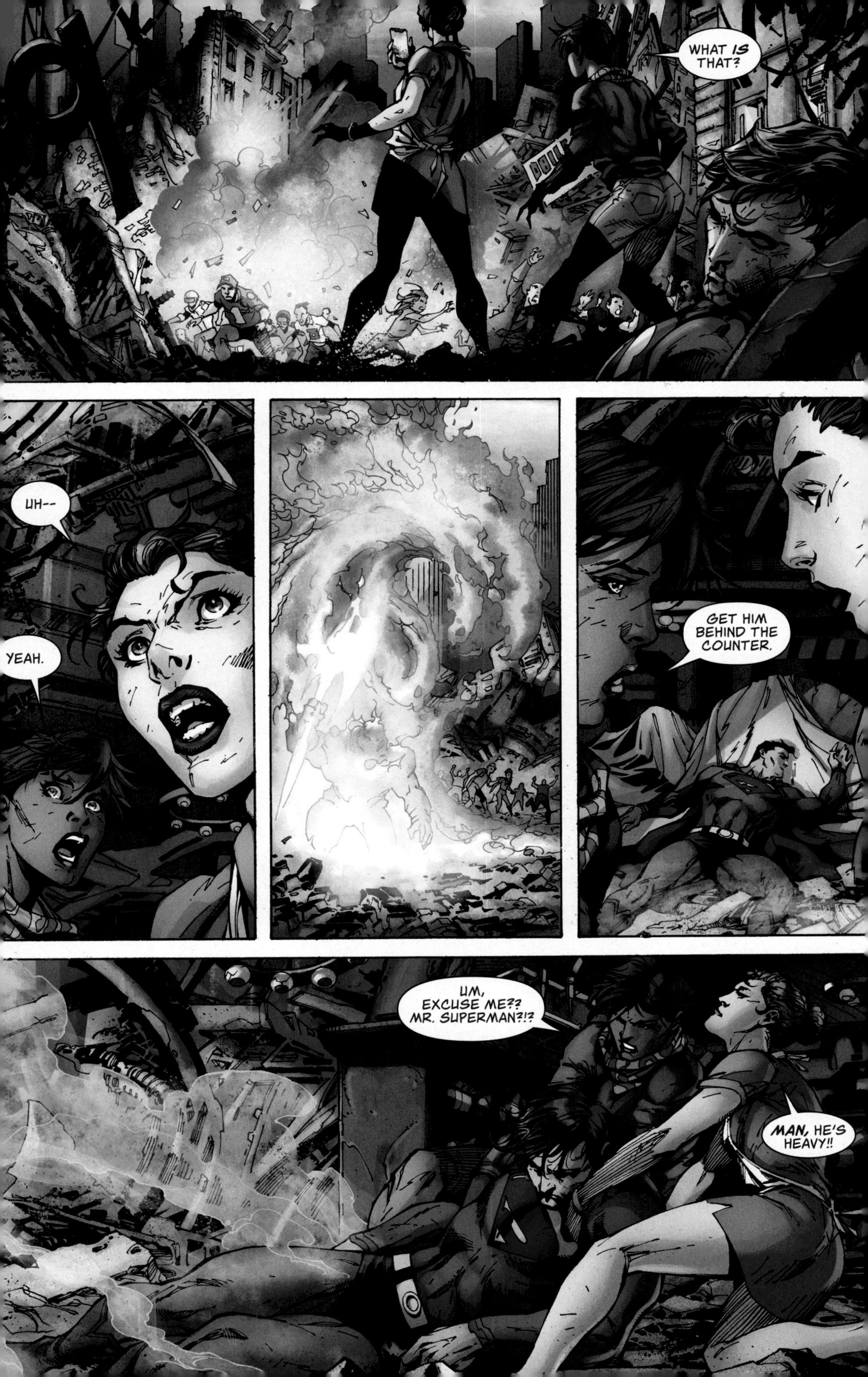
WHAT *IS* THAT?
UH--
YEAH.
GET HIM BEHIND THE COUNTER.
UM, EXCUSE ME?? MR. SUPERMAN?!?
MAN, HE'S HEAVY!!

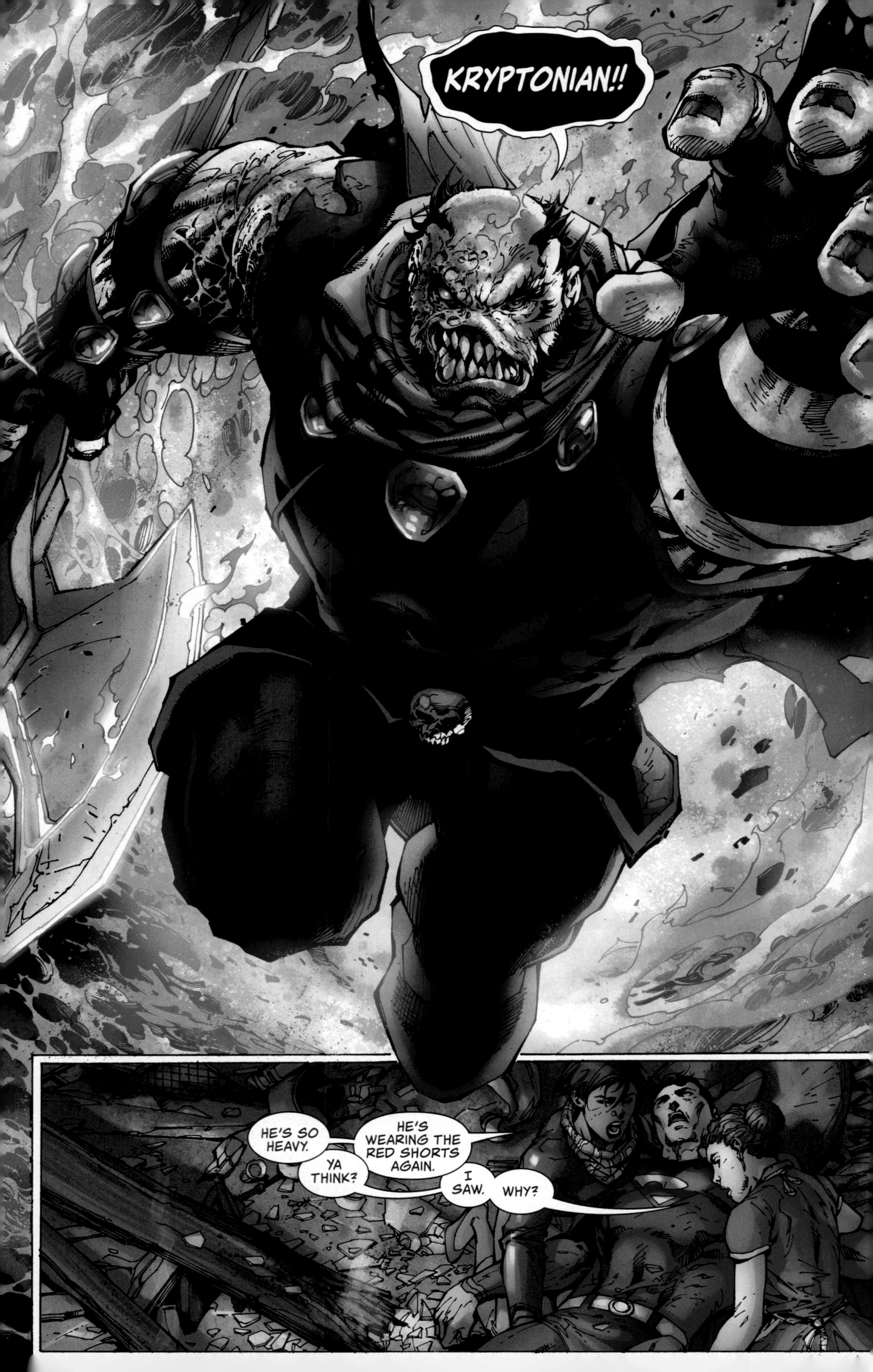
KRYPTONIAN!!
HE'S SO HEAVY.
HE'S WEARING THE RED SHORTS AGAIN.
YA THINK?
I SAW.
WHY?

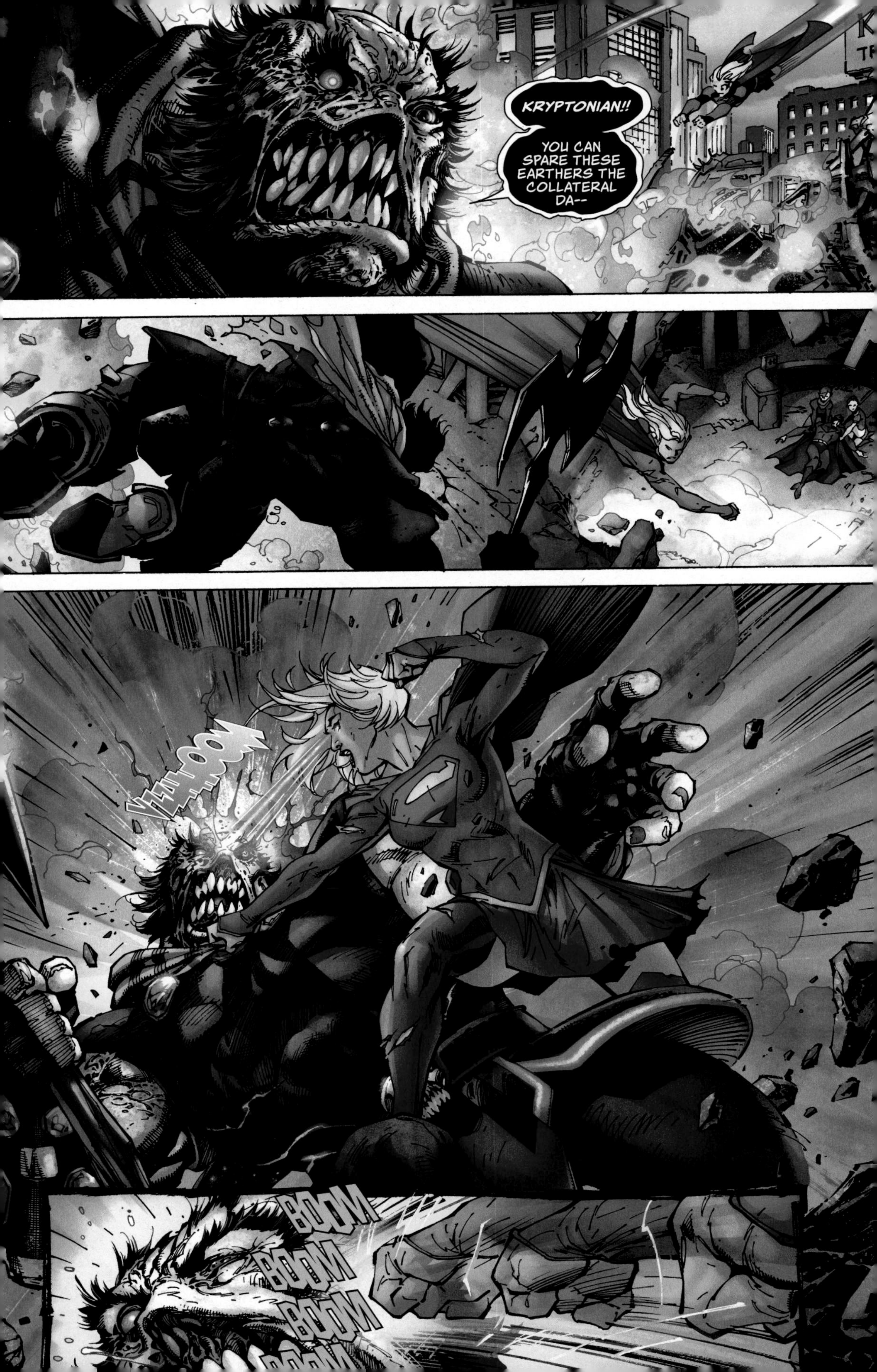
KRYPTONIAN!!
YOU CAN SPARE THESE EARTHERS THE COLLATERAL DA--
BOOM
BOOM
BOOM

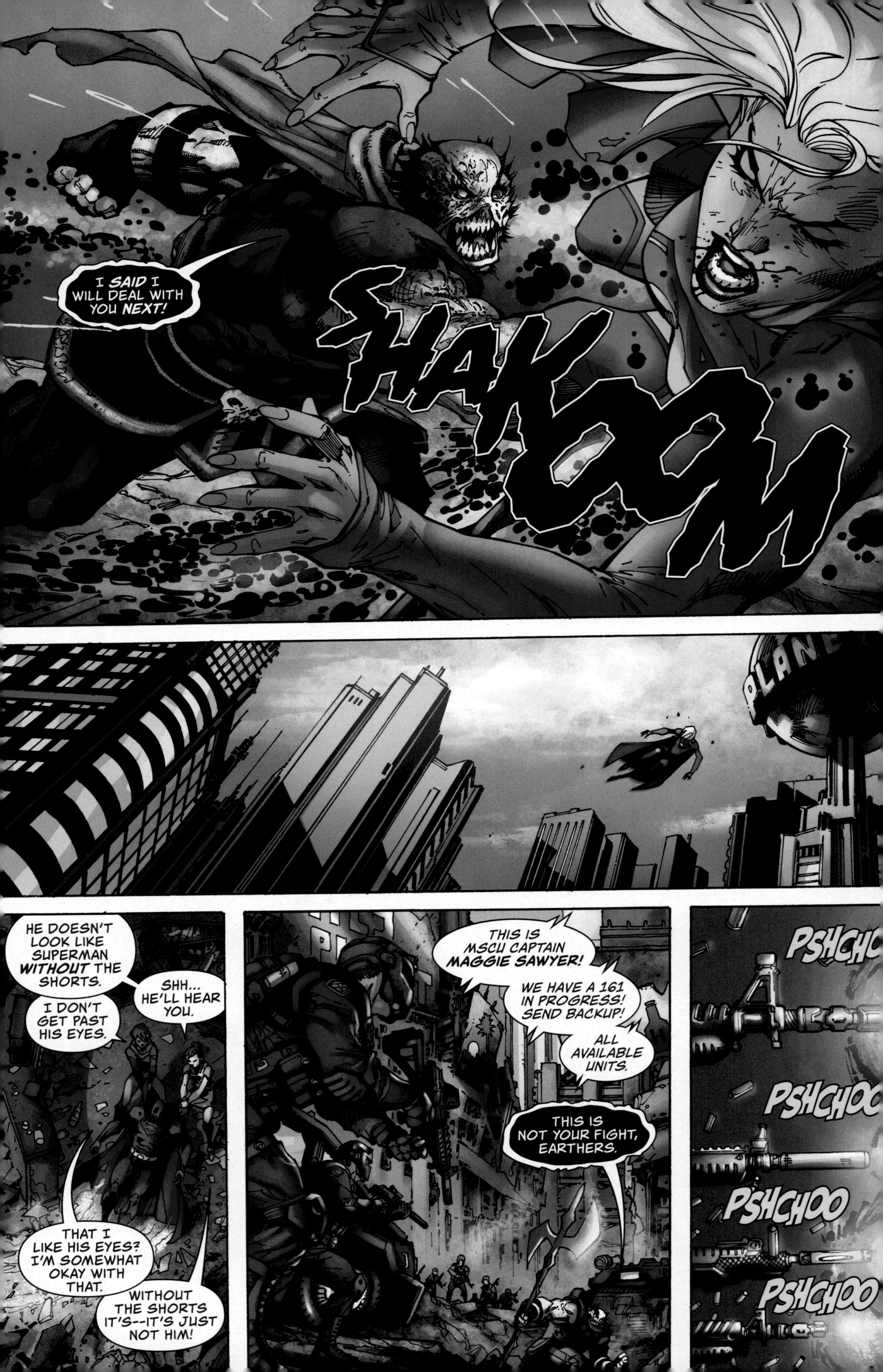
I *SAID* I WILL DEAL WITH YOU *NEXT!*
SHAKOOM
HE DOESN'T LOOK LIKE SUPERMAN *WITHOUT* THE SHORTS.
SHH... HE'LL HEAR YOU.
I DON'T GET PAST HIS EYES.
THAT I LIKE HIS EYES? I'M SOMEWHAT OKAY WITH THAT.
WITHOUT THE SHORTS IT'S--IT'S JUST NOT HIM!
THIS IS MSCU CAPTAIN *MAGGIE SAWYER!*
WE HAVE A 161 IN PROGRESS! SEND BACKUP!
ALL AVAILABLE UNITS.
THIS IS NOT YOUR FIGHT, EARTHERS.
PSHCHOO
PSHCHOO
PSHCHOO
PSHCHOO

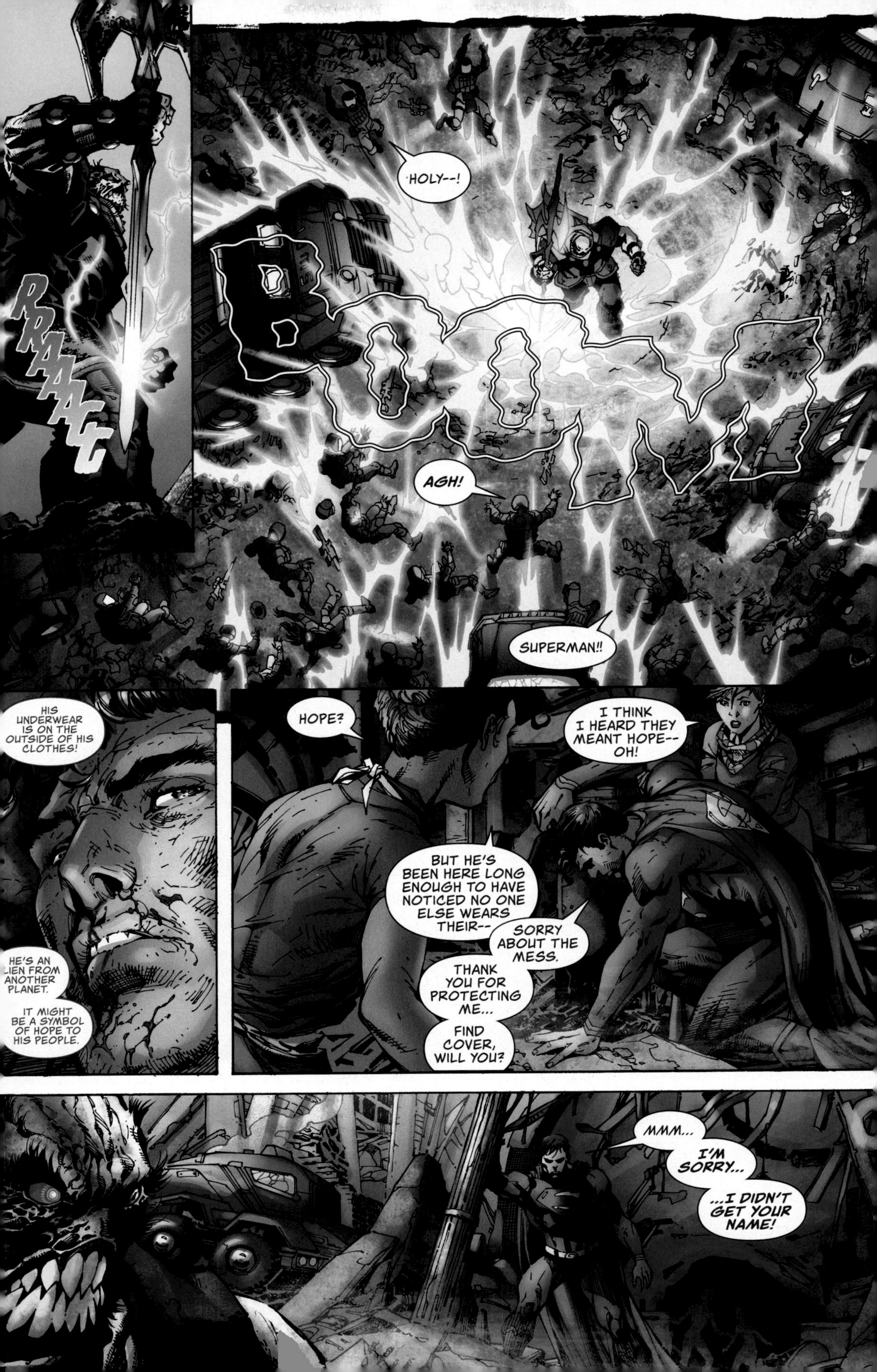
RRAAAACC
HOLY--!
BOOM
AGH!
SUPERMAN!!
HIS UNDERWEAR IS ON THE OUTSIDE OF HIS CLOTHES!
HOPE?
I THINK I HEARD THEY MEANT HOPE-- OH!
BUT HE'S BEEN HERE LONG ENOUGH TO HAVE NOTICED NO ONE ELSE WEARS THEIR--
HE'S AN ALIEN FROM ANOTHER PLANET.
IT MIGHT BE A SYMBOL OF HOPE TO HIS PEOPLE.
SORRY ABOUT THE MESS.
THANK YOU FOR PROTECTING ME...
FIND COVER, WILL YOU?
MMM...
I'M SORRY...
...I DIDN'T GET YOUR NAME!

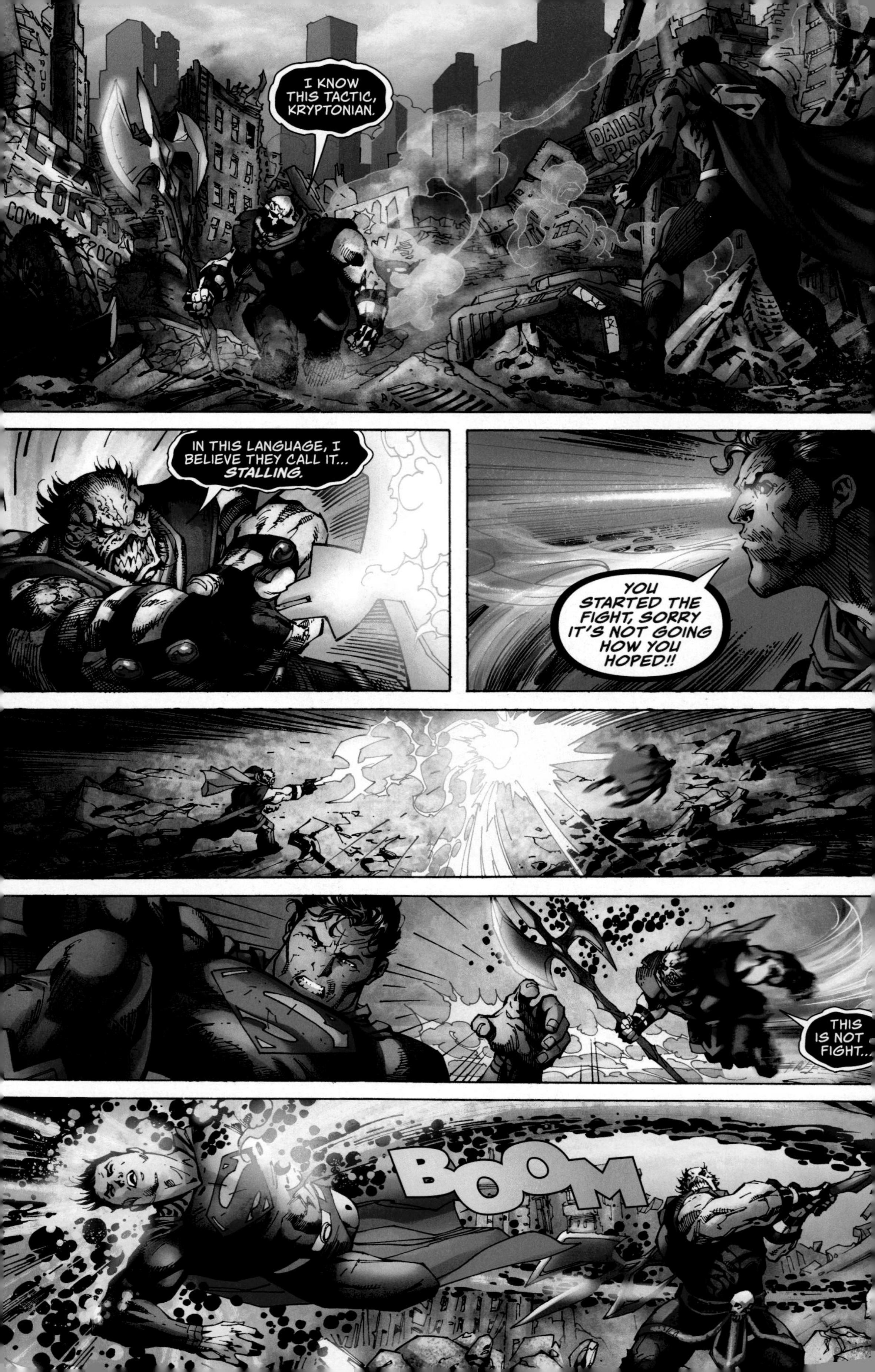
I KNOW THIS TACTIC, KRYPTONIAN.
IN THIS LANGUAGE, I BELIEVE THEY CALL IT... STALLING.
YOU STARTED THE FIGHT, SORRY IT'S NOT GOING HOW YOU HOPED!!
THIS IS NOT FIGHT...
BOOM

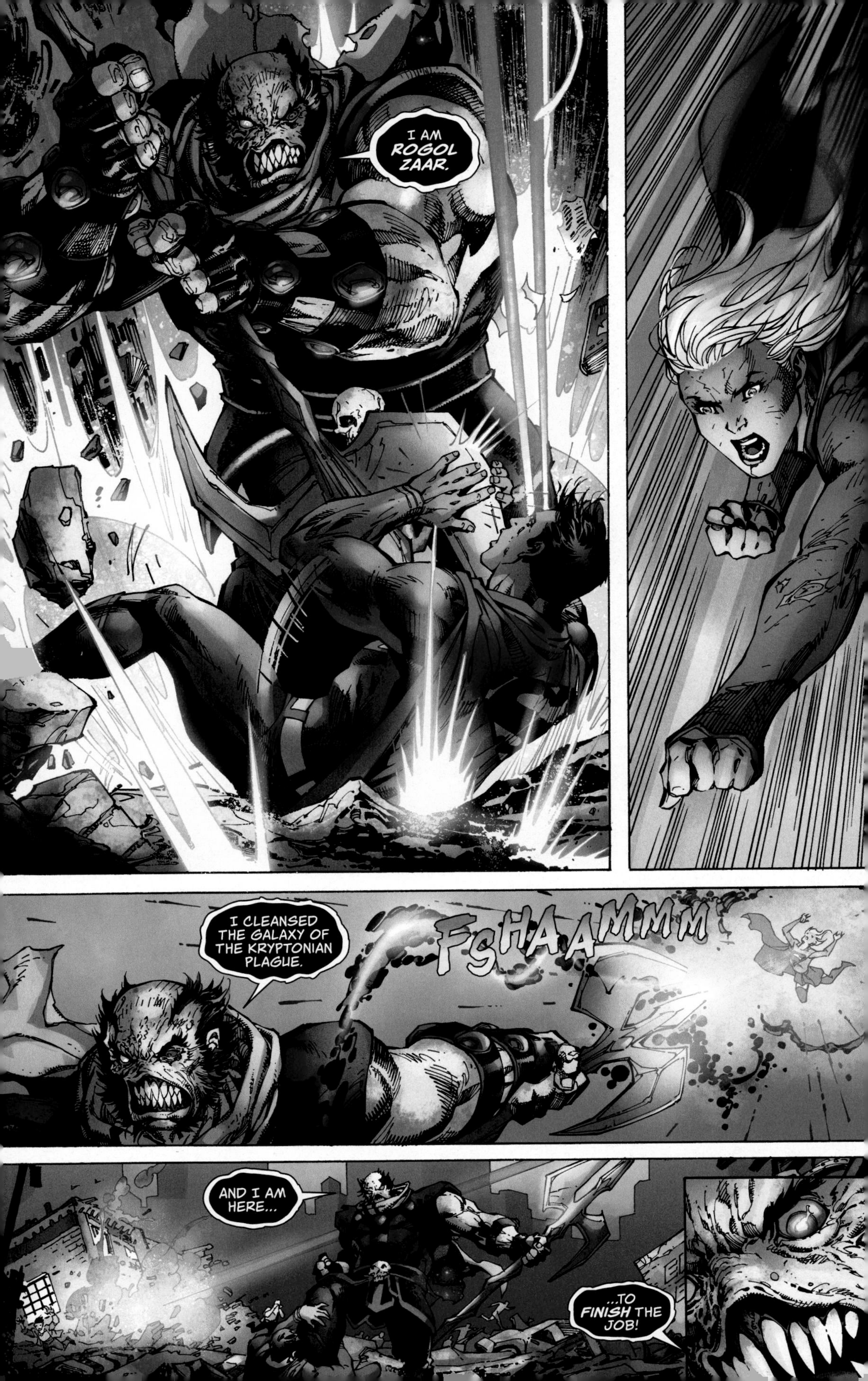

I AM ROGOL ZAAR.
I CLEANSED THE GALAXY OF THE KRYPTONIAN PLAGUE.
FSHAAMMMM
AND I AM HERE...
...TO FINISH THE JOB!

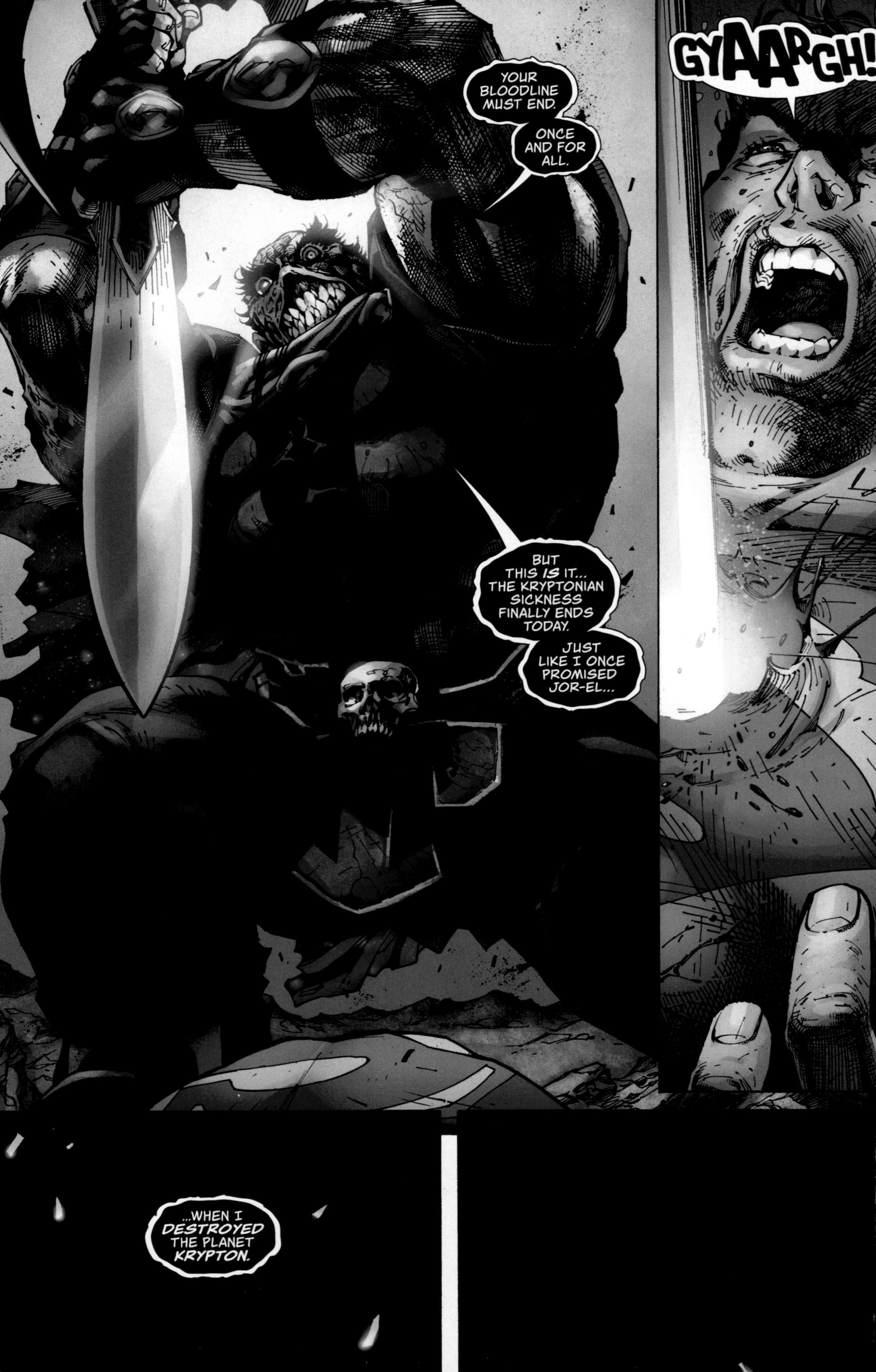
YOUR BLOODLINE MUST END.
ONCE AND FOR ALL.
GYAARGH!
BUT THIS *IS* IT... THE KRYPTONIAN SICKNESS FINALLY ENDS TODAY.
JUST LIKE I ONCE PROMISED JOR-EL...
...WHEN I *DESTROYED* THE PLANET *KRYPTON.*

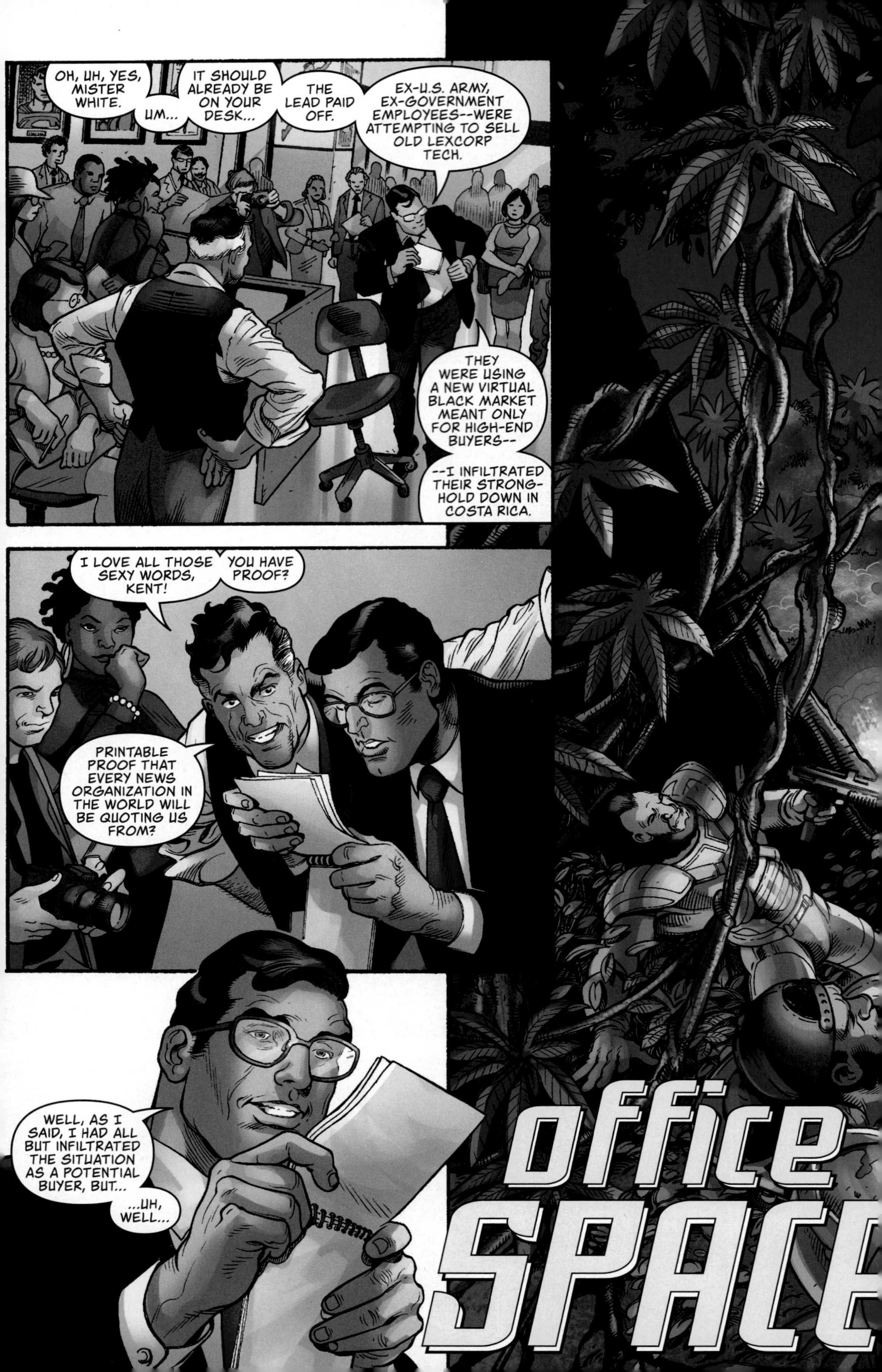
OH, UH, YES, MISTER WHITE.
UM...
IT SHOULD ALREADY BE ON YOUR DESK...
THE LEAD PAID OFF.
EX-U.S. ARMY, EX-GOVERNMENT EMPLOYEES--WERE ATTEMPTING TO SELL OLD LEXCORP TECH.
THEY WERE USING A NEW VIRTUAL BLACK MARKET MEANT ONLY FOR HIGH-END BUYERS--
--I INFILTRATED THEIR STRONG-HOLD DOWN IN COSTA RICA.
I LOVE ALL THOSE SEXY WORDS, KENT!
YOU HAVE PROOF?
PRINTABLE PROOF THAT EVERY NEWS ORGANIZATION IN THE WORLD WILL BE QUOTING US FROM?
WELL, AS I SAID, I HAD ALL BUT INFILTRATED THE SITUATION AS A POTENTIAL BUYER, BUT...
...UH, WELL...
office SPACE

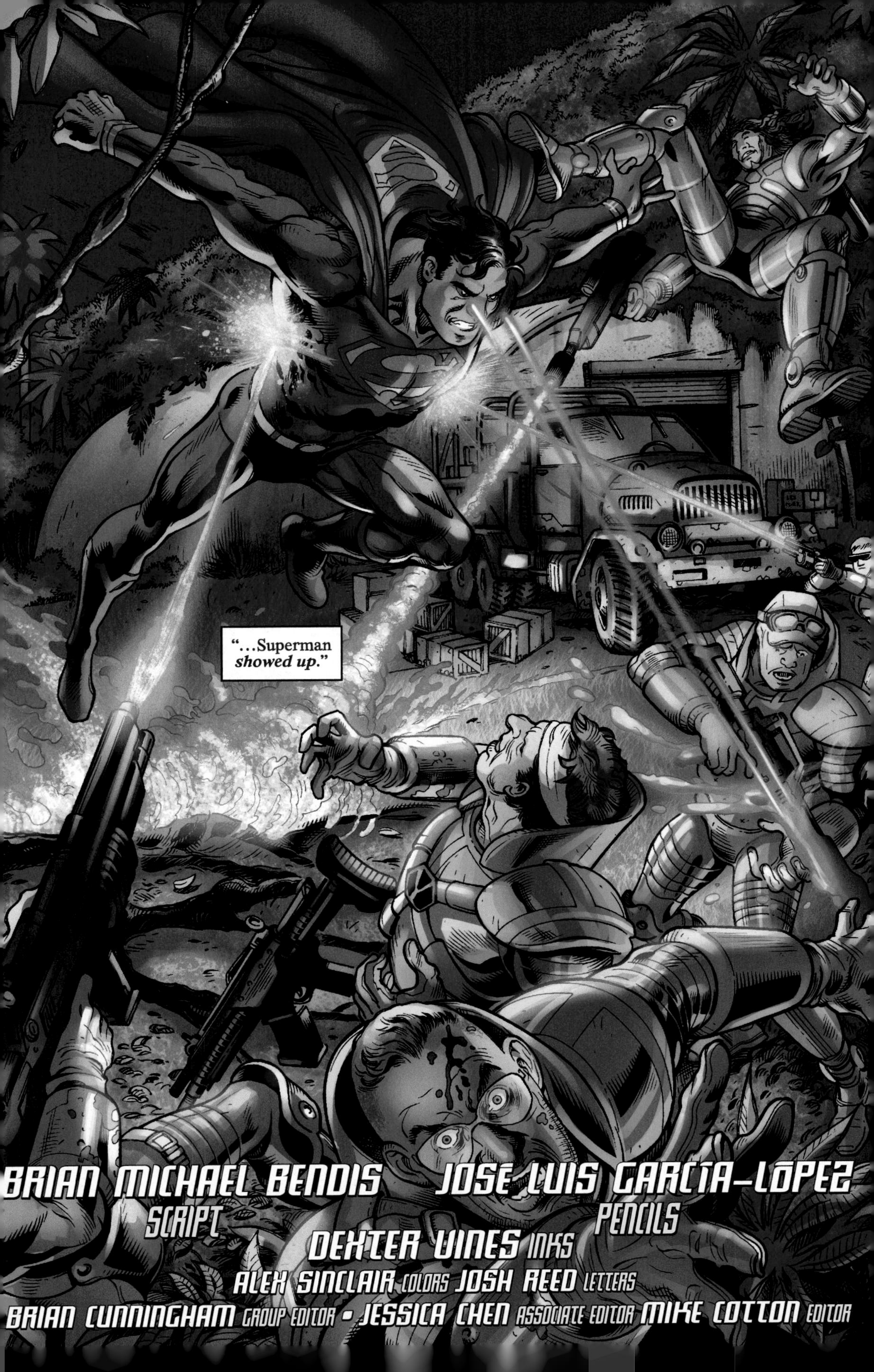
"...Superman *showed up*."
BRIAN MICHAEL BENDIS SCRIPT
JOSE LUIS GARCIA-LÓPEZ PENCILS
DEXTER VINES INKS
ALEX SINCLAIR COLORS JOSH REED LETTERS
BRIAN CUNNINGHAM GROUP EDITOR • JESSICA CHEN ASSOCIATE EDITOR MIKE COTTON EDITOR

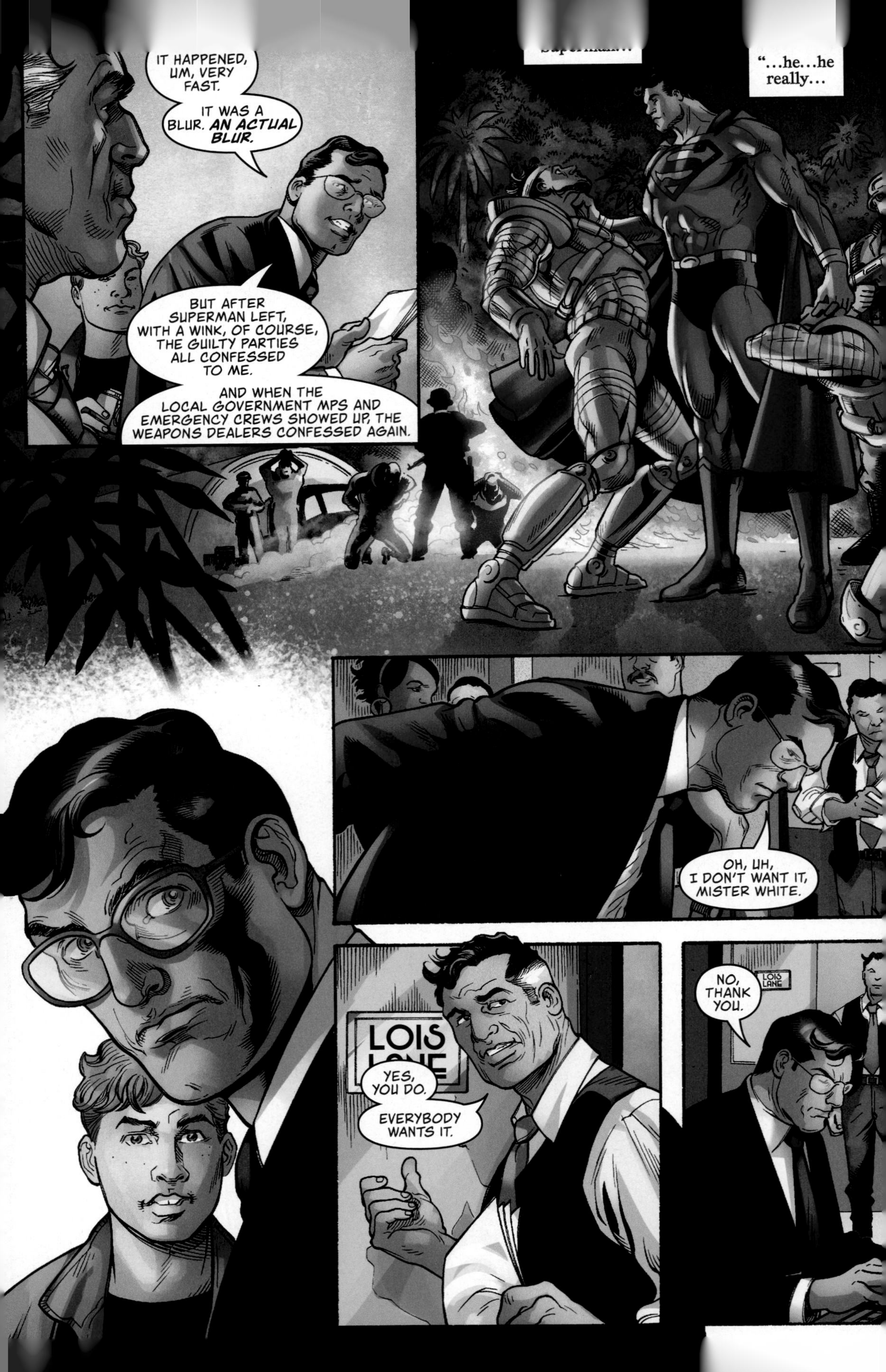
IT HAPPENED, UM, VERY FAST.
IT WAS A BLUR. AN ACTUAL BLUR.
BUT AFTER SUPERMAN LEFT, WITH A WINK, OF COURSE, THE GUILTY PARTIES ALL CONFESSED TO ME.
AND WHEN THE LOCAL GOVERNMENT MPS AND EMERGENCY CREWS SHOWED UP, THE WEAPONS DEALERS CONFESSED AGAIN.
"...he...he really...
OH, UH, I DON'T WANT IT, MISTER WHITE.
LOIS LANE
YES, YOU DO.
EVERYBODY WANTS IT.
LOIS LANE
NO, THANK YOU.

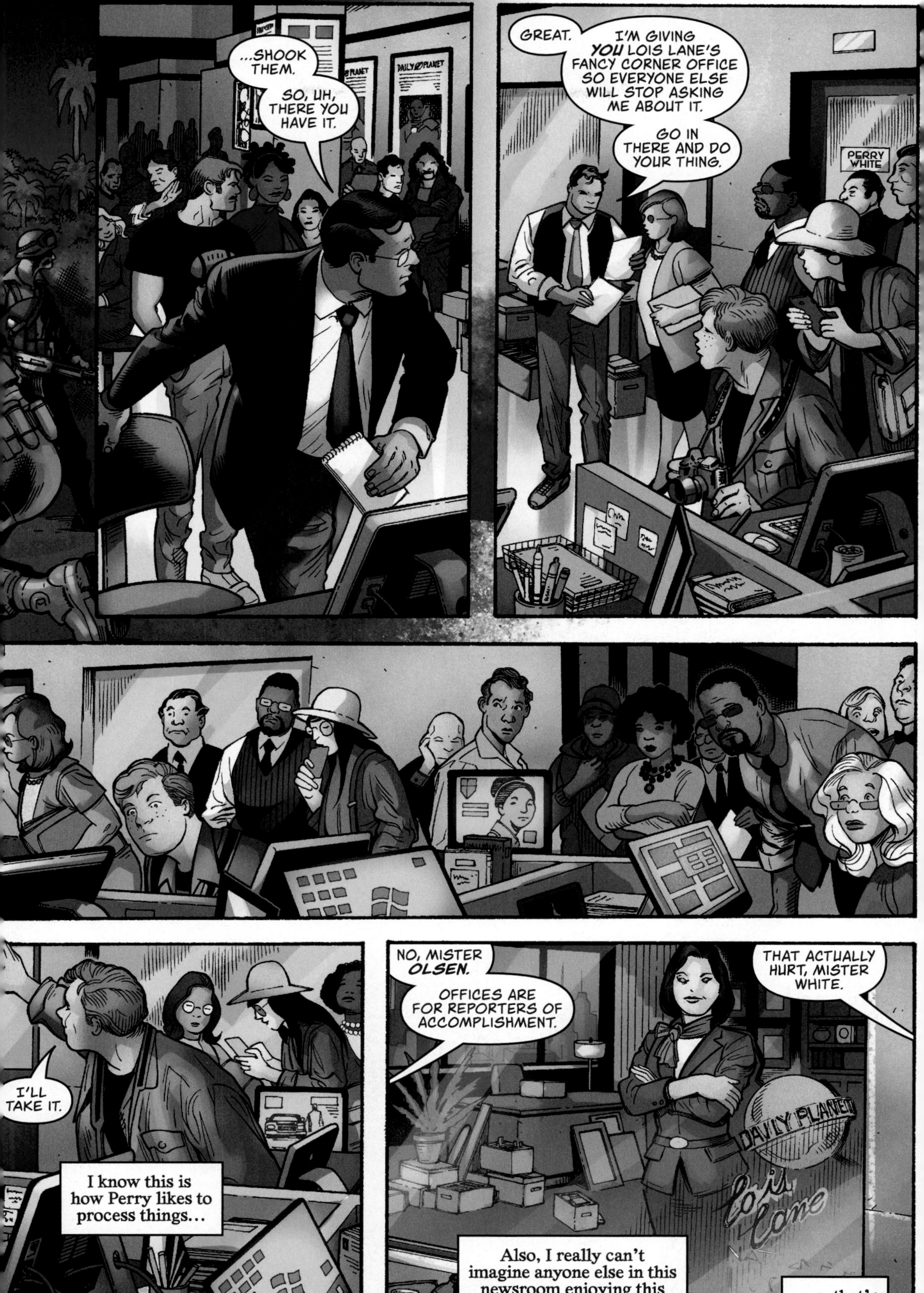
...SHOOK THEM.
SO, UH, THERE YOU HAVE IT.
GREAT.
I'M GIVING YOU LOIS LANE'S FANCY CORNER OFFICE SO EVERYONE ELSE WILL STOP ASKING ME ABOUT IT.
GO IN THERE AND DO YOUR THING.
PERRY WHITE
I'LL TAKE IT.
I know this is how Perry likes to process things…
NO, MISTER OLSEN.
OFFICES ARE FOR REPORTERS OF ACCOMPLISHMENT.
THAT ACTUALLY HURT, MISTER WHITE.
DAILY PLANET
Lois Lane
Also, I really can't imagine anyone else in this newsroom enjoying this awkward display of--
--no, that's not true…

...Trish Q over at Page Six is about to faint from joy.

This gossip has been sniffing around me for a month.

Red Kryptonite, Gold Kryptonite--and now I might have found my HUMAN Kryptonite.

SO, OKAY, YES, FOR THOSE OF YOU JUST JOINING US, OR GLEEFULLY DISCONNECTED TO THE GOSSIP AROUND HERE...

...LOIS LANE, OUR BEST REPORTER, NO LONGER WORKS HERE.

NO OFFENSE TO THE REST OF YOU...

MISTER WHITE...

I KEPT HER OUT OF JAIL!

I'VE KEPT HER OUT OF POLITICAL PRISONS AROUND THE WORLD!! I HAVE DONE EVERYTHING...

I have to remind myself.

This is his version of "having my back."

BUT I GATHERED YOU HERE NOT ONLY TO PUT YOUR FEET TO THE FIRE AND SAVE THE GOOD SOUL OF AMERICAN JOURNALISM...

...BUT BECAUSE WE CAN ANNOUNCE A NEW HIRE.

AND NOW SHE HAS GONE OFF TO WRITE HER BIG BEST-SELLING, PEOPLE PLEASING...

Please, Perry, stop.

MY POINT IS, LADIES AND GENTLEMEN OF THE FREE PRESS:

TODAY IS NOT THE DAY TO ASK ME FOR FAVORS, OR DEADLINE EXTENSIONS, OR ANYTHING ELSE.

THIS IS OUR NEW CITY BEAT REPORTER, STRAIGHT FROM THE STAR CITY SENTINEL...

...MISS ROBINSON GOODE.

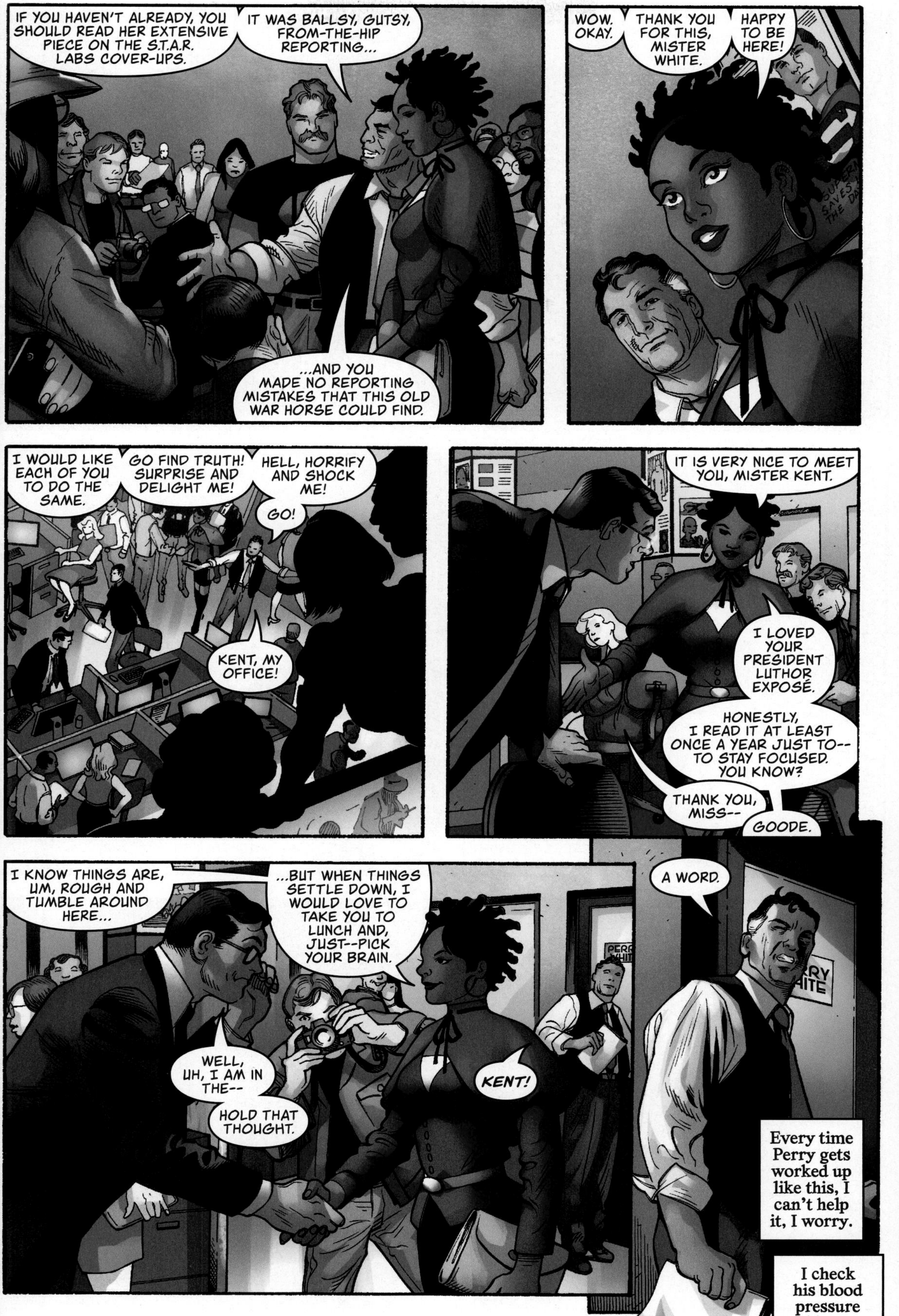
IF YOU HAVEN'T ALREADY, YOU SHOULD READ HER EXTENSIVE PIECE ON THE S.T.A.R. LABS COVER-UPS.
IT WAS BALLSY, GUTSY, FROM-THE-HIP REPORTING...
...AND YOU MADE NO REPORTING MISTAKES THAT THIS OLD WAR HORSE COULD FIND.
WOW. OKAY.
THANK YOU FOR THIS, MISTER WHITE.
HAPPY TO BE HERE!
I WOULD LIKE EACH OF YOU TO DO THE SAME.
GO FIND TRUTH! SURPRISE AND DELIGHT ME!
HELL, HORRIFY AND SHOCK ME!
GO!
KENT, MY OFFICE!
IT IS VERY NICE TO MEET YOU, MISTER KENT.
I LOVED YOUR PRESIDENT LUTHOR EXPOSÉ.
HONESTLY, I READ IT AT LEAST ONCE A YEAR JUST TO-- TO STAY FOCUSED. YOU KNOW?
THANK YOU, MISS--
GOODE.
I KNOW THINGS ARE, UM, ROUGH AND TUMBLE AROUND HERE...
...BUT WHEN THINGS SETTLE DOWN, I WOULD LOVE TO TAKE YOU TO LUNCH AND, JUST--PICK YOUR BRAIN.
WELL, UH, I AM IN THE--
HOLD THAT THOUGHT.
KENT!
A WORD.
Every time Perry gets worked up like this, I can't help it, I worry.
I check his blood pressure and heart…

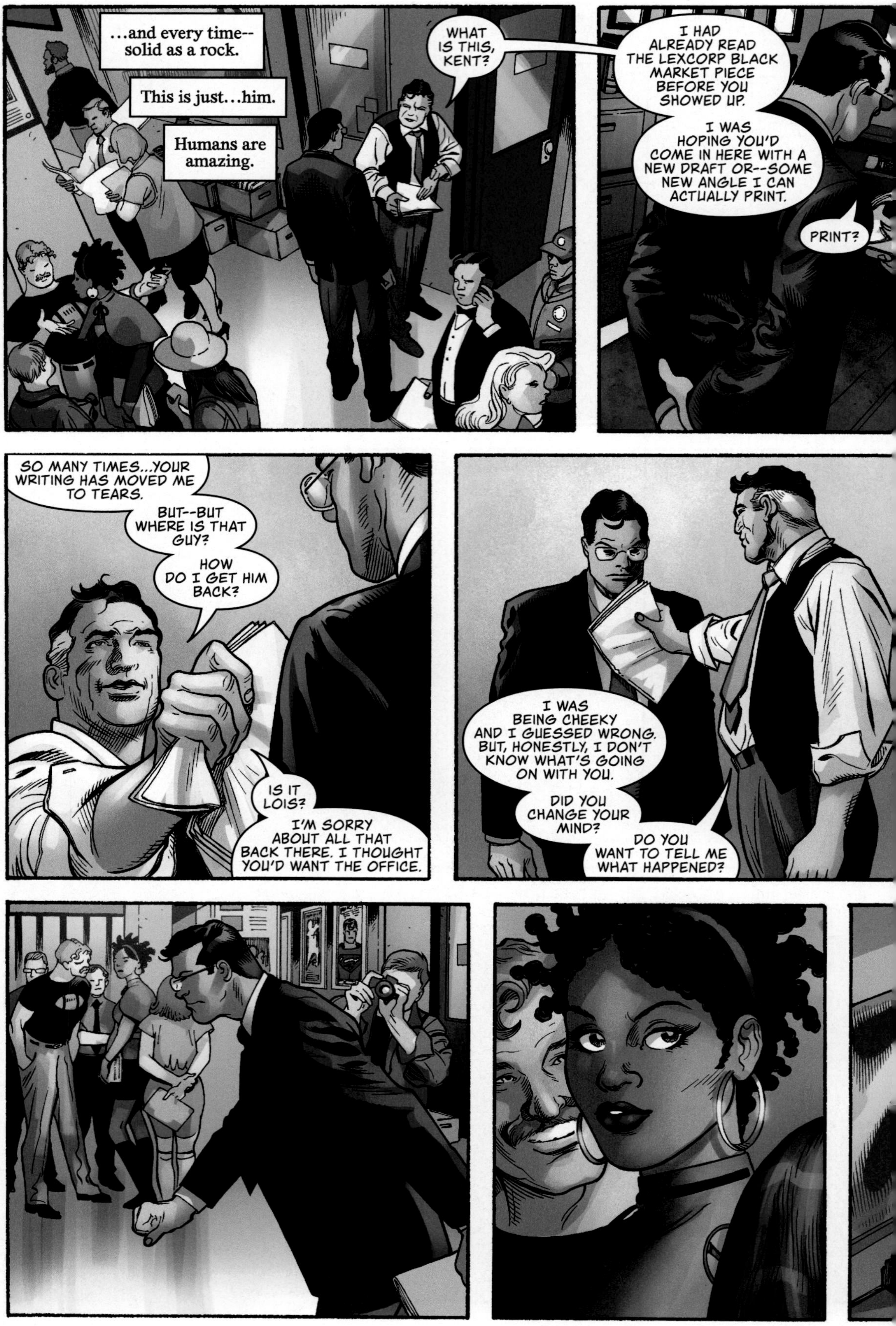
...and every time--solid as a rock.
This is just...him.
Humans are amazing.
WHAT IS THIS, KENT?
I HAD ALREADY READ THE LEXCORP BLACK MARKET PIECE BEFORE YOU SHOWED UP.
I WAS HOPING YOU'D COME IN HERE WITH A NEW DRAFT OR--SOME NEW ANGLE I CAN ACTUALLY PRINT.
PRINT?
SO MANY TIMES...YOUR WRITING HAS MOVED ME TO TEARS.
BUT--BUT WHERE IS THAT GUY?
HOW DO I GET HIM BACK?
IS IT LOIS?
I'M SORRY ABOUT ALL THAT BACK THERE. I THOUGHT YOU'D WANT THE OFFICE.
I WAS BEING CHEEKY AND I GUESSED WRONG. BUT, HONESTLY, I DON'T KNOW WHAT'S GOING ON WITH YOU.
DID YOU CHANGE YOUR MIND?
DO YOU WANT TO TELL ME WHAT HAPPENED?

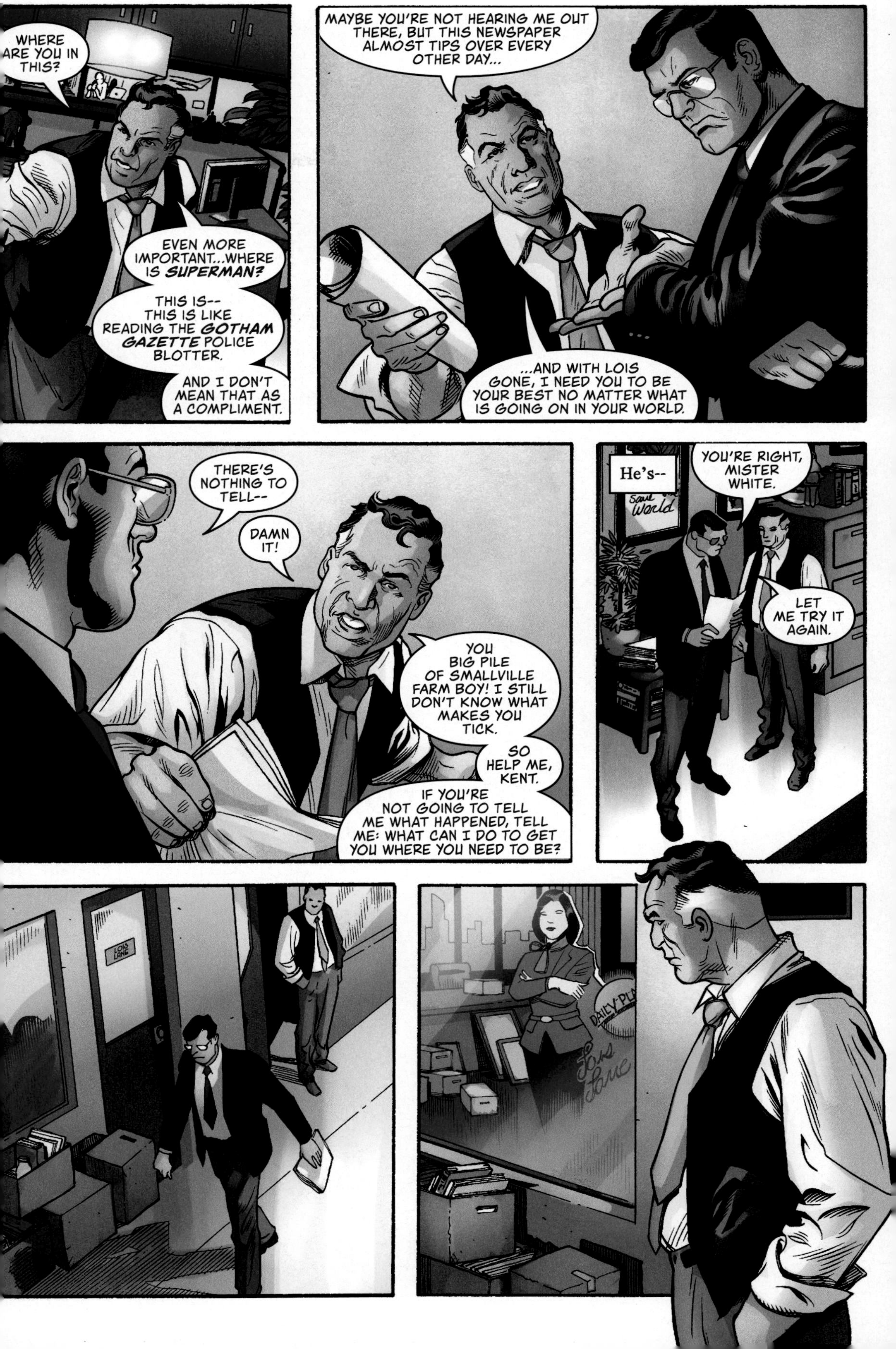
WHERE ARE YOU IN THIS?
EVEN MORE IMPORTANT...WHERE IS SUPERMAN?
THIS IS-- THIS IS LIKE READING THE GOTHAM GAZETTE POLICE BLOTTER.
AND I DON'T MEAN THAT AS A COMPLIMENT.
MAYBE YOU'RE NOT HEARING ME OUT THERE, BUT THIS NEWSPAPER ALMOST TIPS OVER EVERY OTHER DAY...
...AND WITH LOIS GONE, I NEED YOU TO BE YOUR BEST NO MATTER WHAT IS GOING ON IN YOUR WORLD.
THERE'S NOTHING TO TELL--
DAMN IT!
YOU BIG PILE OF SMALLVILLE FARM BOY! I STILL DON'T KNOW WHAT MAKES YOU TICK.
SO HELP ME, KENT.
IF YOU'RE NOT GOING TO TELL ME WHAT HAPPENED, TELL ME: WHAT CAN I DO TO GET YOU WHERE YOU NEED TO BE?
He's--
YOU'RE RIGHT, MISTER WHITE.
LET ME TRY IT AGAIN.
LOIS LANE
DAILY PLA
Lois Lane

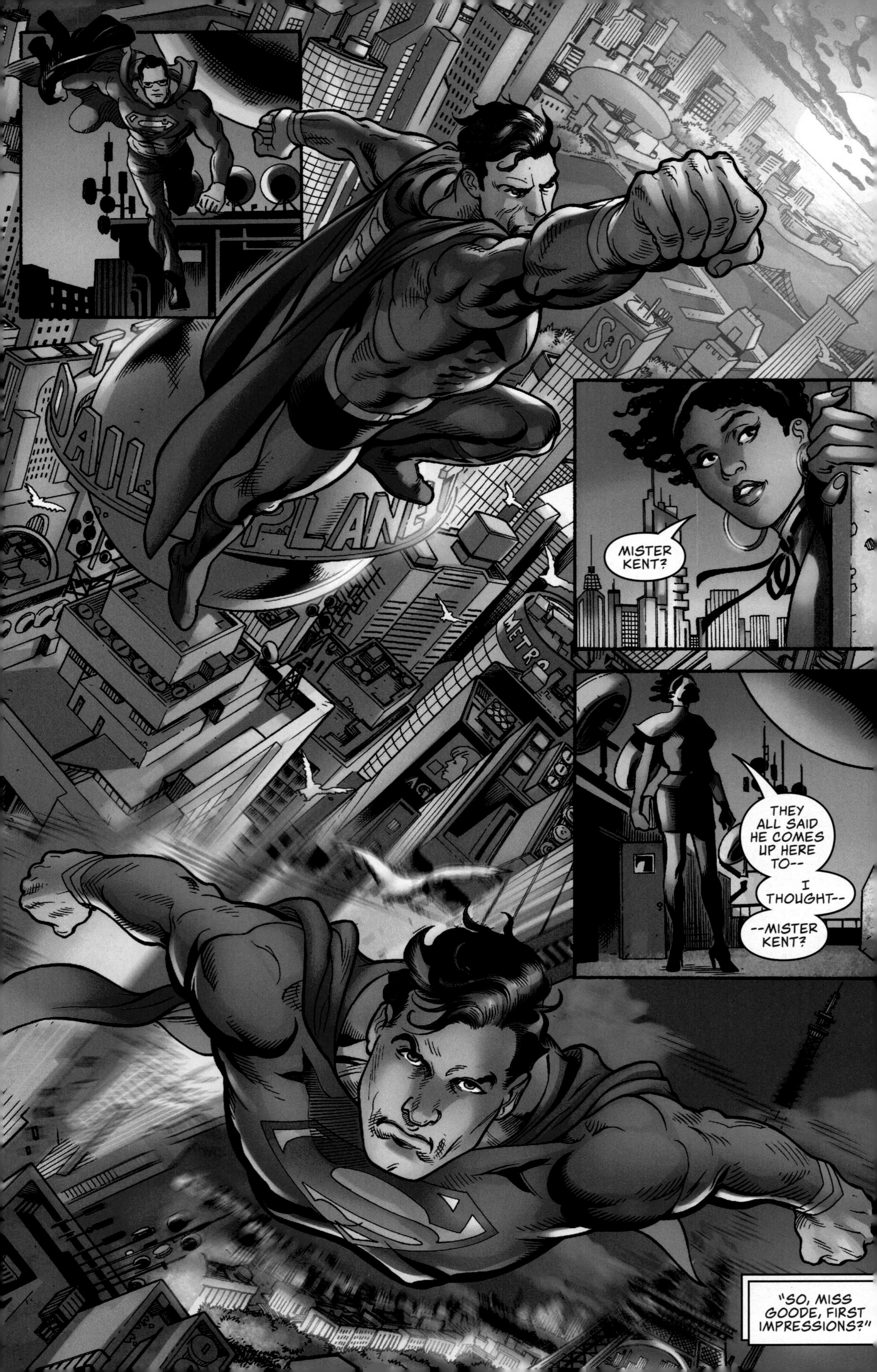
MISTER KENT?
THEY ALL SAID HE COMES UP HERE TO--
I THOUGHT--
--MISTER KENT?
"SO, MISS GOODE, FIRST IMPRESSIONS?"

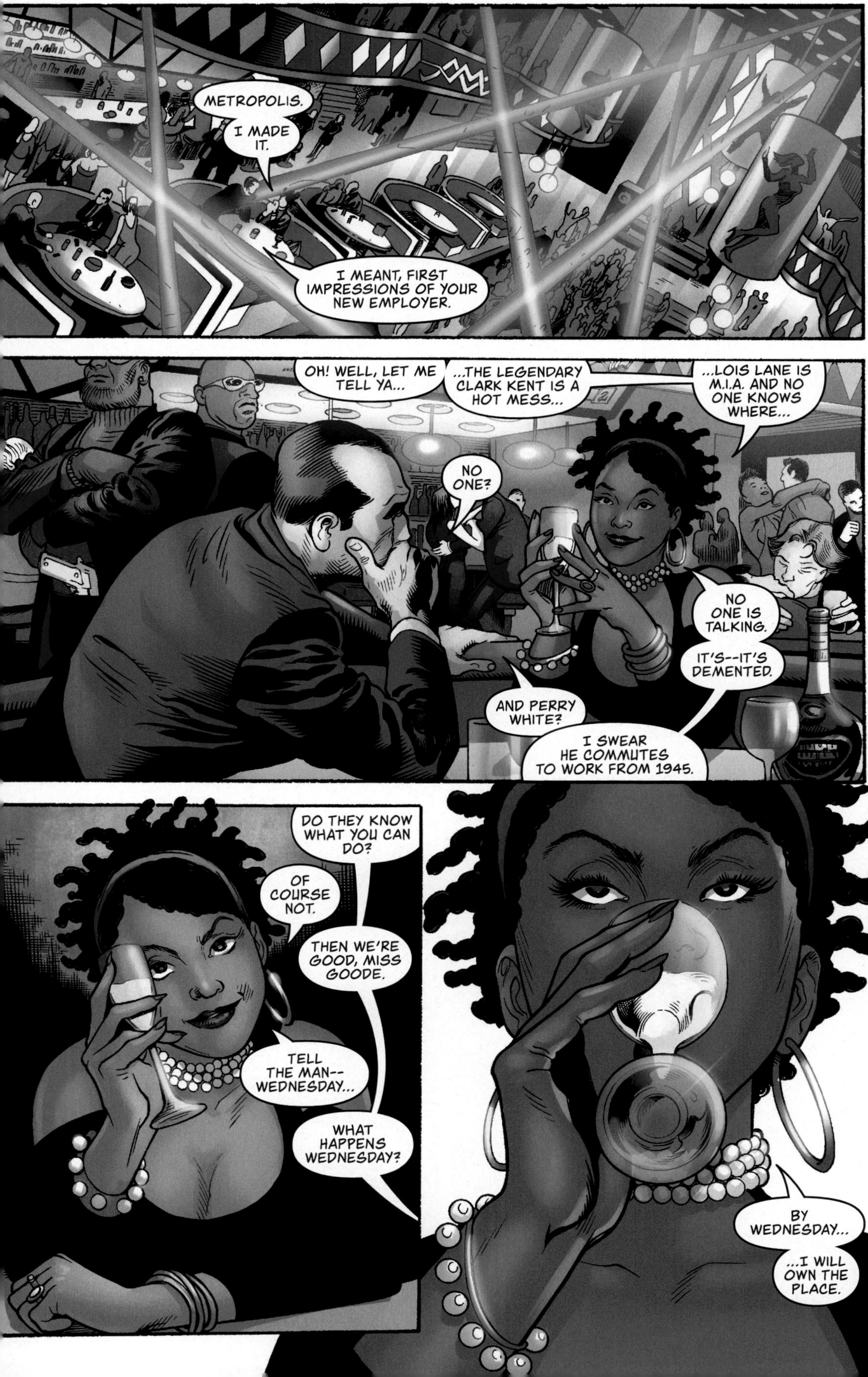
METROPOLIS.
I MADE IT.
I MEANT, FIRST IMPRESSIONS OF YOUR NEW EMPLOYER.
OH! WELL, LET ME TELL YA...
...THE LEGENDARY CLARK KENT IS A HOT MESS...
...LOIS LANE IS M.I.A. AND NO ONE KNOWS WHERE...
NO ONE?
NO ONE IS TALKING.
IT'S--IT'S DEMENTED.
AND PERRY WHITE?
I SWEAR HE COMMUTES TO WORK FROM 1945.
DO THEY KNOW WHAT YOU CAN DO?
OF COURSE NOT.
THEN WE'RE GOOD, MISS GOODE.
TELL THE MAN-- WEDNESDAY...
WHAT HAPPENS WEDNESDAY?
BY WEDNESDAY...
...I WILL OWN THE PLACE.

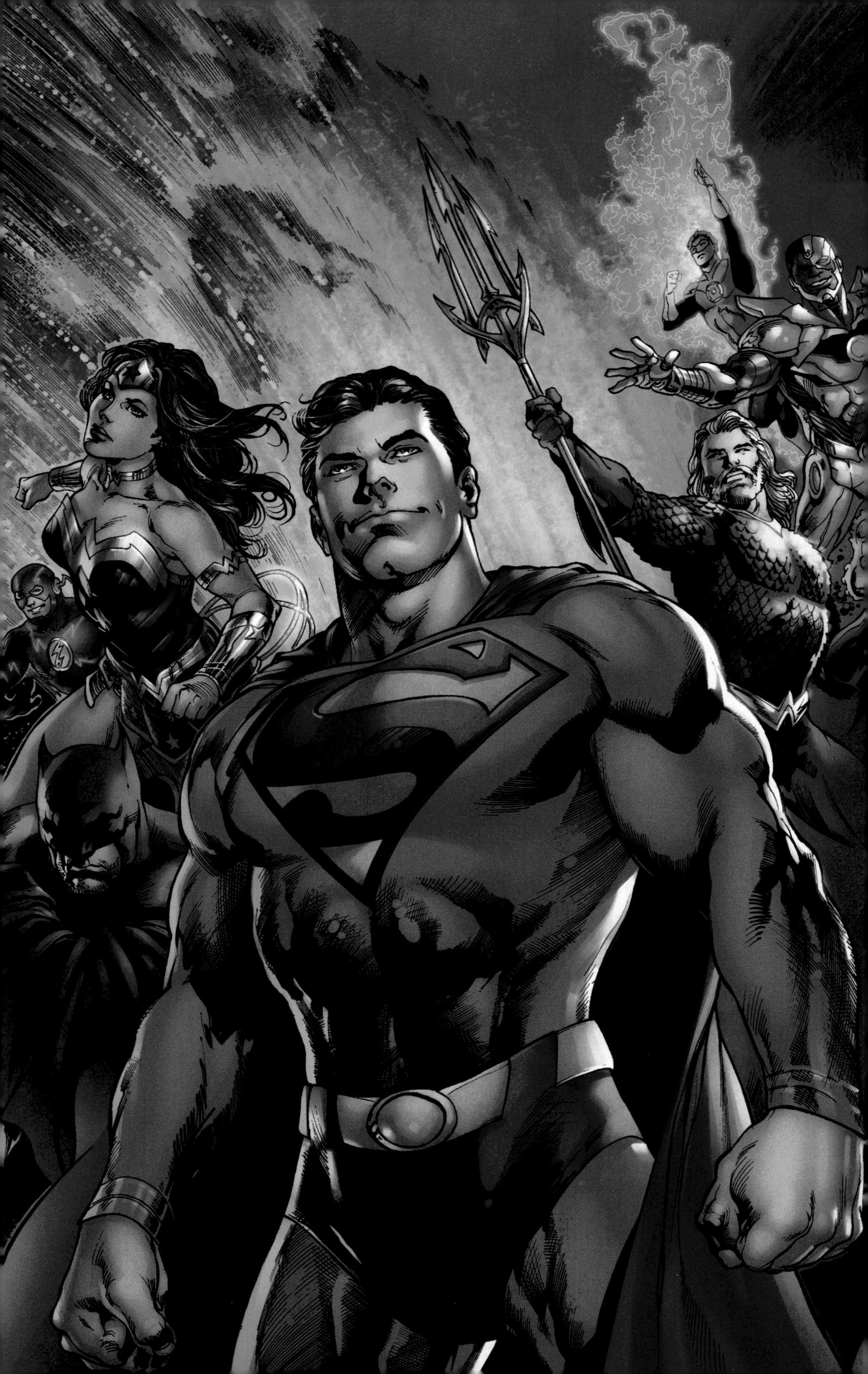

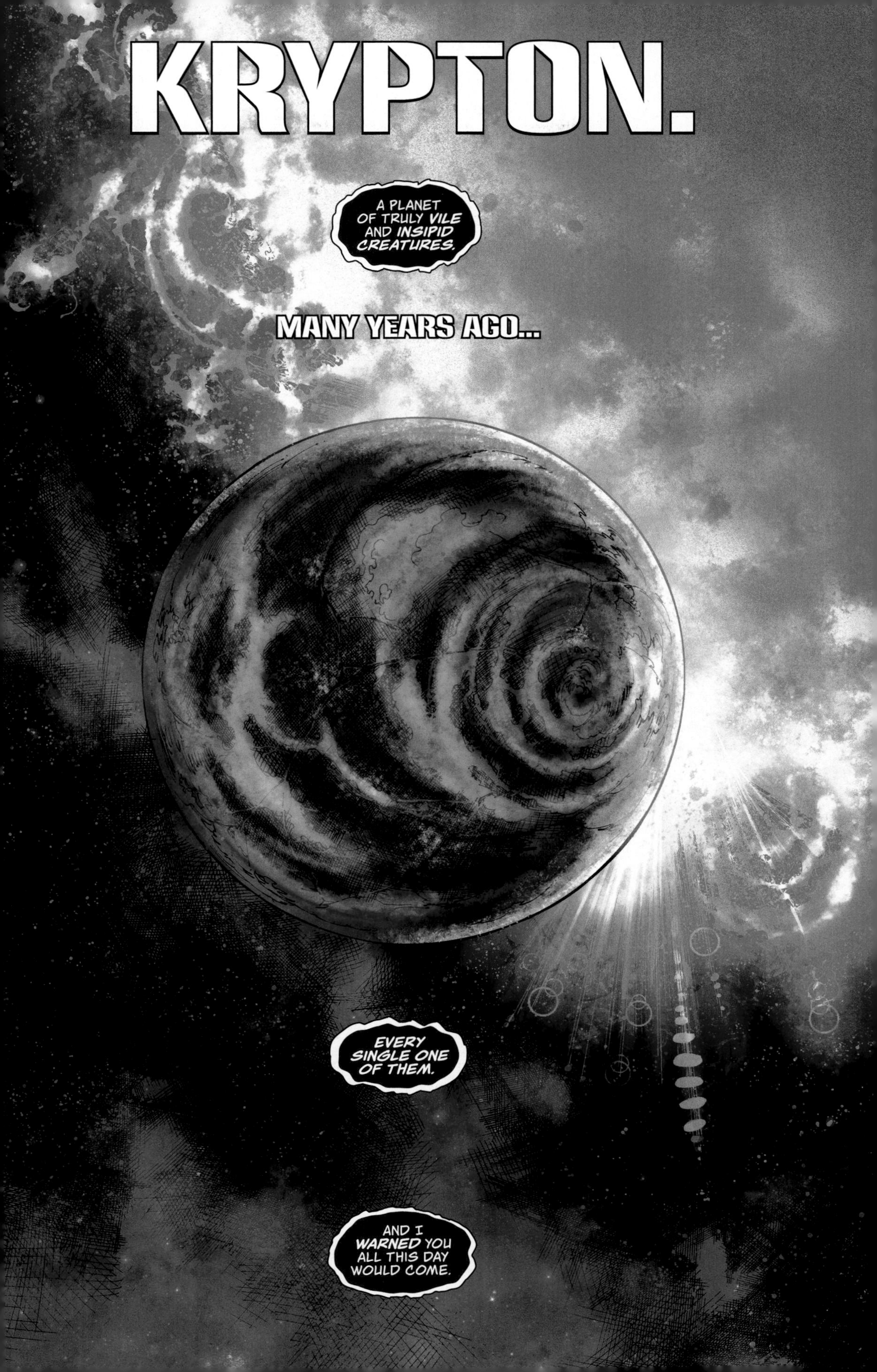
KRYPTON.
A PLANET OF TRULY VILE AND INSIPID CREATURES.
MANY YEARS AGO...
EVERY SINGLE ONE OF THEM.
AND I WARNED YOU ALL THIS DAY WOULD COME.

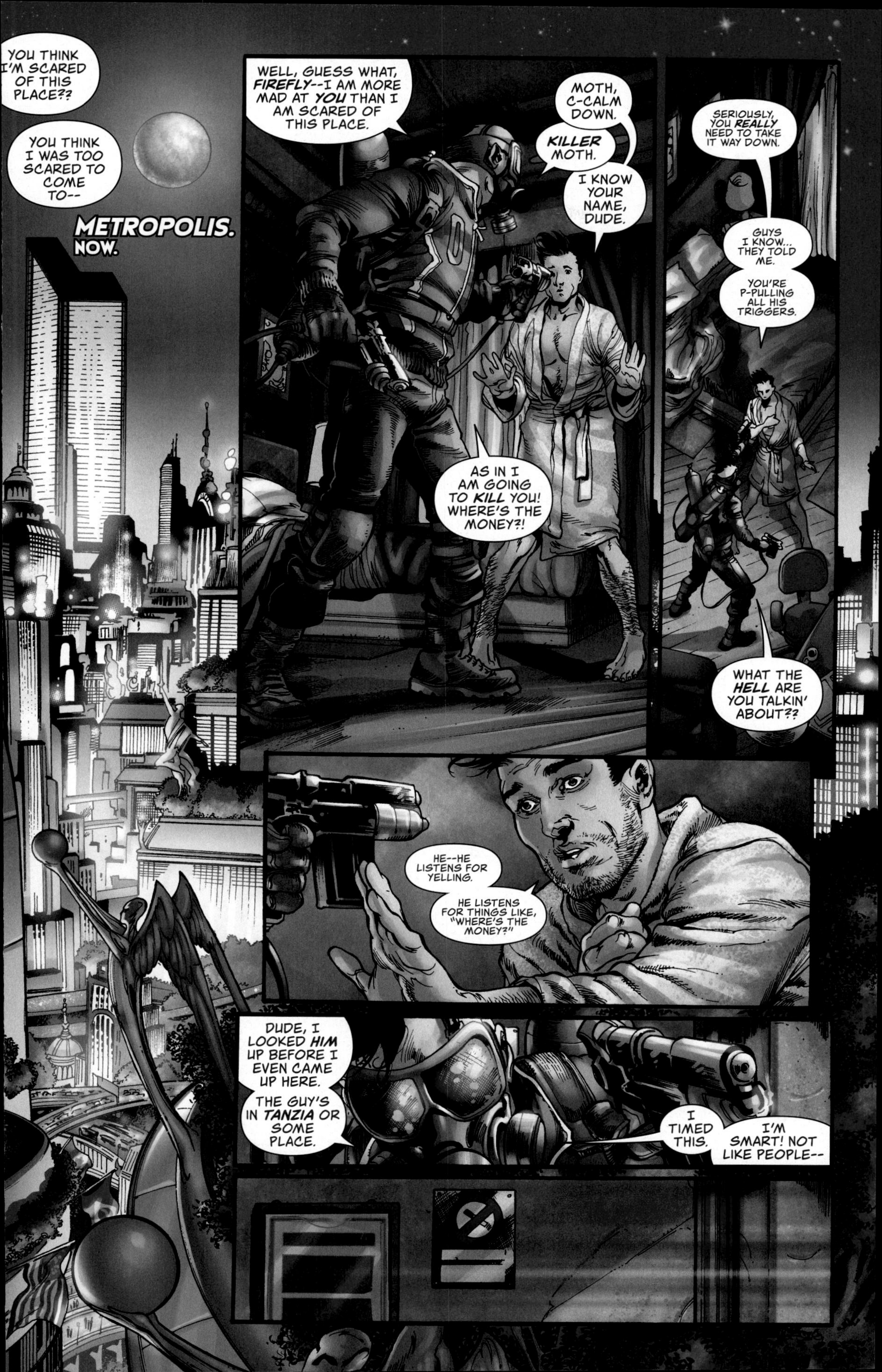

YOU THINK I'M SCARED OF THIS PLACE??
YOU THINK I WAS TOO SCARED TO COME TO--
METROPOLIS. NOW.
WELL, GUESS WHAT, FIREFLY--I AM MORE MAD AT YOU THAN I AM SCARED OF THIS PLACE.
MOTH, C-CALM DOWN.
KILLER MOTH.
I KNOW YOUR NAME, DUDE.
AS IN I AM GOING TO KILL YOU! WHERE'S THE MONEY?!
SERIOUSLY, YOU REALLY NEED TO TAKE IT WAY DOWN.
GUYS I KNOW... THEY TOLD ME.
YOU'RE P-PULLING ALL HIS TRIGGERS.
WHAT THE HELL ARE YOU TALKIN' ABOUT??
HE--HE LISTENS FOR YELLING.
HE LISTENS FOR THINGS LIKE, "WHERE'S THE MONEY?"
DUDE, I LOOKED HIM UP BEFORE I EVEN CAME UP HERE.
THE GUY'S IN TANZIA OR SOME PLACE.
I TIMED THIS.
I'M SMART! NOT LIKE PEOPLE--

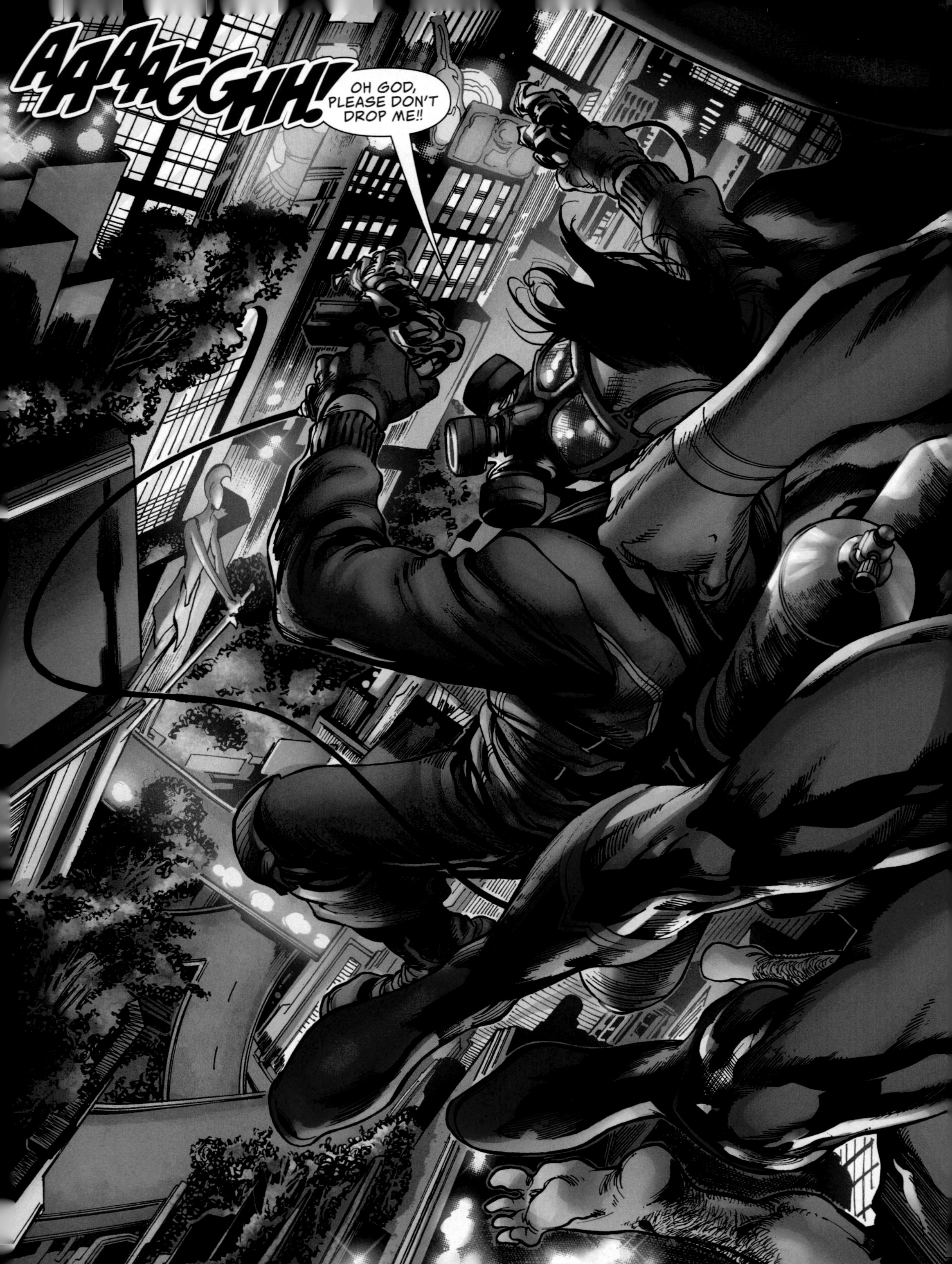
AAAAGGHH!
OH GOD, PLEASE DON'T DROP ME!!

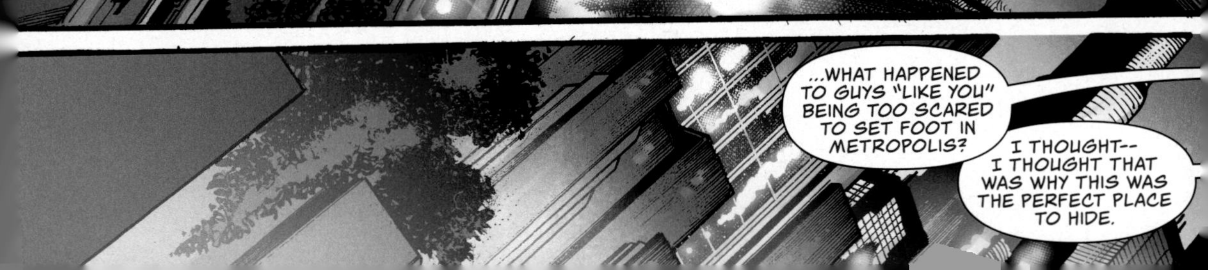
...WHAT HAPPENED TO GUYS "LIKE YOU" BEING TOO SCARED TO SET FOOT IN METROPOLIS?
I THOUGHT-- I THOUGHT THAT WAS WHY THIS WAS THE PERFECT PLACE TO HIDE.

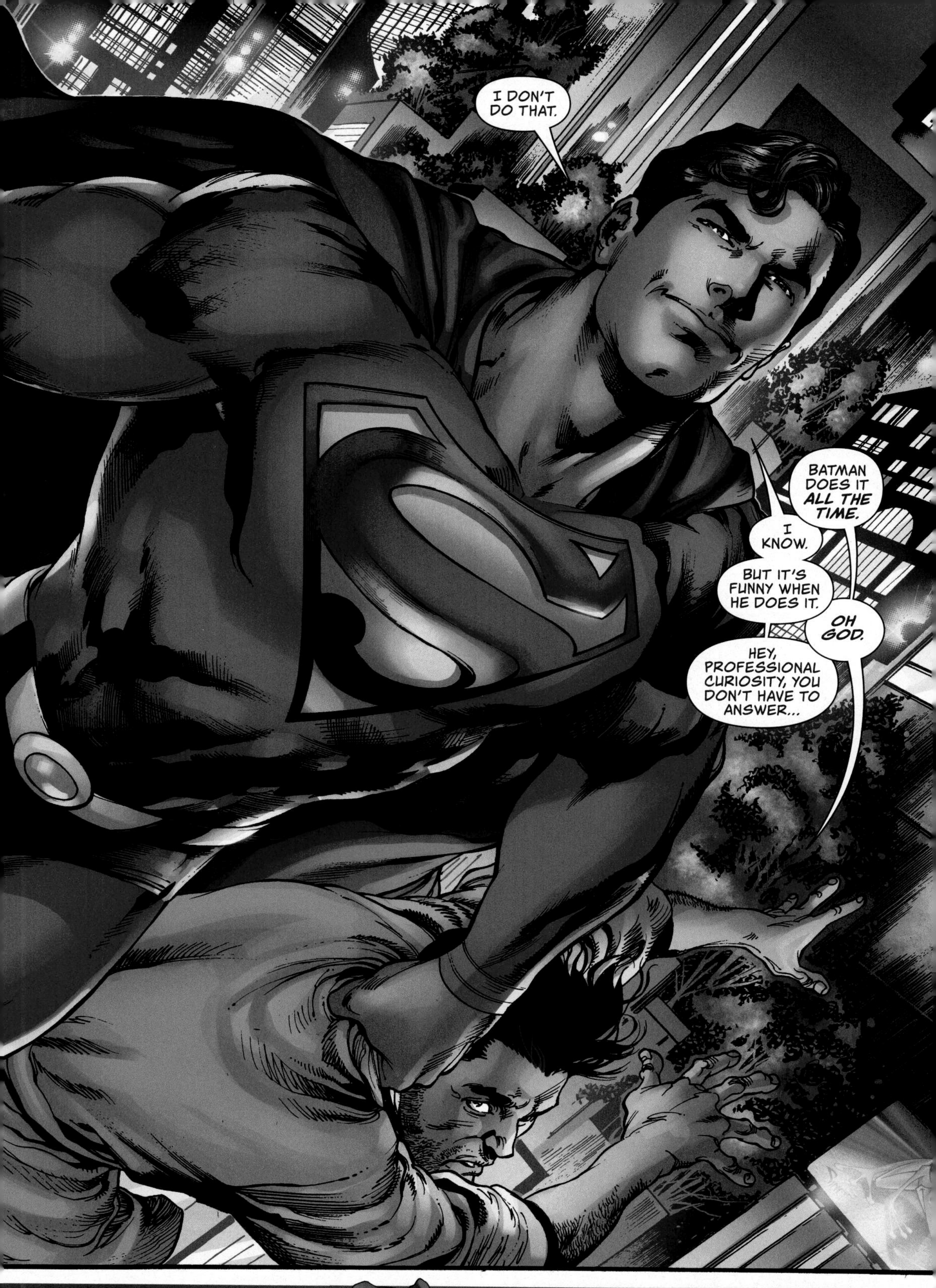
I DON'T DO THAT.
BATMAN DOES IT *ALL THE TIME.*
I KNOW.
BUT IT'S FUNNY WHEN HE DOES IT.
OH GOD.
HEY, PROFESSIONAL CURIOSITY, YOU DON'T HAVE TO ANSWER...

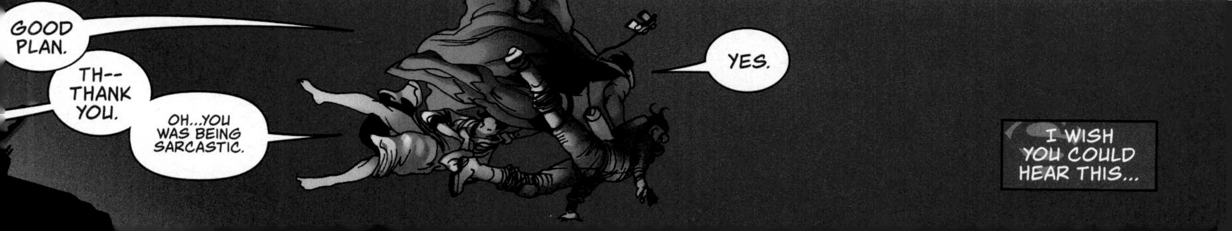
GOOD PLAN.
TH-- THANK YOU.
OH...YOU WAS BEING SARCASTIC.
YES.
I WISH YOU COULD HEAR THIS...

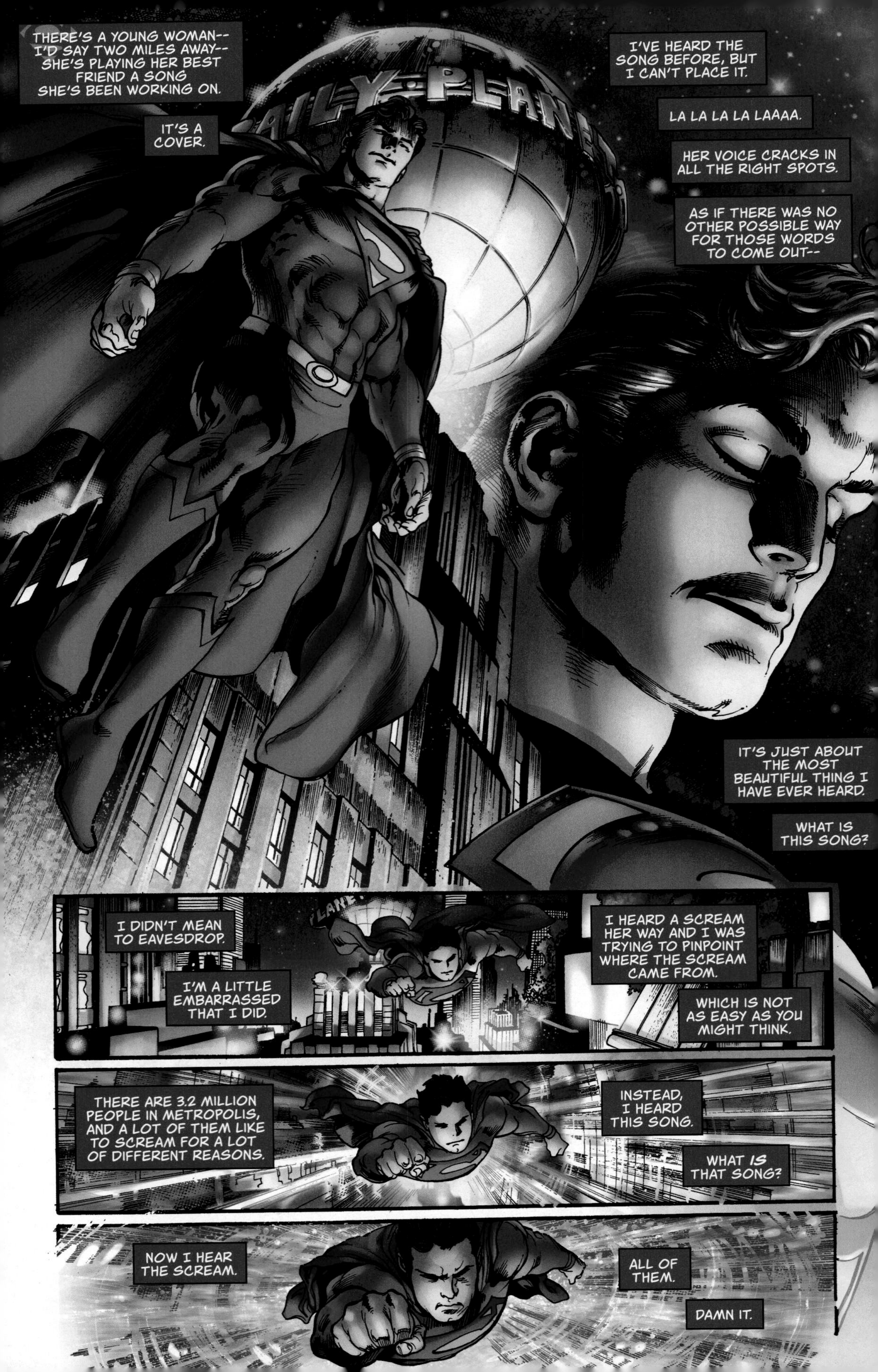
THERE'S A YOUNG WOMAN-- I'D SAY TWO MILES AWAY-- SHE'S PLAYING HER BEST FRIEND A SONG SHE'S BEEN WORKING ON.
IT'S A COVER.
I'VE HEARD THE SONG BEFORE, BUT I CAN'T PLACE IT.
LA LA LA LA LAAAA.
HER VOICE CRACKS IN ALL THE RIGHT SPOTS.
AS IF THERE WAS NO OTHER POSSIBLE WAY FOR THOSE WORDS TO COME OUT--
IT'S JUST ABOUT THE MOST BEAUTIFUL THING I HAVE EVER HEARD.
WHAT IS THIS SONG?
I DIDN'T MEAN TO EAVESDROP.
I'M A LITTLE EMBARRASSED THAT I DID.
I HEARD A SCREAM HER WAY AND I WAS TRYING TO PINPOINT WHERE THE SCREAM CAME FROM.
WHICH IS NOT AS EASY AS YOU MIGHT THINK.
THERE ARE 3.2 MILLION PEOPLE IN METROPOLIS, AND A LOT OF THEM LIKE TO SCREAM FOR A LOT OF DIFFERENT REASONS.
INSTEAD, I HEARD THIS SONG.
WHAT IS THAT SONG?
NOW I HEAR THE SCREAM.
ALL OF THEM.
DAMN IT.

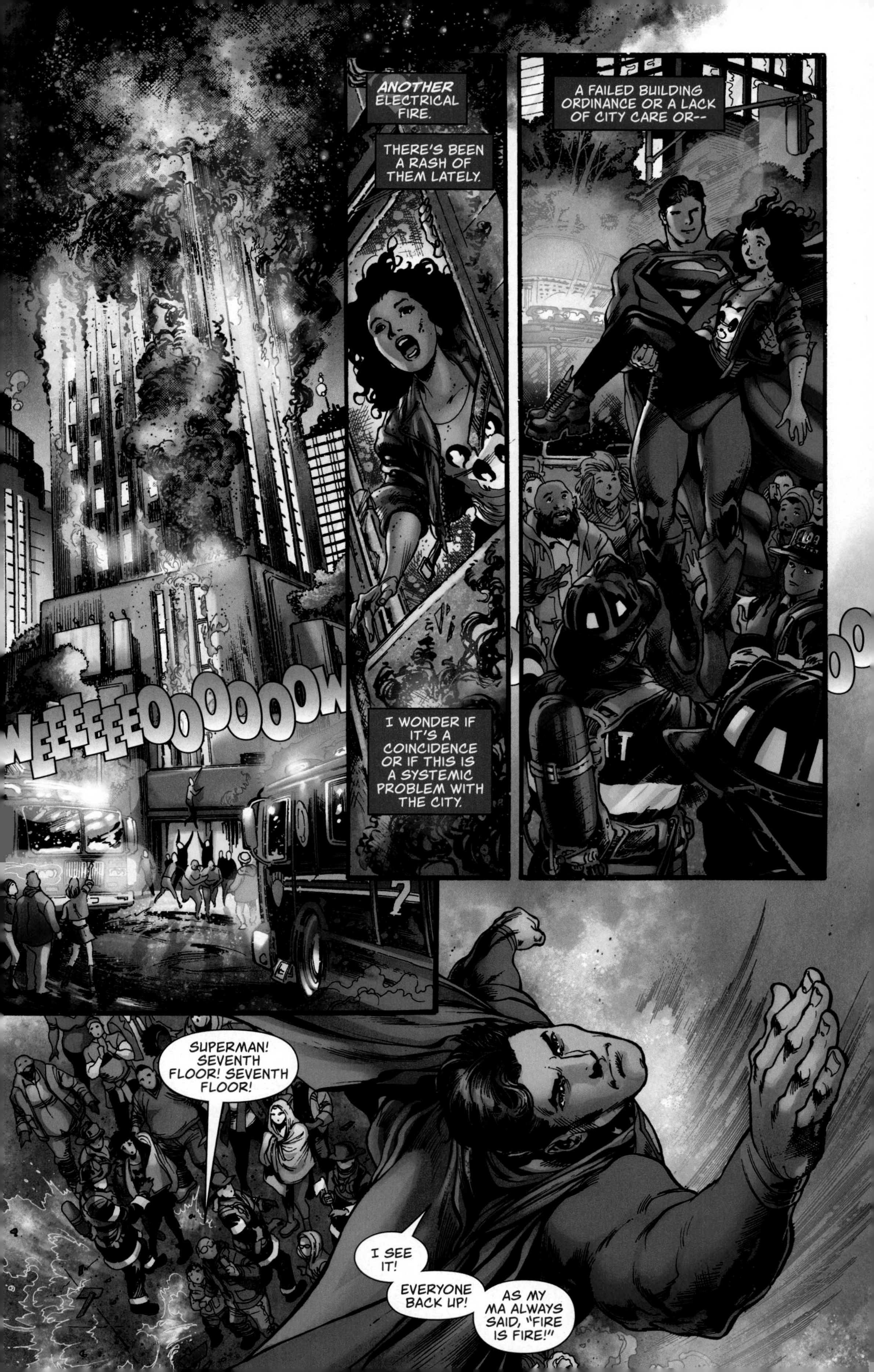
WEEEEEOOOOOOW
ANOTHER ELECTRICAL FIRE.
THERE'S BEEN A RASH OF THEM LATELY.
I WONDER IF IT'S A COINCIDENCE OR IF THIS IS A SYSTEMIC PROBLEM WITH THE CITY.
A FAILED BUILDING ORDINANCE OR A LACK OF CITY CARE OR--
SUPERMAN! SEVENTH FLOOR! SEVENTH FLOOR!
I SEE IT!
EVERYONE BACK UP!
AS MY MA ALWAYS SAID, "FIRE IS FIRE!"

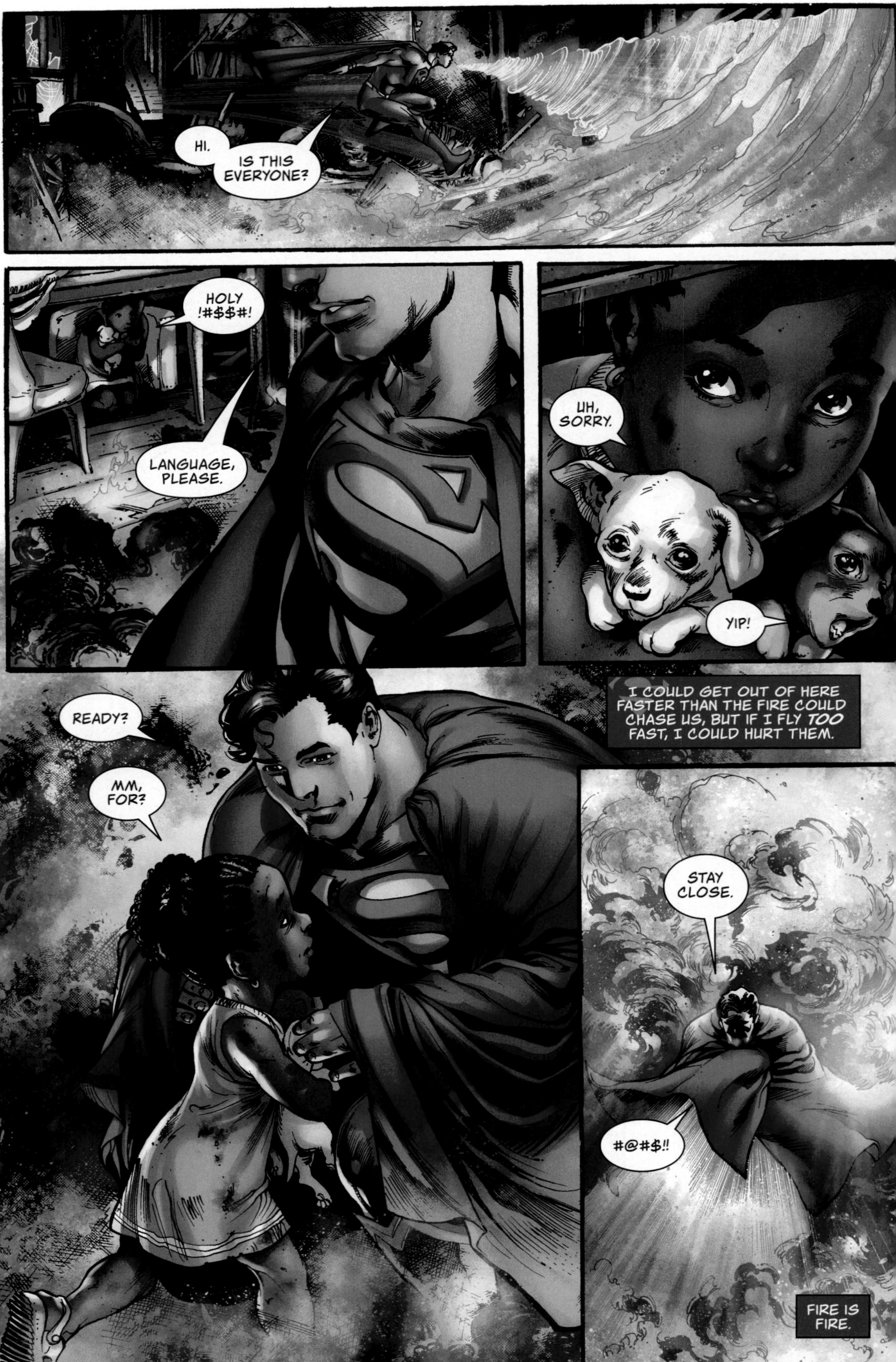
HI.
IS THIS EVERYONE?
HOLY !#$$#!
LANGUAGE, PLEASE.
UH, SORRY.
YIP!
READY?
MM, FOR?
I COULD GET OUT OF HERE FASTER THAN THE FIRE COULD CHASE US, BUT IF I FLY *TOO* FAST, I COULD HURT THEM.
STAY CLOSE.
#@#$!!
FIRE IS FIRE.

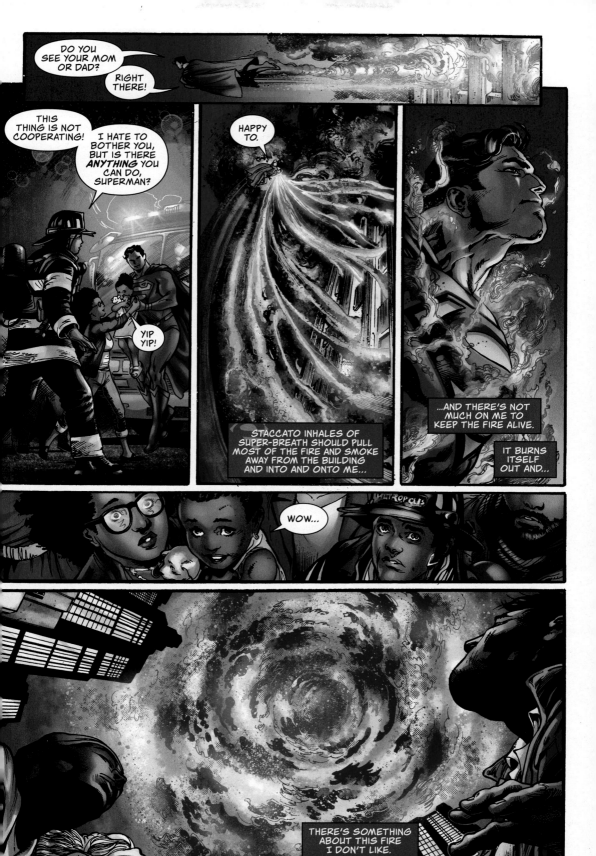

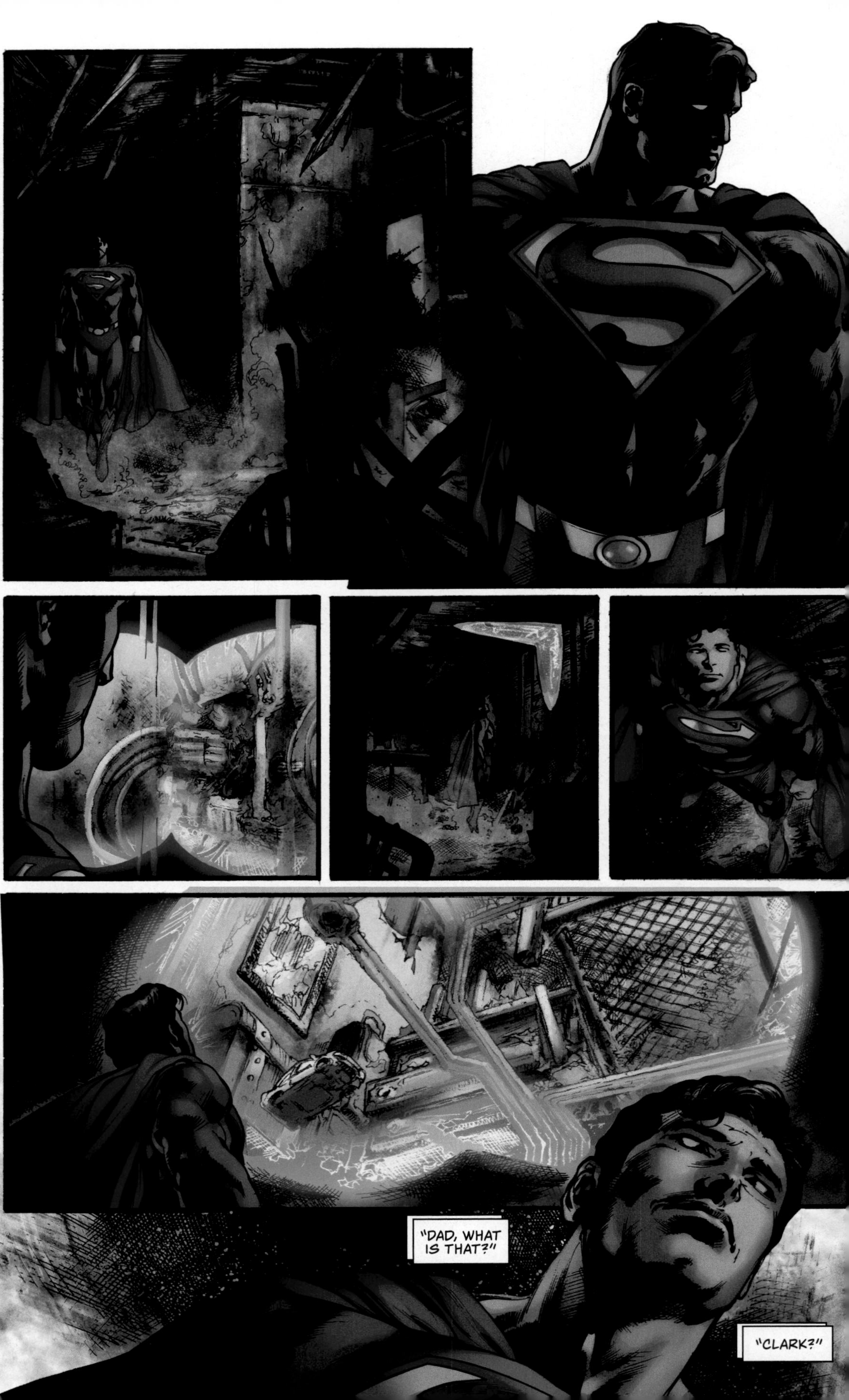
"DAD, WHAT IS THAT?"
"CLARK?"

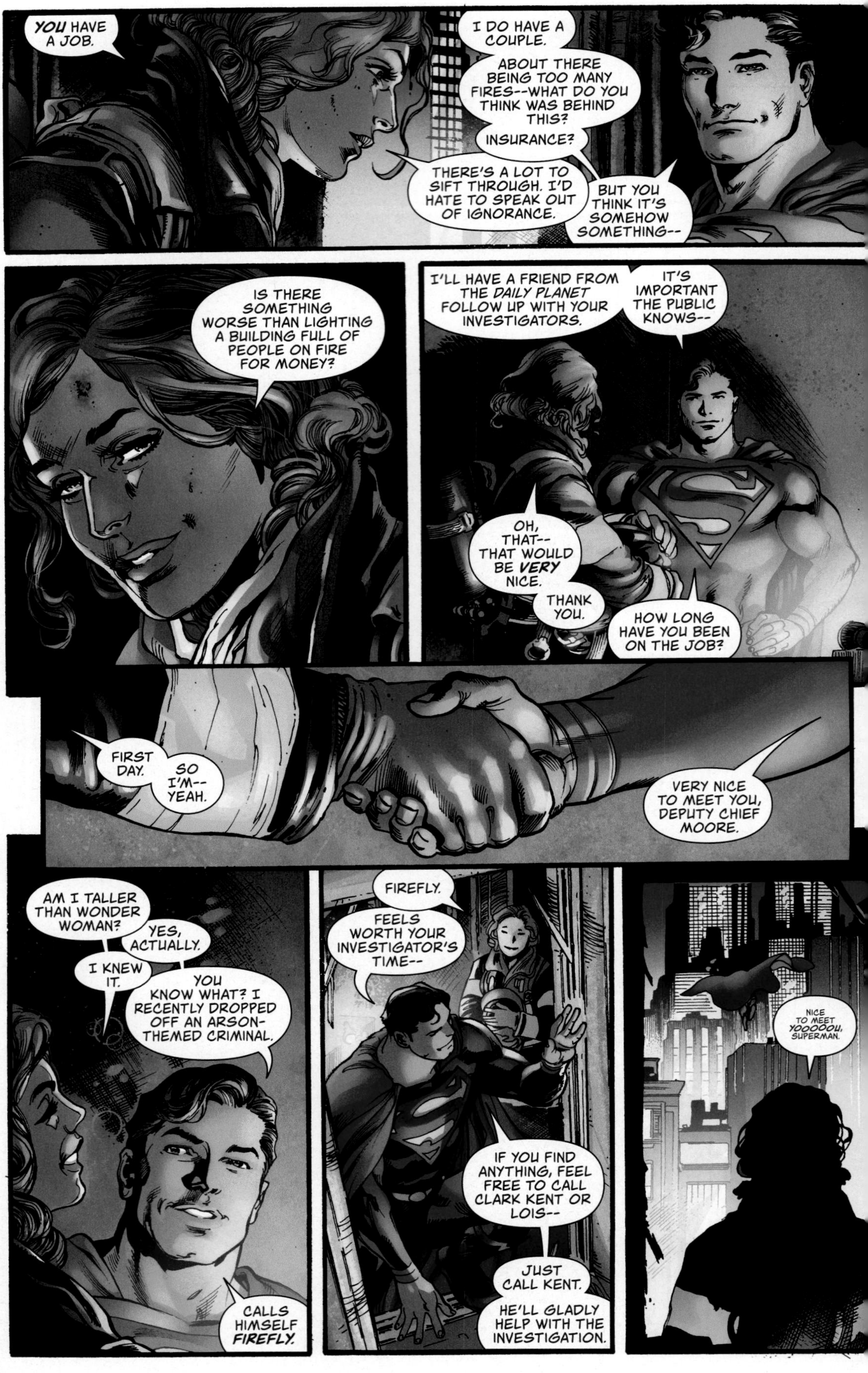
YOU HAVE A JOB.
I DO HAVE A COUPLE.
ABOUT THERE BEING TOO MANY FIRES--WHAT DO YOU THINK WAS BEHIND THIS?
INSURANCE?
THERE'S A LOT TO SIFT THROUGH. I'D HATE TO SPEAK OUT OF IGNORANCE.
BUT YOU THINK IT'S SOMEHOW SOMETHING--
IS THERE SOMETHING WORSE THAN LIGHTING A BUILDING FULL OF PEOPLE ON FIRE FOR MONEY?
I'LL HAVE A FRIEND FROM THE DAILY PLANET FOLLOW UP WITH YOUR INVESTIGATORS.
IT'S IMPORTANT THE PUBLIC KNOWS--
OH, THAT--THAT WOULD BE VERY NICE.
THANK YOU.
HOW LONG HAVE YOU BEEN ON THE JOB?
FIRST DAY.
SO I'M--YEAH.
VERY NICE TO MEET YOU, DEPUTY CHIEF MOORE.
AM I TALLER THAN WONDER WOMAN?
YES, ACTUALLY.
I KNEW IT.
YOU KNOW WHAT? I RECENTLY DROPPED OFF AN ARSON-THEMED CRIMINAL.
CALLS HIMSELF FIREFLY.
FIREFLY.
FEELS WORTH YOUR INVESTIGATOR'S TIME--
IF YOU FIND ANYTHING, FEEL FREE TO CALL CLARK KENT OR LOIS--
JUST CALL KENT.
HE'LL GLADLY HELP WITH THE INVESTIGATION.
NICE TO MEET YOOOOOU, SUPERMAN.

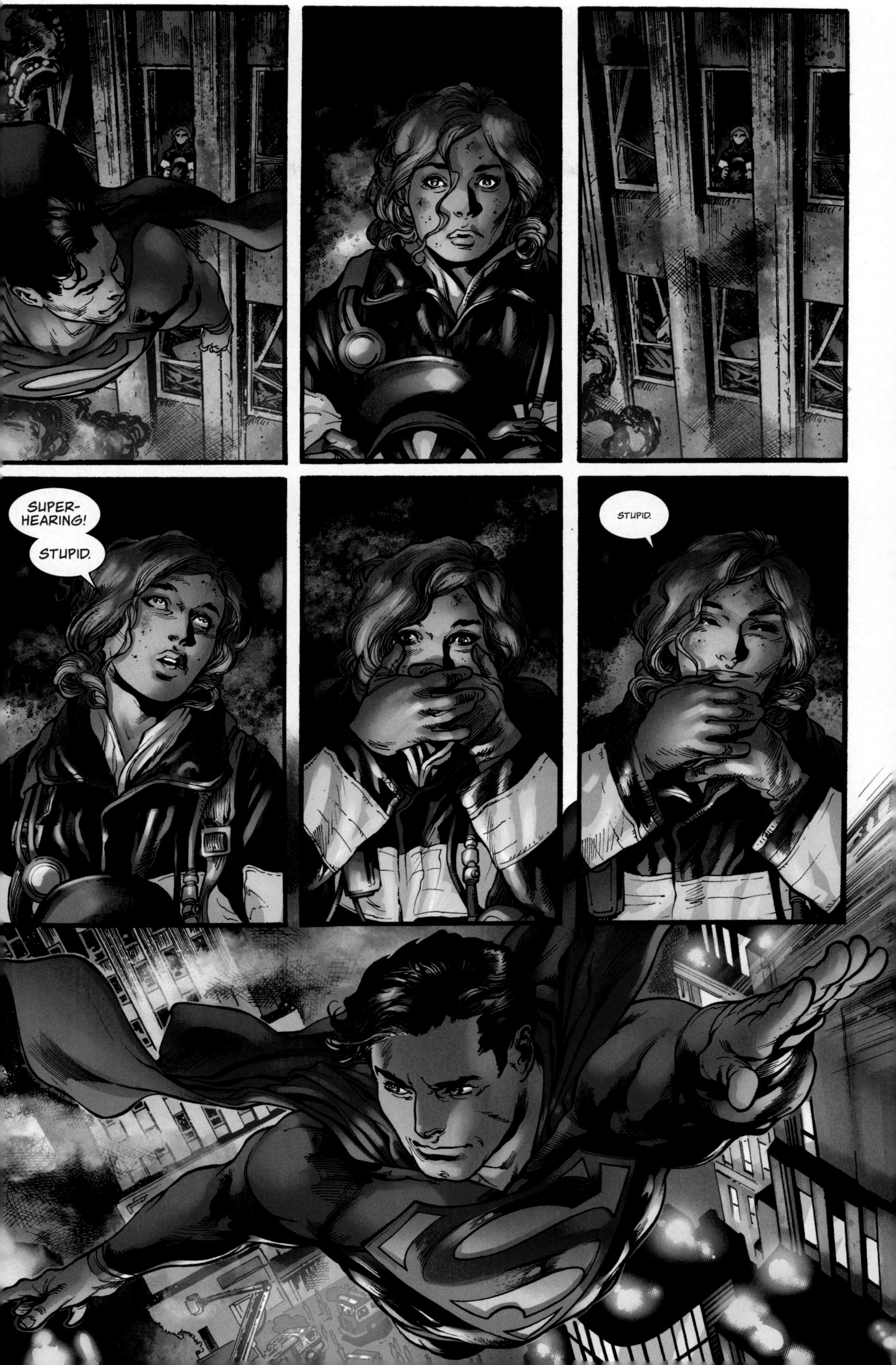
SUPER-HEARING!
STUPID.
STUPID.

THEN.
GNYAARGH!
GYAAAGGH!
CHUUNNKK
HUAAGHH!
YOU ARE MY FIRST VISITOR HERE...

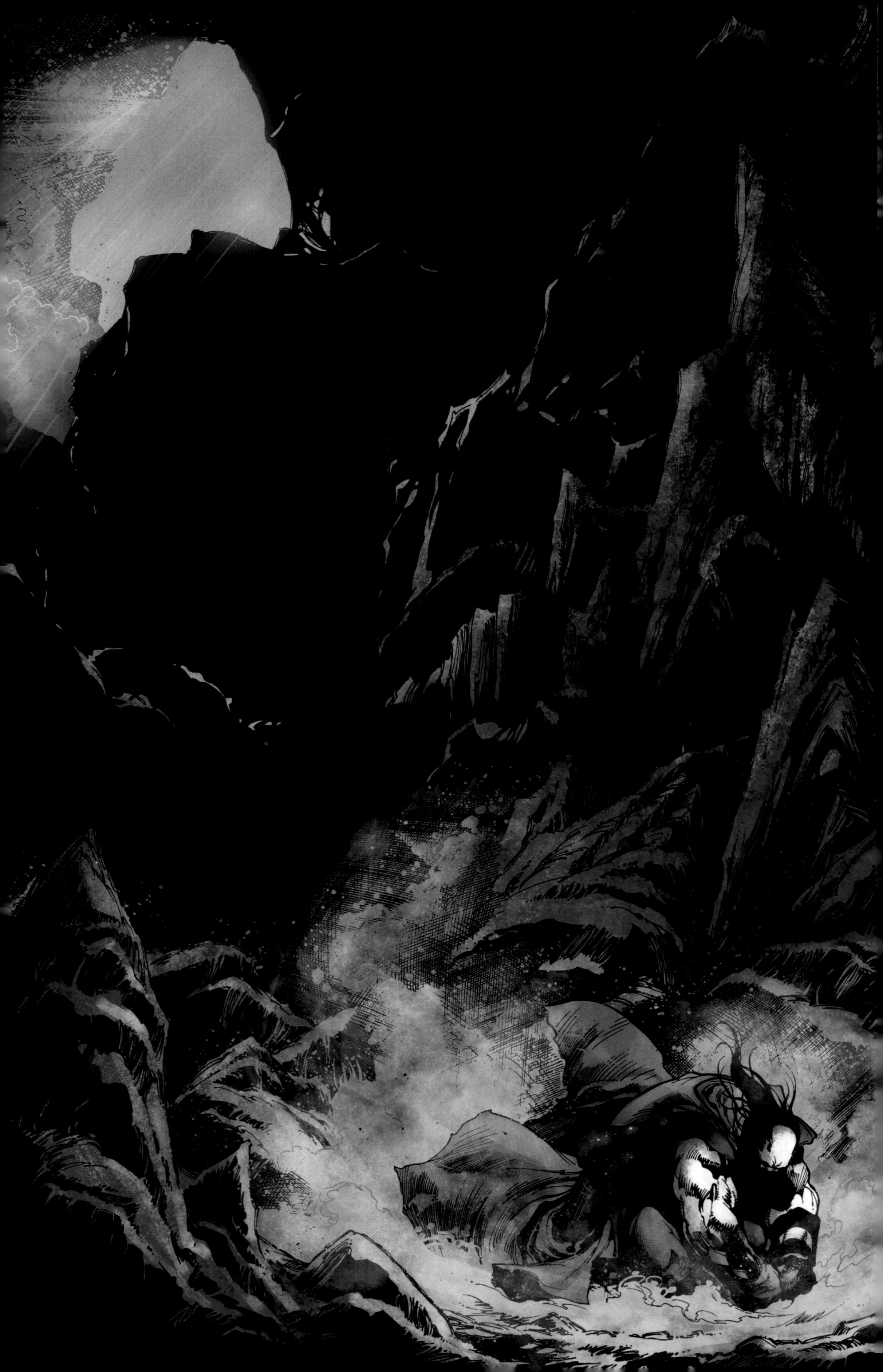

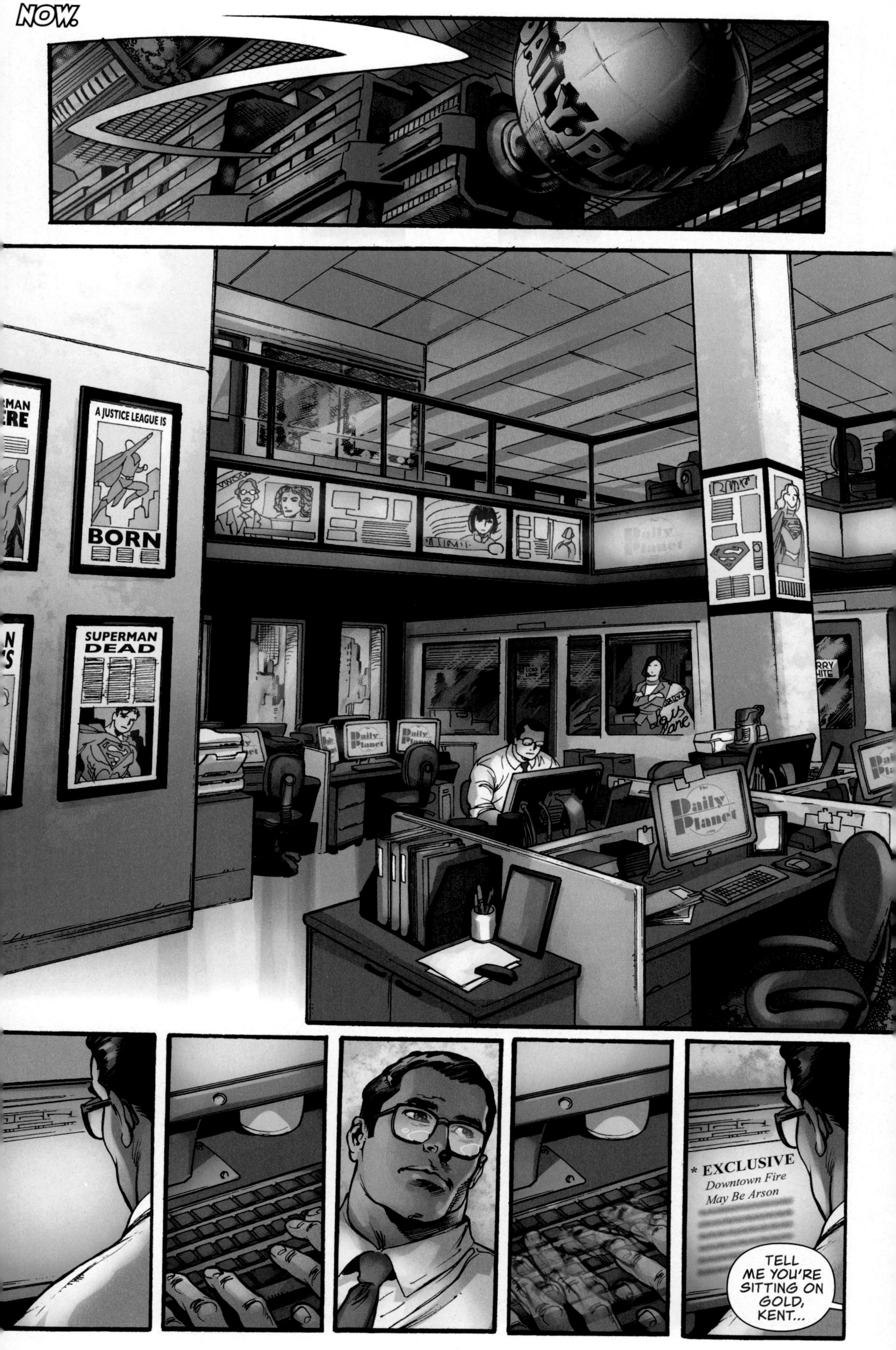
NOW.
A JUSTICE LEAGUE IS BORN
SUPERMAN DEAD
EXCLUSIVE
Downtown Fire May Be Arson
TELL ME YOU'RE SITTING ON GOLD, KENT...

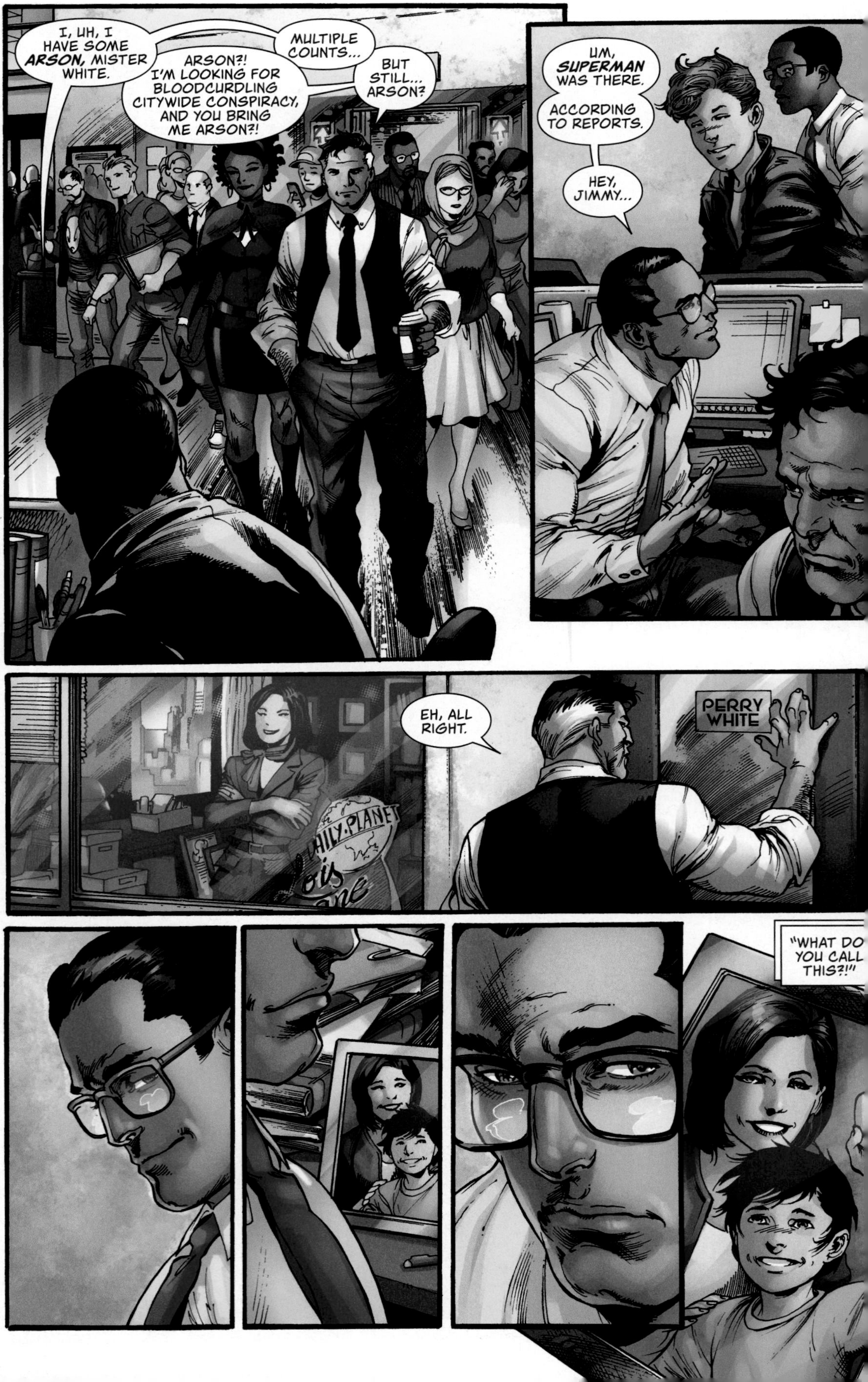
I, UH, I HAVE SOME ARSON, MISTER WHITE.
ARSON?! I'M LOOKING FOR BLOODCURDLING CITYWIDE CONSPIRACY, AND YOU BRING ME ARSON?!
MULTIPLE COUNTS...
BUT STILL... ARSON?
UM, SUPERMAN WAS THERE.
ACCORDING TO REPORTS.
HEY, JIMMY...
EH, ALL RIGHT.
PERRY WHITE
DAILY PLANET
Lois Lane
"WHAT DO YOU CALL THIS?!"

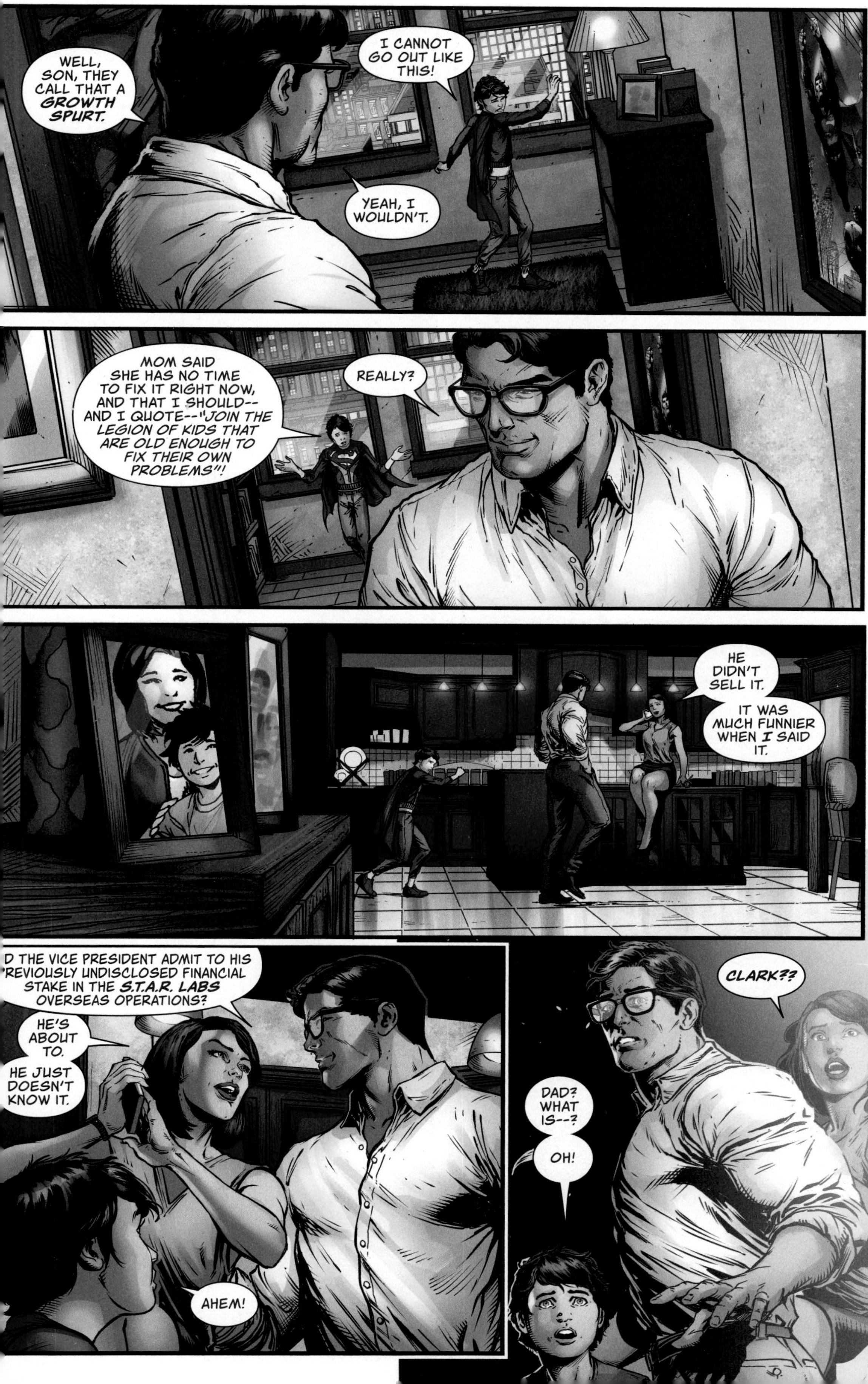
WELL, SON, THEY CALL THAT A GROWTH SPURT.
I CANNOT GO OUT LIKE THIS!
YEAH, I WOULDN'T.
MOM SAID SHE HAS NO TIME TO FIX IT RIGHT NOW, AND THAT I SHOULD-- AND I QUOTE--"JOIN THE LEGION OF KIDS THAT ARE OLD ENOUGH TO FIX THEIR OWN PROBLEMS"!
REALLY?
HE DIDN'T SELL IT.
IT WAS MUCH FUNNIER WHEN I SAID IT.
D THE VICE PRESIDENT ADMIT TO HIS 'REVIOUSLY UNDISCLOSED FINANCIAL STAKE IN THE S.T.A.R. LABS OVERSEAS OPERATIONS?
HE'S ABOUT TO.
HE JUST DOESN'T KNOW IT.
AHEM!
CLARK??
DAD? WHAT IS--?
OH!

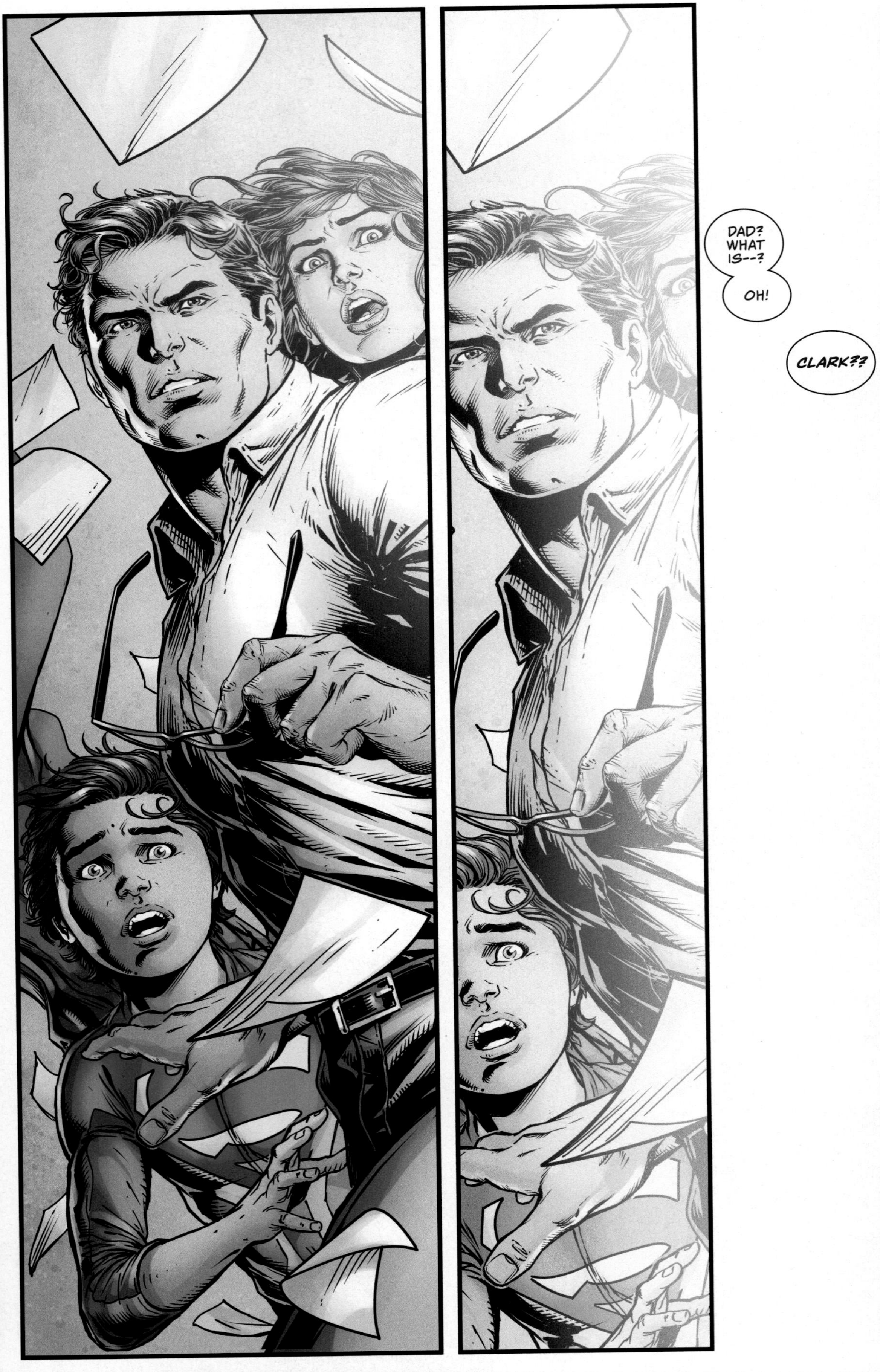
DAD? WHAT IS--?
OH!
CLARK??

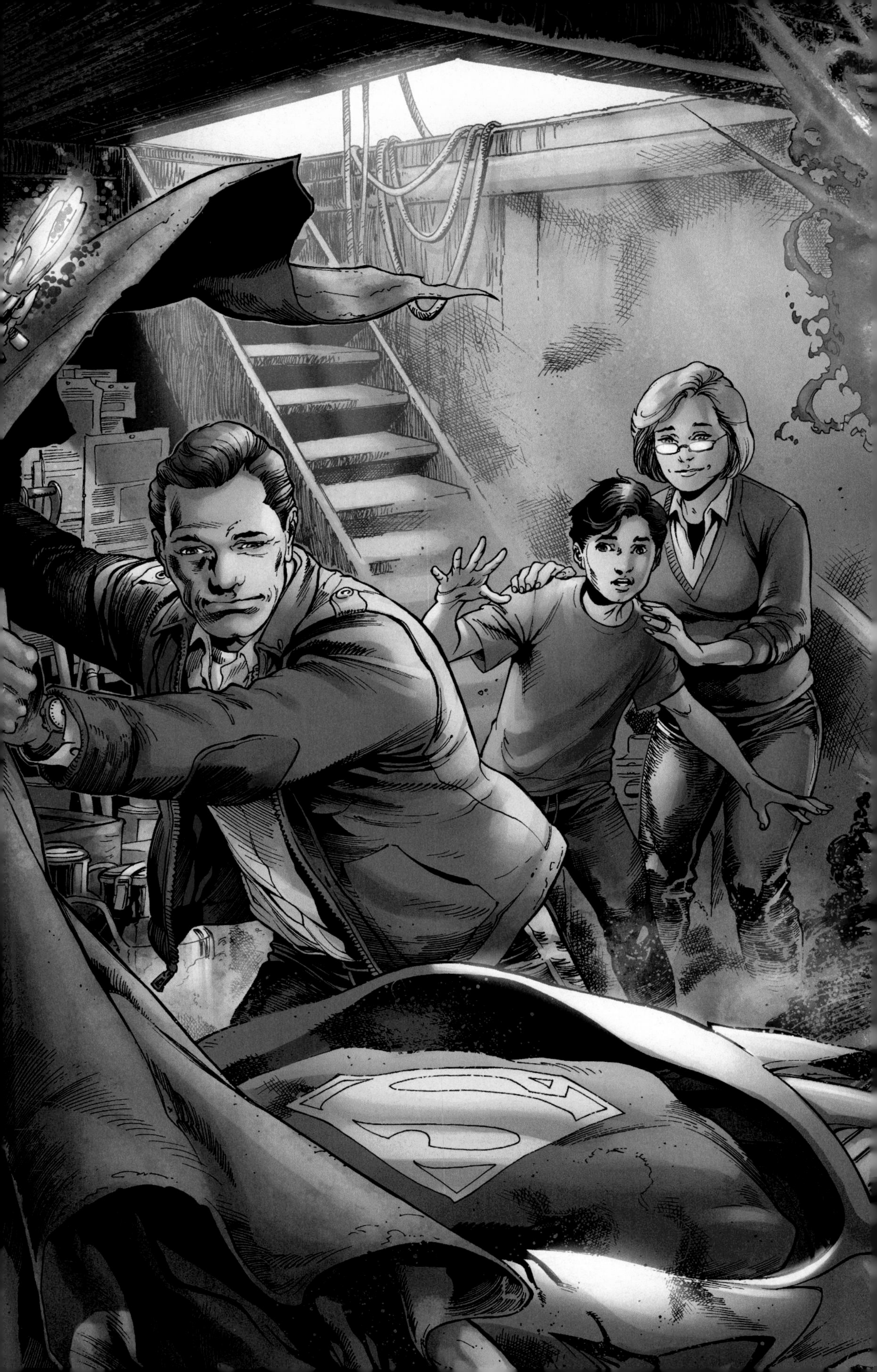

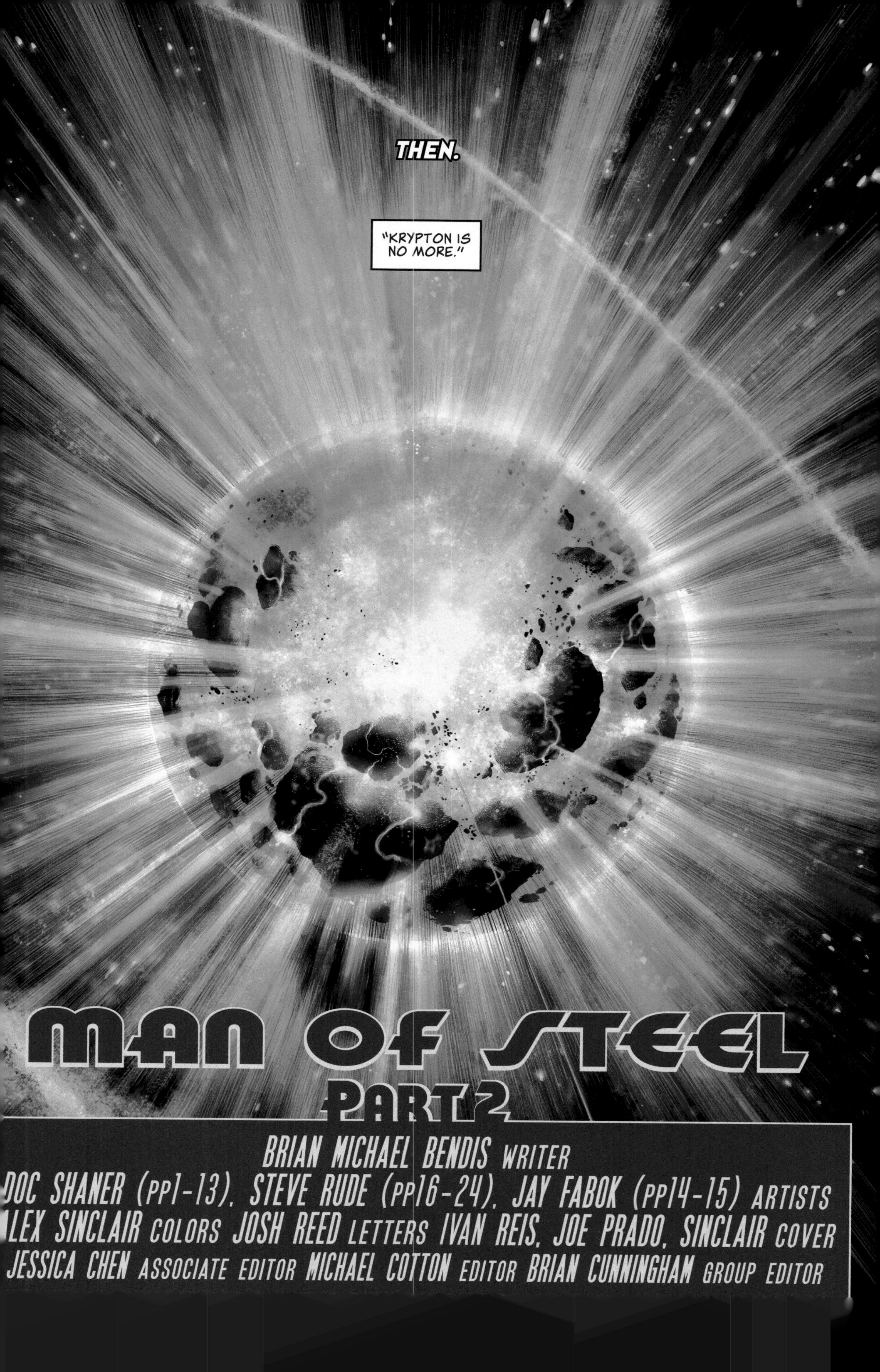
THEN.
"KRYPTON IS NO MORE."
MAN OF STEEL
PART 2
BRIAN MICHAEL BENDIS WRITER
DOC SHANER (PP1-13), STEVE RUDE (PP16-24), JAY FABOK (PP14-15) ARTISTS
ALEX SINCLAIR COLORS JOSH REED LETTERS IVAN REIS, JOE PRADO, SINCLAIR COVER
JESSICA CHEN ASSOCIATE EDITOR MICHAEL COTTON EDITOR BRIAN CUNNINGHAM GROUP EDITOR

I AM AWARE.

YOU'RE GOING TO FLOAT THERE AND PRETEND YOU HAD *NOTHING* TO DO WITH IT?

I *HAD* NOTHING TO DO WITH IT.

YOU KNEW *NOTHING* ABOUT THIS?

I *STILL* DON'T, LORD GANDELO.

FROM WHAT THE GUARDIANS' INVESTIGATION COULD GATHER, IT WAS AN UNSTABLE PLANET.

IT HAPPENS.

IT *HAPPENS??*

WHEN DOES IT *HAPPEN?!*

I RULE OVER 42 STAR SYSTEMS, APPA ALI APSA, AND TO MY KNOWLEDGE, *IT NEVER HAPPENS.*

IT *JUST* HAPPENED.

WHERE WAS THE *GREEN LANTERN* OF THAT SECTOR?

IT'S A BIG SECTOR. *I'M* NOT SURE THERE WAS SUFFICIENT WARNING--

YOU, APPA ALI APSA, ARE IN *CHARGE* OF THE GREEN LANTERN-- WHERE *WAS* THE GREEN LANTERN?

WHERE *WAS* IT?

ROGOL ZAAR COMES TO US WITH THE *GROTESQUE* IDEA TO "CLEANSE" KRYPTON...

HE ASKS PERMISSION. WE *UNANIMOUSLY* VOTE NO.

YOU GO TELL HIM...

...AND NOW KRYPTON, SUDDENLY, IS *NO MORE.*

I WILL NOT ENTERTAIN THIS ONE MOMENT--

WE'LL SEE WHAT KING MYAND'R OR SARDATH THINKS OF THIS.

ACTUALLY, IF WHAT YOU SAY IS TRUE...

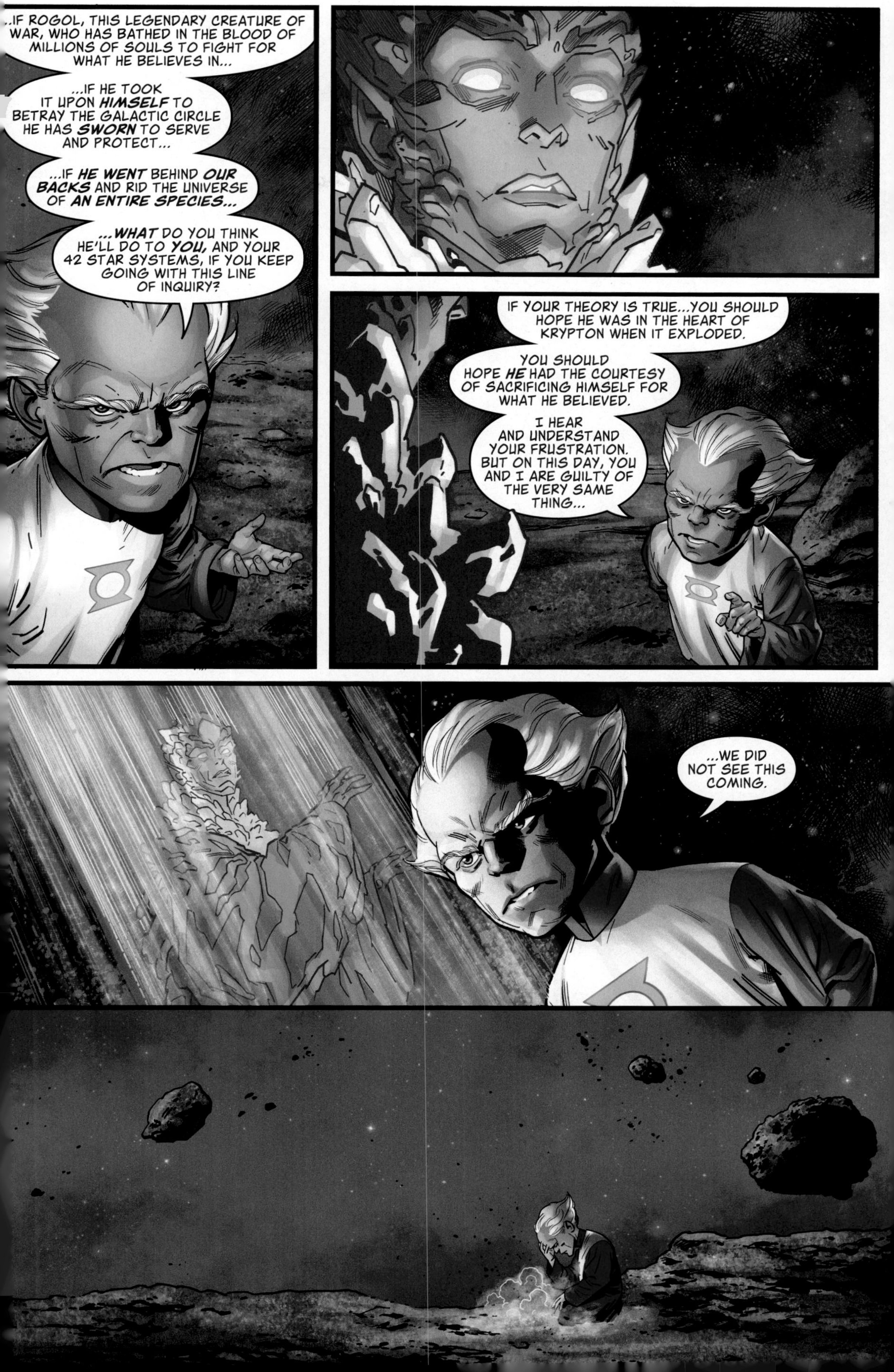
...IF ROGOL, THIS LEGENDARY CREATURE OF WAR, WHO HAS BATHED IN THE BLOOD OF MILLIONS OF SOULS TO FIGHT FOR WHAT HE BELIEVES IN...
...IF HE TOOK IT UPON HIMSELF TO BETRAY THE GALACTIC CIRCLE HE HAS SWORN TO SERVE AND PROTECT...
...IF HE WENT BEHIND OUR BACKS AND RID THE UNIVERSE OF AN ENTIRE SPECIES...
...WHAT DO YOU THINK HE'LL DO TO YOU, AND YOUR 42 STAR SYSTEMS, IF YOU KEEP GOING WITH THIS LINE OF INQUIRY?
IF YOUR THEORY IS TRUE...YOU SHOULD HOPE HE WAS IN THE HEART OF KRYPTON WHEN IT EXPLODED.
YOU SHOULD HOPE HE HAD THE COURTESY OF SACRIFICING HIMSELF FOR WHAT HE BELIEVED.
I HEAR AND UNDERSTAND YOUR FRUSTRATION. BUT ON THIS DAY, YOU AND I ARE GUILTY OF THE VERY SAME THING...
...WE DID NOT SEE THIS COMING.

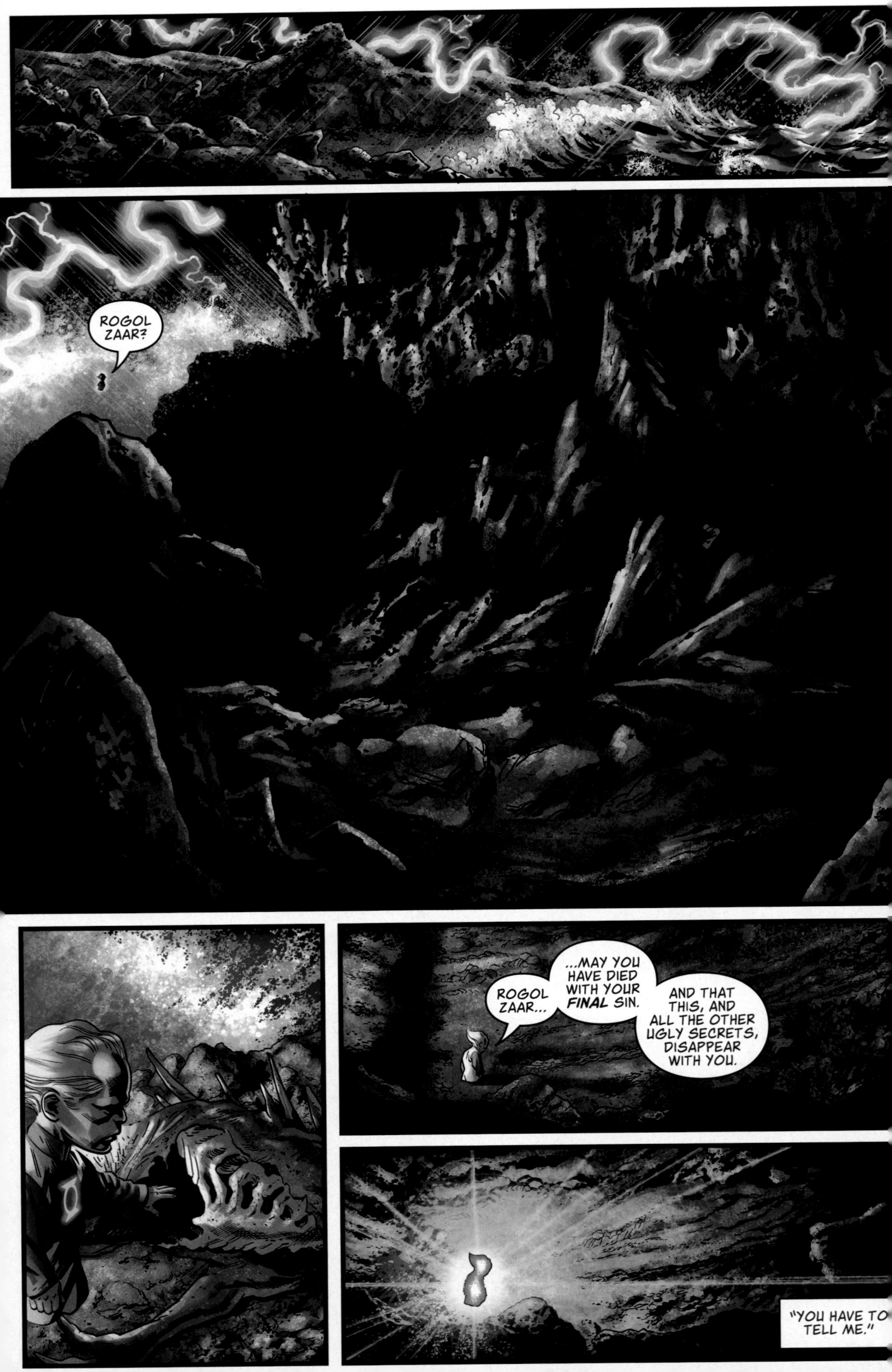
ROGOL ZAAR?
ROGOL ZAAR...
...MAY YOU HAVE DIED WITH YOUR FINAL SIN.
AND THAT THIS, AND ALL THE OTHER UGLY SECRETS, DISAPPEAR WITH YOU.
"YOU HAVE TO TELL ME."

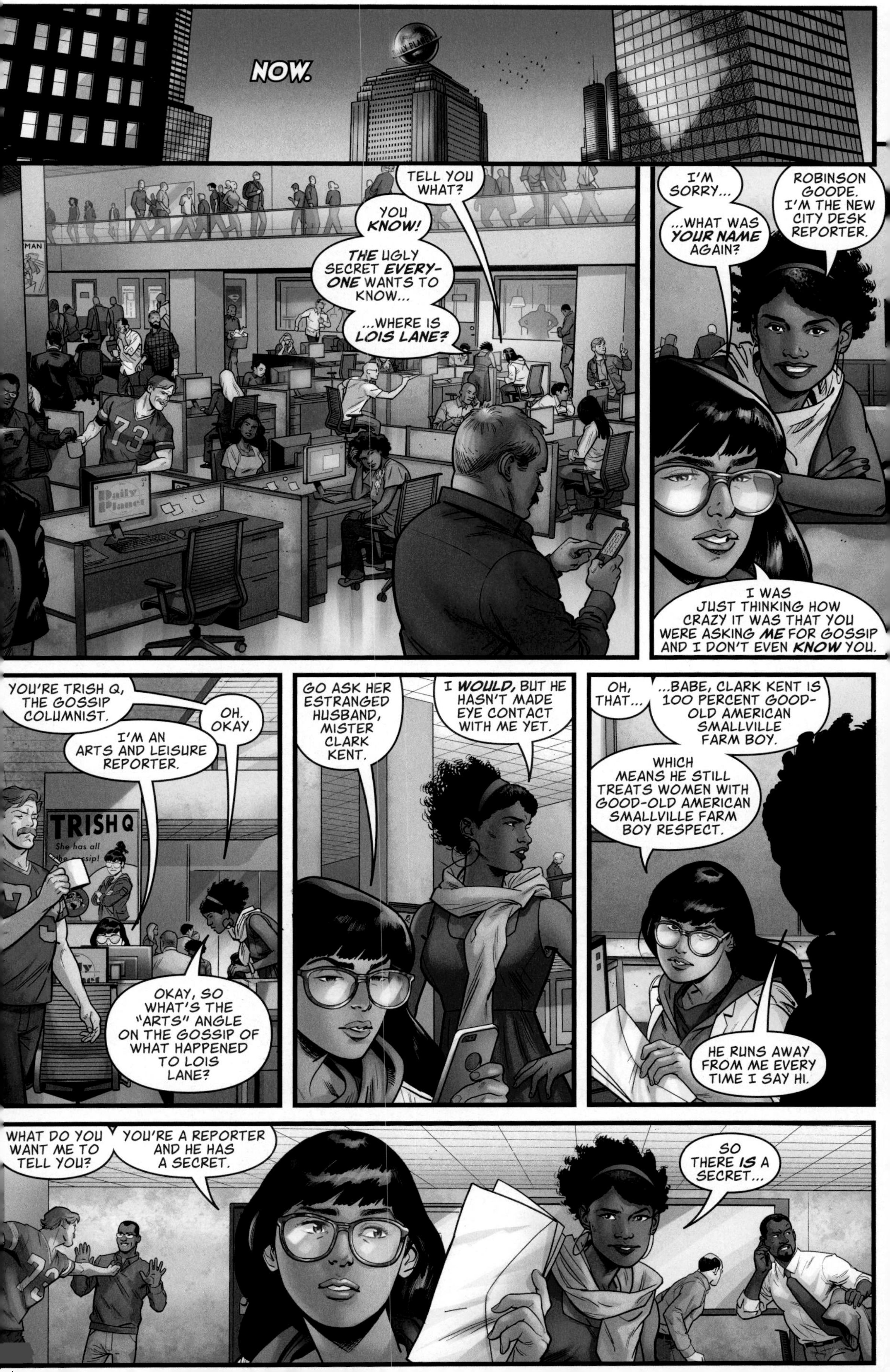
NOW.
TELL YOU WHAT?
YOU KNOW!
THE UGLY SECRET EVERY-ONE WANTS TO KNOW...
...WHERE IS LOIS LANE?
MAN
Daily Planet
I'M SORRY...
...WHAT WAS YOUR NAME AGAIN?
ROBINSON GOODE. I'M THE NEW CITY DESK REPORTER.
I WAS JUST THINKING HOW CRAZY IT WAS THAT YOU WERE ASKING ME FOR GOSSIP AND I DON'T EVEN KNOW YOU.
YOU'RE TRISH Q, THE GOSSIP COLUMNIST.
OH. OKAY.
I'M AN ARTS AND LEISURE REPORTER.
TRISH Q
OKAY, SO WHAT'S THE "ARTS" ANGLE ON THE GOSSIP OF WHAT HAPPENED TO LOIS LANE?
GO ASK HER ESTRANGED HUSBAND, MISTER CLARK KENT.
I WOULD, BUT HE HASN'T MADE EYE CONTACT WITH ME YET.
OH, THAT...
...BABE, CLARK KENT IS 100 PERCENT GOOD-OLD AMERICAN SMALLVILLE FARM BOY.
WHICH MEANS HE STILL TREATS WOMEN WITH GOOD-OLD AMERICAN SMALLVILLE FARM BOY RESPECT.
HE RUNS AWAY FROM ME EVERY TIME I SAY HI.
WHAT DO YOU WANT ME TO TELL YOU?
YOU'RE A REPORTER AND HE HAS A SECRET.
SO THERE IS A SECRET...

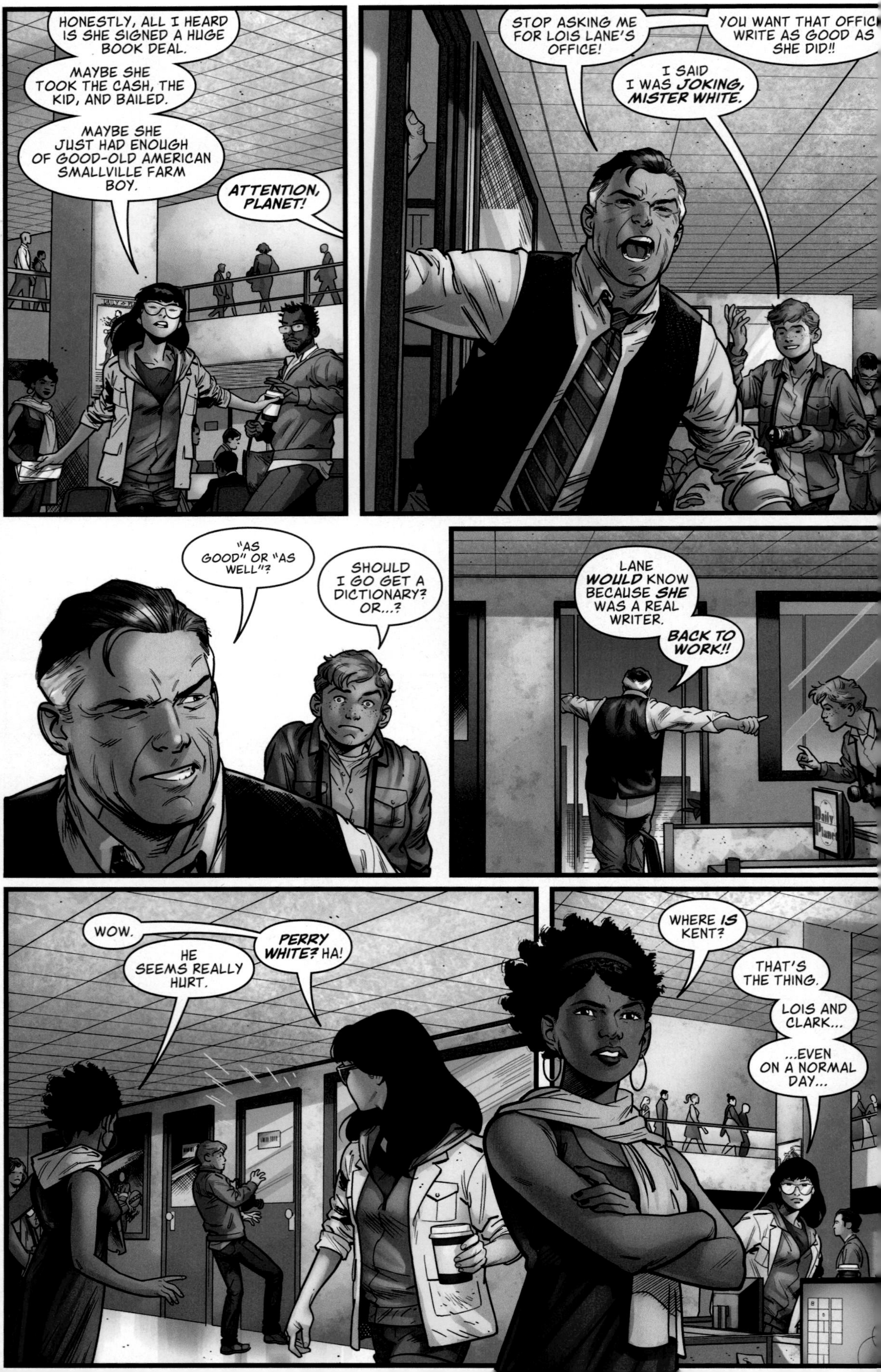
HONESTLY, ALL I HEARD IS SHE SIGNED A HUGE BOOK DEAL.
MAYBE SHE TOOK THE CASH, THE KID, AND BAILED.
MAYBE SHE JUST HAD ENOUGH OF GOOD-OLD AMERICAN SMALLVILLE FARM BOY.
ATTENTION, PLANET!
STOP ASKING ME FOR LOIS LANE'S OFFICE!
YOU WANT THAT OFFIC WRITE AS GOOD AS SHE DID!!
I SAID I WAS JOKING, MISTER WHITE.
"AS GOOD" OR "AS WELL"?
SHOULD I GO GET A DICTIONARY? OR...?
LANE WOULD KNOW BECAUSE SHE WAS A REAL WRITER.
BACK TO WORK!!
WOW.
PERRY WHITE? HA!
HE SEEMS REALLY HURT.
WHERE IS KENT?
THAT'S THE THING.
LOIS AND CLARK...
...EVEN ON A NORMAL DAY...

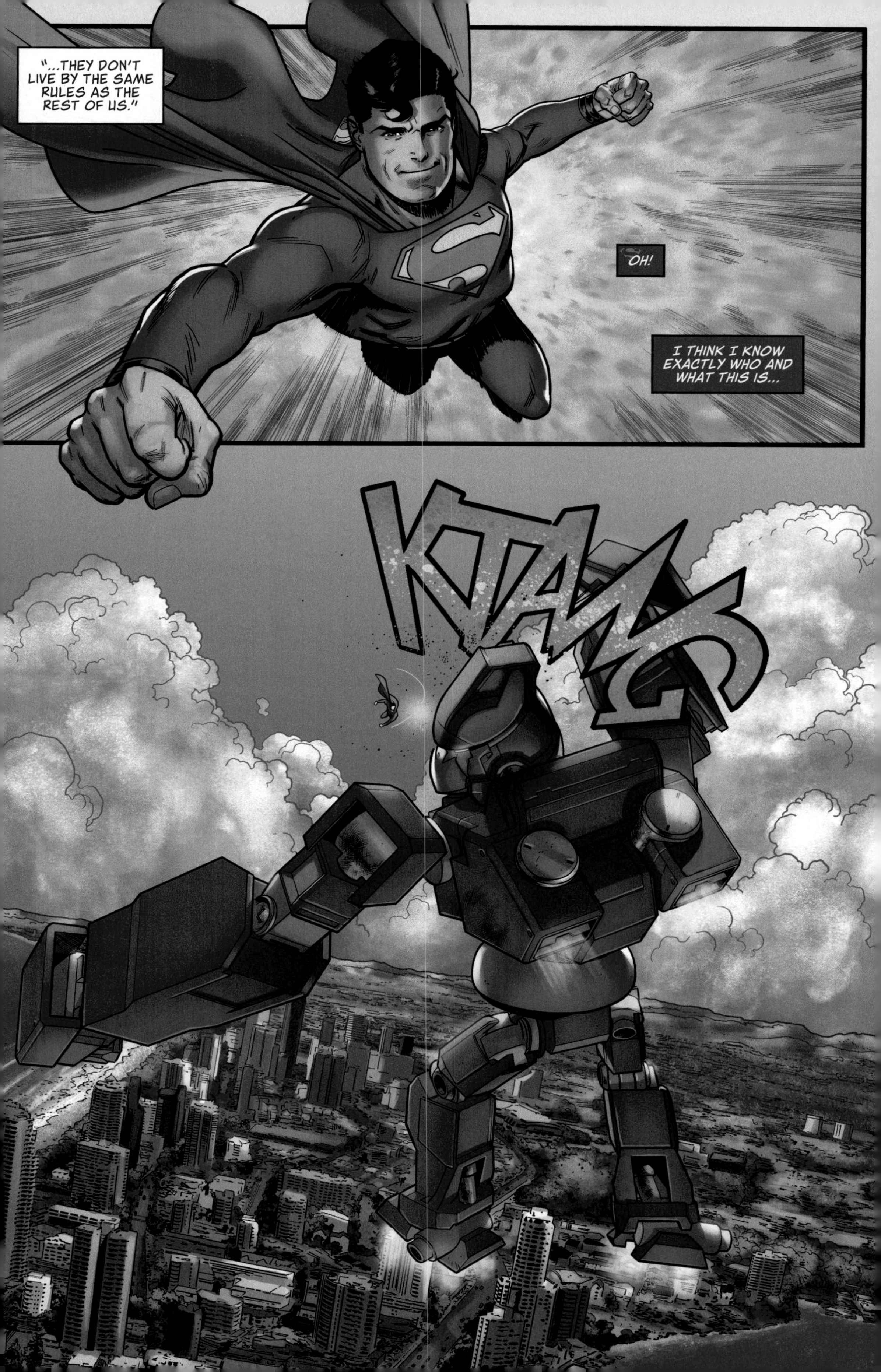
"...THEY DON'T LIVE BY THE SAME RULES AS THE REST OF US."
OH!
I THINK I KNOW EXACTLY WHO AND WHAT THIS IS...
KTANG

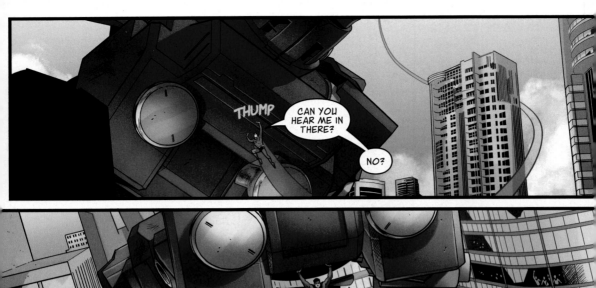

THUMP

CAN YOU HEAR ME IN THERE?

NO?

IT'S OKAY, I CAN WAIT.

NOT SURE WHY HE'S ALL THE WAY OUT HERE IN COAST CITY.

FUMPP

I JUST HAPPENED TO BE FLYING BACK FROM THE ALASKAN TSUNAMI OR I WOULD HAVE MISSED THIS...

SUPERMAN!

NOT FAIR!

ZZATTTT

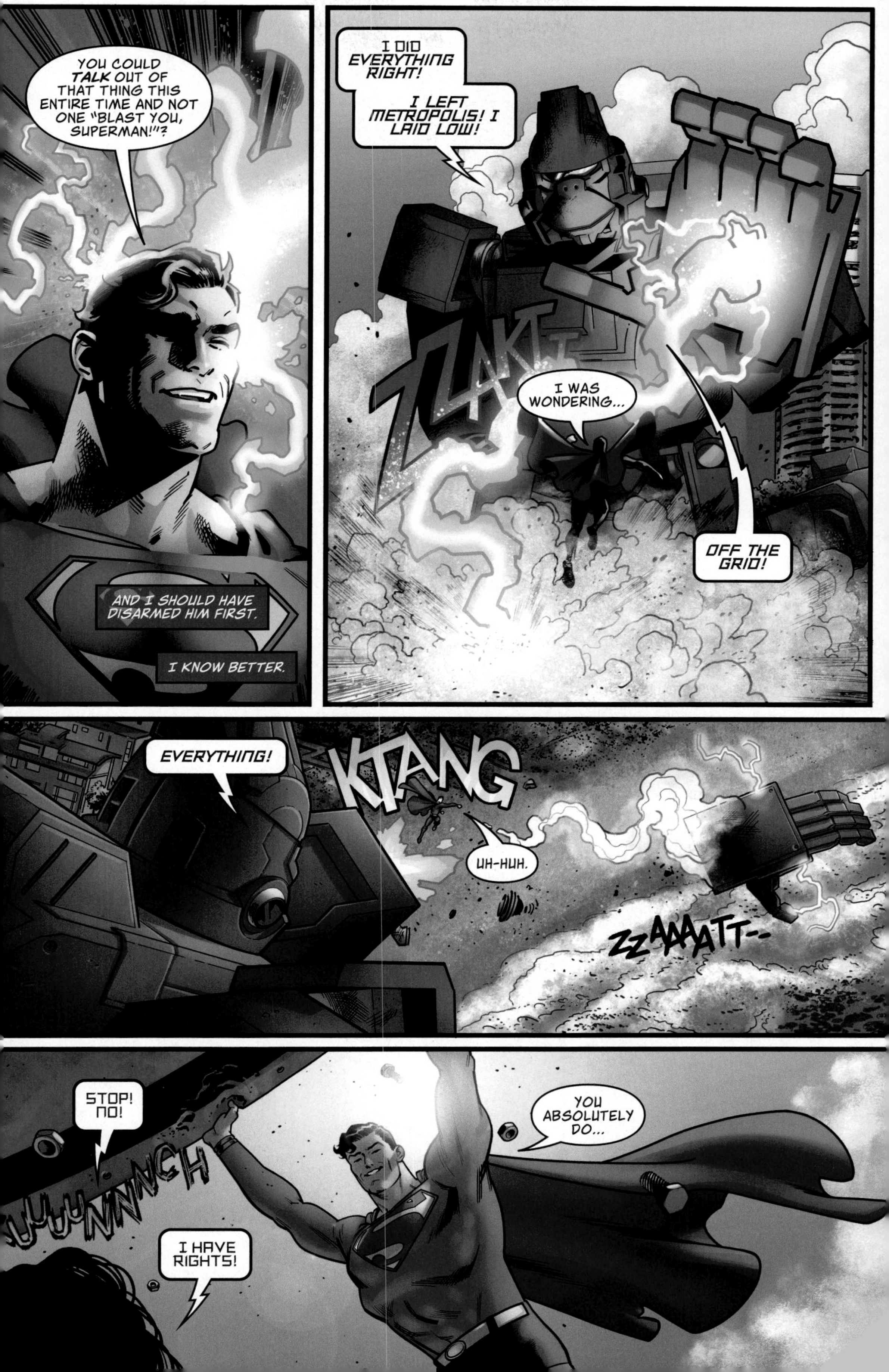
YOU COULD TALK OUT OF THAT THING THIS ENTIRE TIME AND NOT ONE "BLAST YOU, SUPERMAN!"?
AND I SHOULD HAVE DISARMED HIM FIRST.
I KNOW BETTER.
I DID EVERYTHING RIGHT!
I LEFT METROPOLIS! I LAID LOW!
ZZAKT
I WAS WONDERING...
OFF THE GRID!
EVERYTHING!
KTANG
UH-HUH.
ZZAAAATT--
STOP! NO!
YOU ABSOLUTELY DO...
SUUUNNNCH
I HAVE RIGHTS!

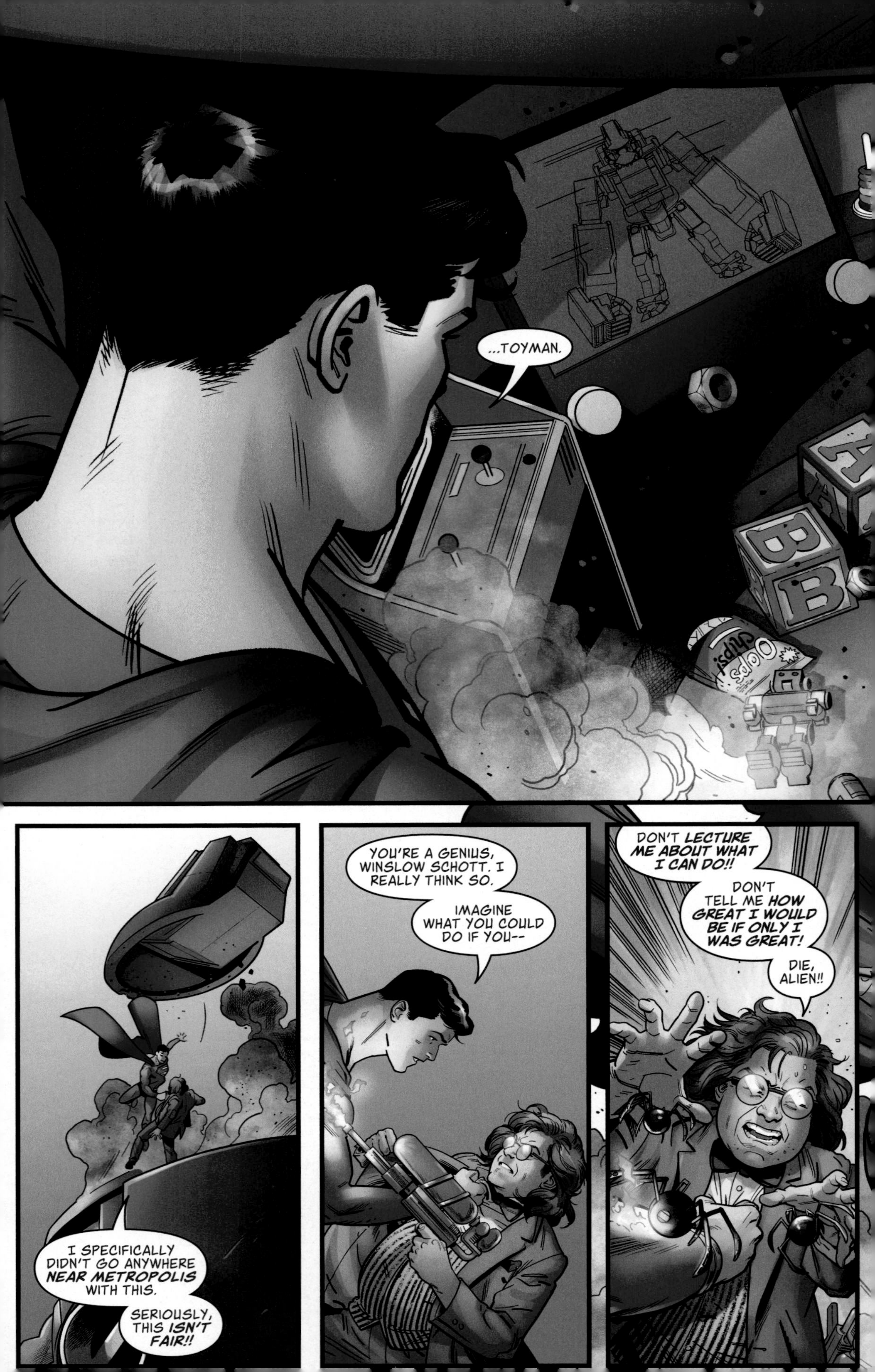
...TOYMAN.
Chips
I SPECIFICALLY DIDN'T GO ANYWHERE NEAR METROPOLIS WITH THIS.
SERIOUSLY, THIS ISN'T FAIR!!
YOU'RE A GENIUS, WINSLOW SCHOTT. I REALLY THINK SO.
IMAGINE WHAT YOU COULD DO IF YOU--
DON'T LECTURE ME ABOUT WHAT I CAN DO!!
DON'T TELL ME HOW GREAT I WOULD BE IF ONLY I WAS GREAT!
DIE, ALIEN!!

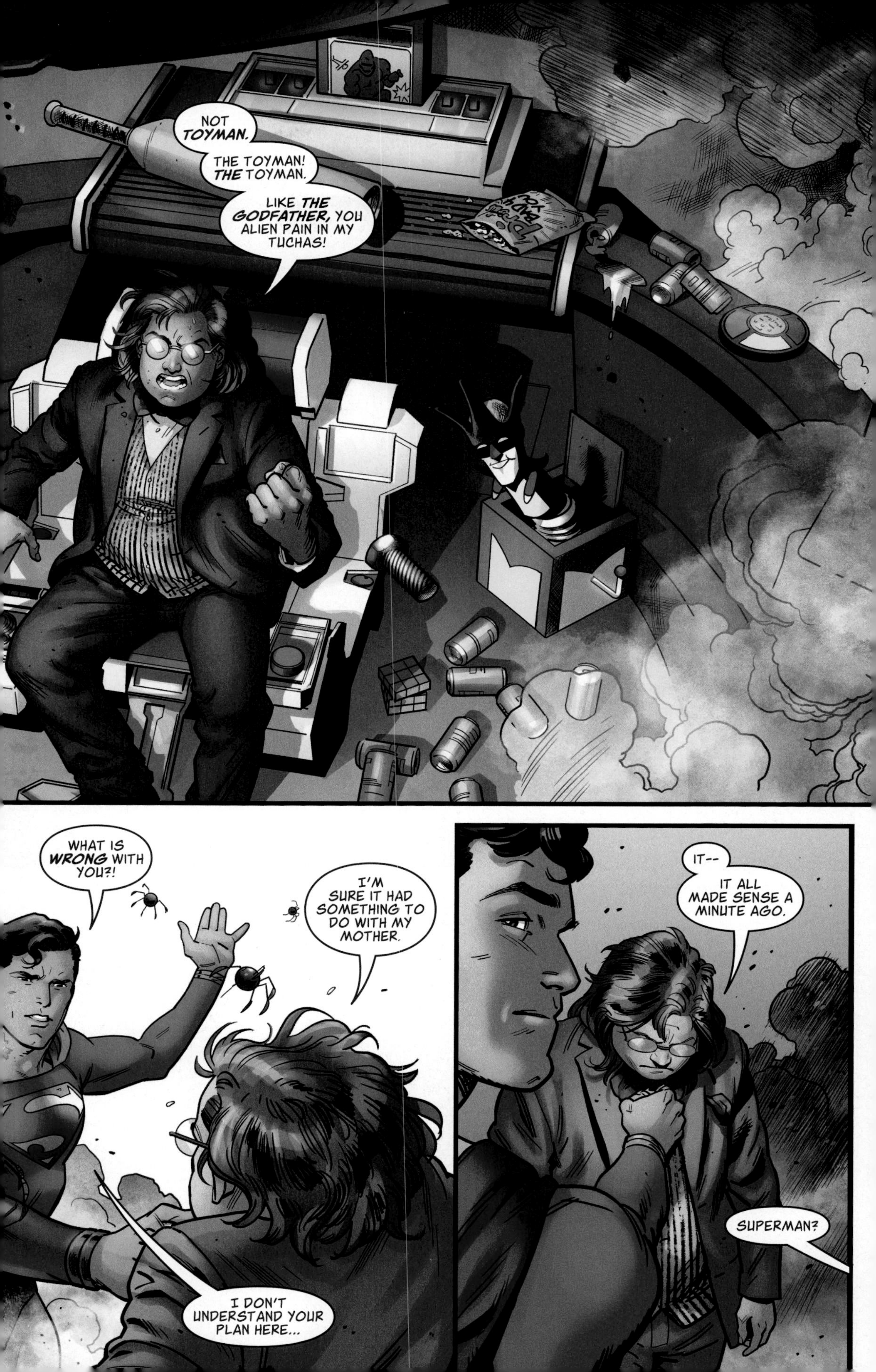

NOT TOYMAN.
THE TOYMAN! THE TOYMAN.
LIKE THE GODFATHER, YOU ALIEN PAIN IN MY TUCHAS!
WHAT IS WRONG WITH YOU?!
I'M SURE IT HAD SOMETHING TO DO WITH MY MOTHER.
I DON'T UNDERSTAND YOUR PLAN HERE...
IT--
IT ALL MADE SENSE A MINUTE AGO.
SUPERMAN?

REALLY GOOD TO SEE YOU, **GREEN LANTERN**

I CALLED YOU TO HAVE DINNER LAST WEEK, I DIDN'T HEAR BACK.

SEE? I SHOULD HAVE MADE A GIANT ROBOT ATTACK SOMETHING, *THEN* YOU'D SHOW RIGHT UP.

UGH!! ANOTHER PUPPET!

YOU COULD MAKE SO MANY PEOPLE SO HAPPY, SO MANY--

YOU CAN'T EVEN SEE THAT THE ENTIRE THING IS A SICK AND TWISTED GAME.

THE *ENTIRE* THING!! PUPPET!!

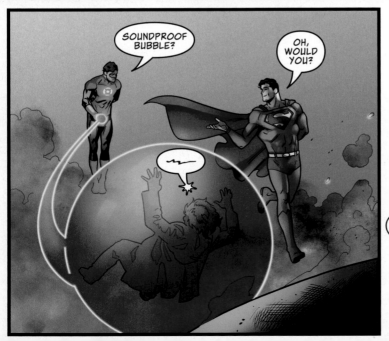

SOUNDPROOF BUBBLE?

OH, WOULD YOU?

~~~

HEY, WHAT'S BEEN HAPPENING WITH YOU?

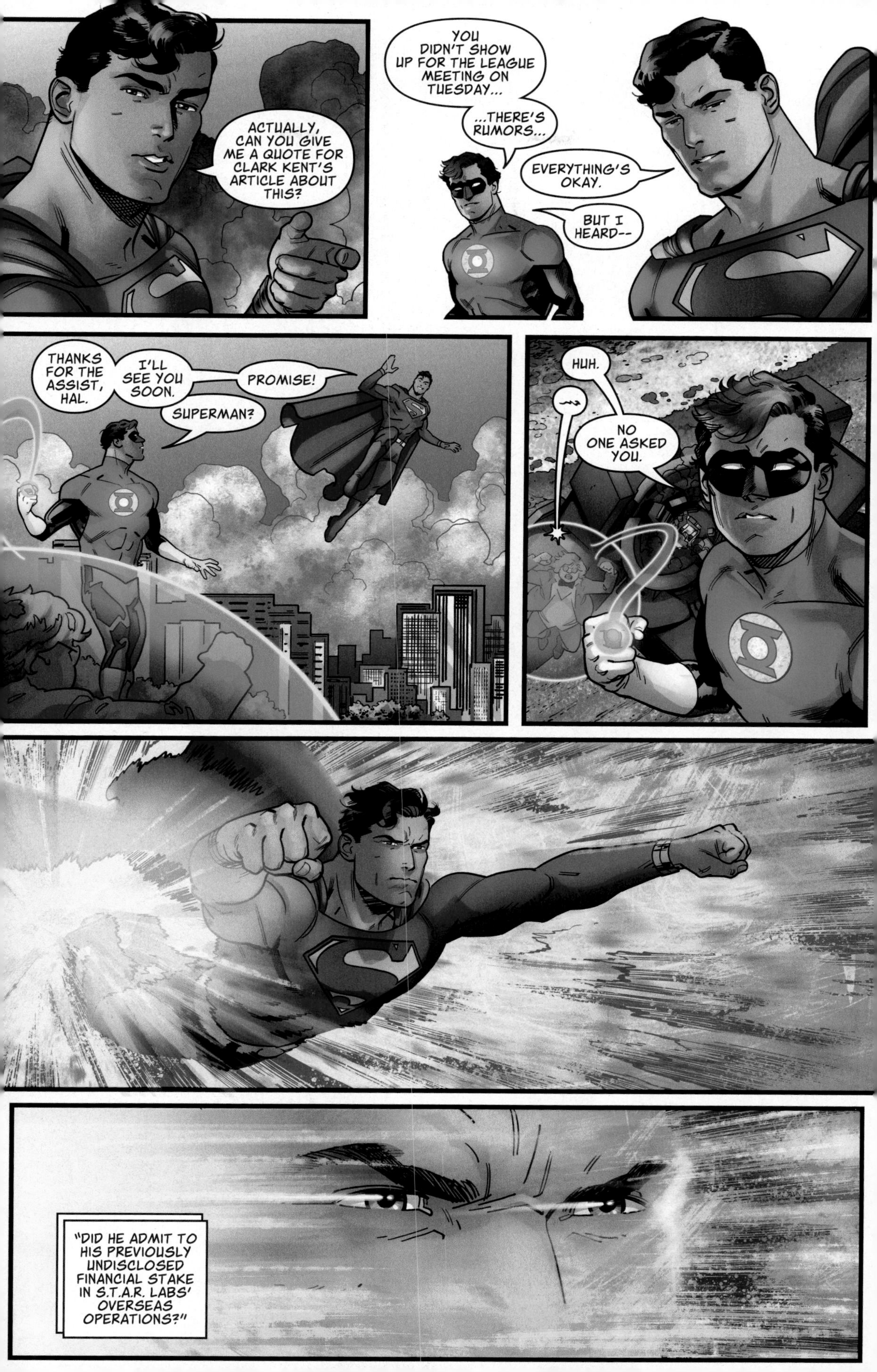
ACTUALLY, CAN YOU GIVE ME A QUOTE FOR CLARK KENT'S ARTICLE ABOUT THIS?
YOU DIDN'T SHOW UP FOR THE LEAGUE MEETING ON TUESDAY...
...THERE'S RUMORS...
EVERYTHING'S OKAY.
BUT I HEARD--
THANKS FOR THE ASSIST, HAL.
I'LL SEE YOU SOON.
PROMISE!
SUPERMAN?
HUH.
NO ONE ASKED YOU.
"DID HE ADMIT TO HIS PREVIOUSLY UNDISCLOSED FINANCIAL STAKE IN S.T.A.R. LABS' OVERSEAS OPERATIONS?"

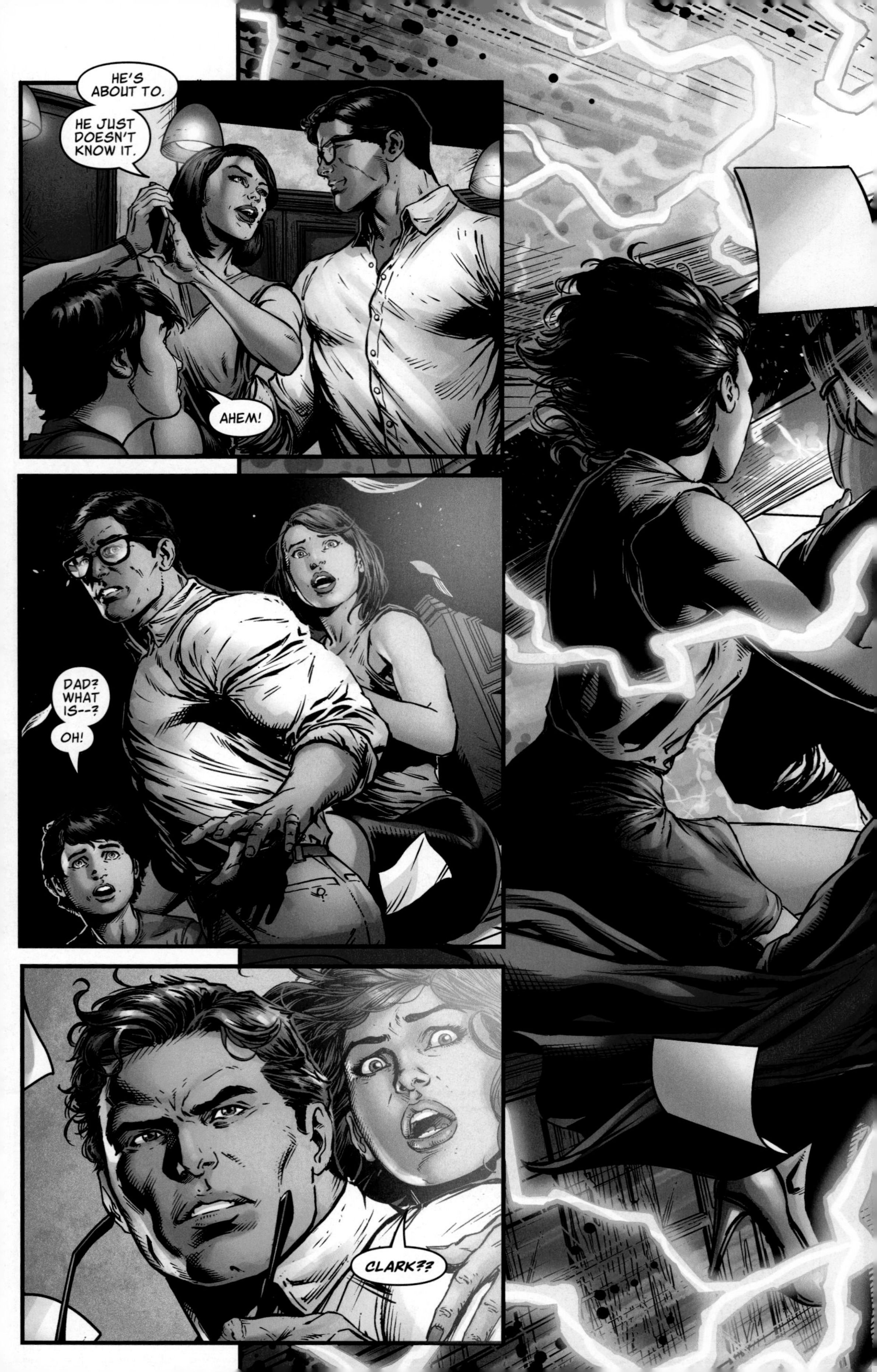
HE'S ABOUT TO.
HE JUST DOESN'T KNOW IT.
AHEM!
DAD? WHAT IS--?
OH!
CLARK??

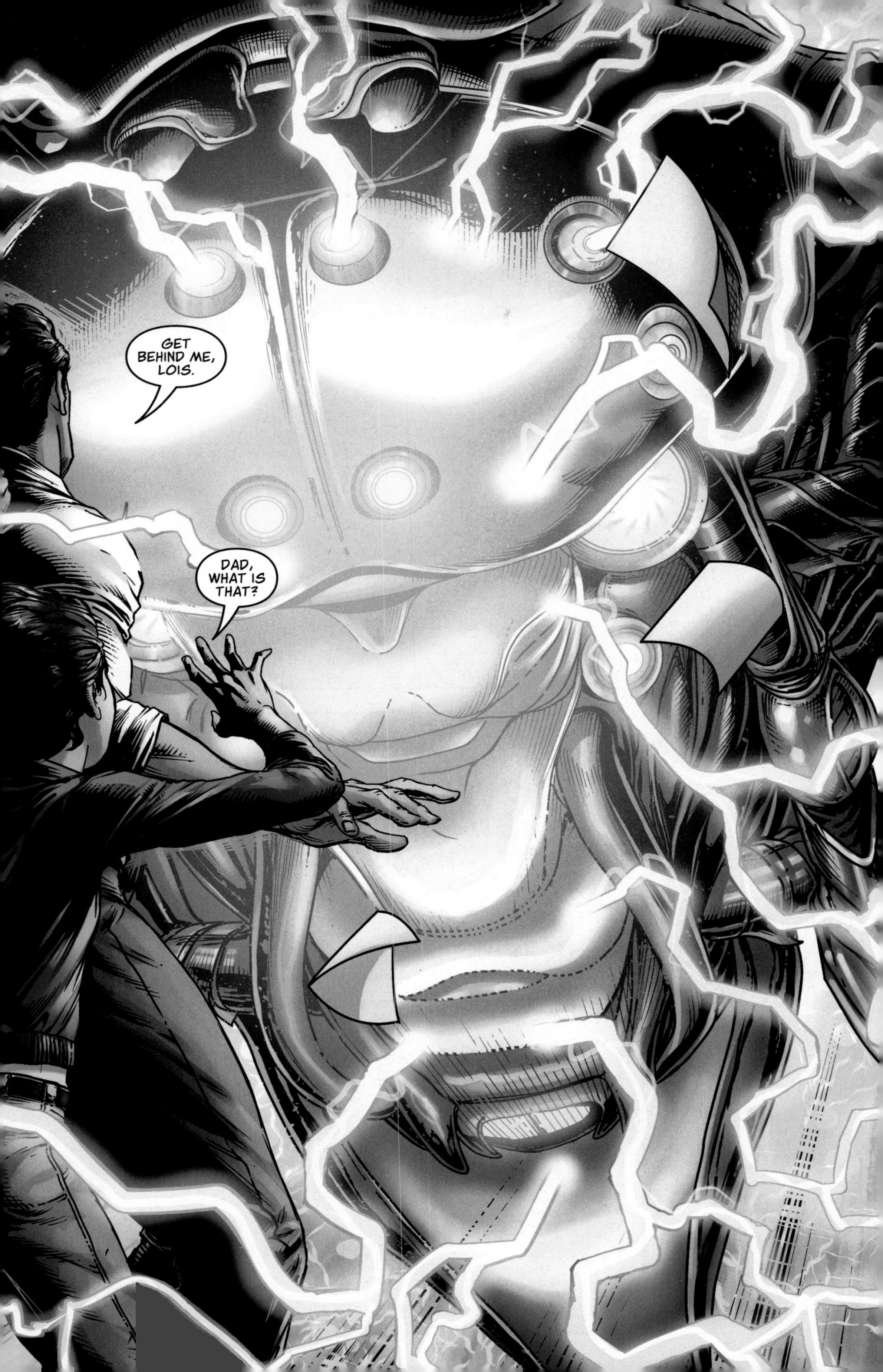
GET BEHIND ME, LOIS.
DAD, WHAT IS THAT?

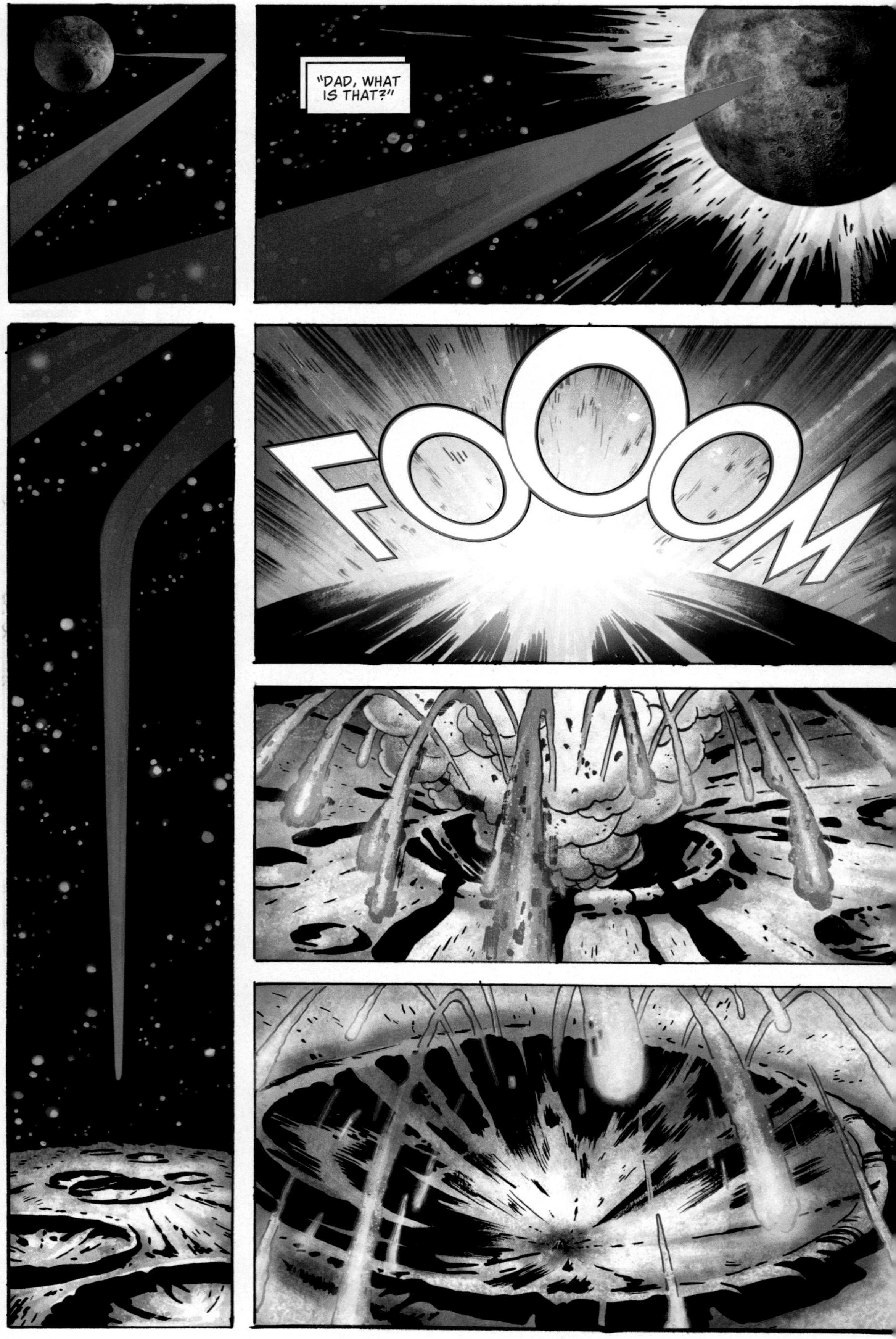
"DAD, WHAT IS THAT?"
FOOOM

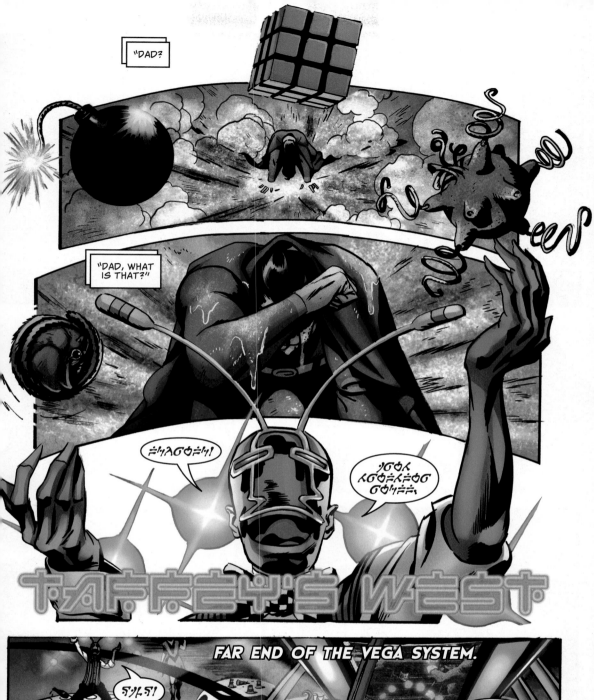

"DAD?"

"DAD, WHAT IS THAT?"

TAFFEY'S WEST

FAR END OF THE VEGA SYSTEM.

OICHIO! OVER HERE, YOU! YOU COME RIGHT HERE AND SIT DOWN AT THE BAR.

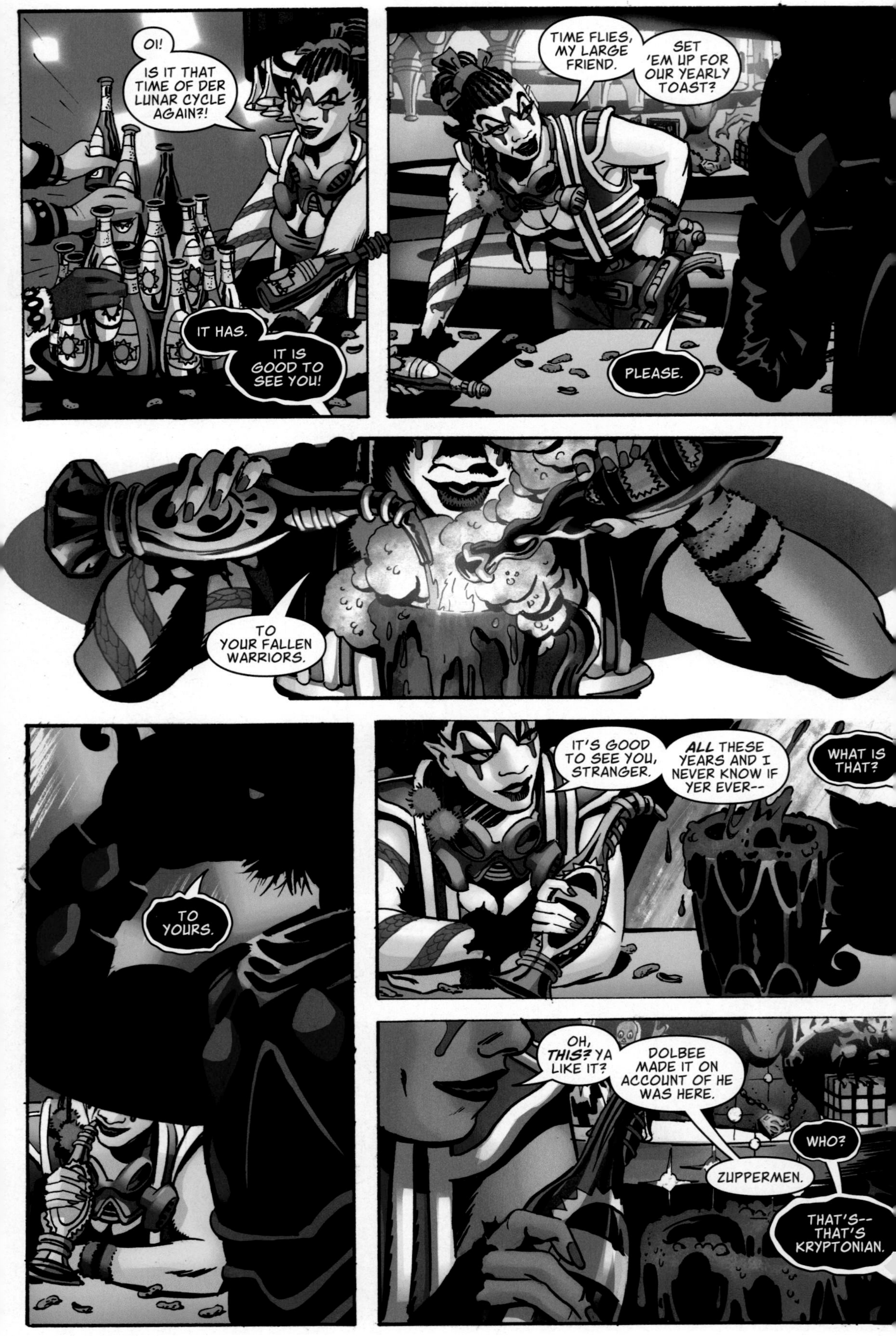
OI!
IS IT THAT TIME OF DER LUNAR CYCLE AGAIN?!
IT HAS.
IT IS GOOD TO SEE YOU!
TIME FLIES, MY LARGE FRIEND.
SET 'EM UP FOR OUR YEARLY TOAST?
PLEASE.
TO YOUR FALLEN WARRIORS.
TO YOURS.
IT'S GOOD TO SEE YOU, STRANGER.
ALL THESE YEARS AND I NEVER KNOW IF YER EVER--
WHAT IS THAT?
OH, THIS? YA LIKE IT?
DOLBEE MADE IT ON ACCOUNT OF HE WAS HERE.
ZUPPERMEN.
WHO?
THAT'S-- THAT'S KRYPTONIAN.

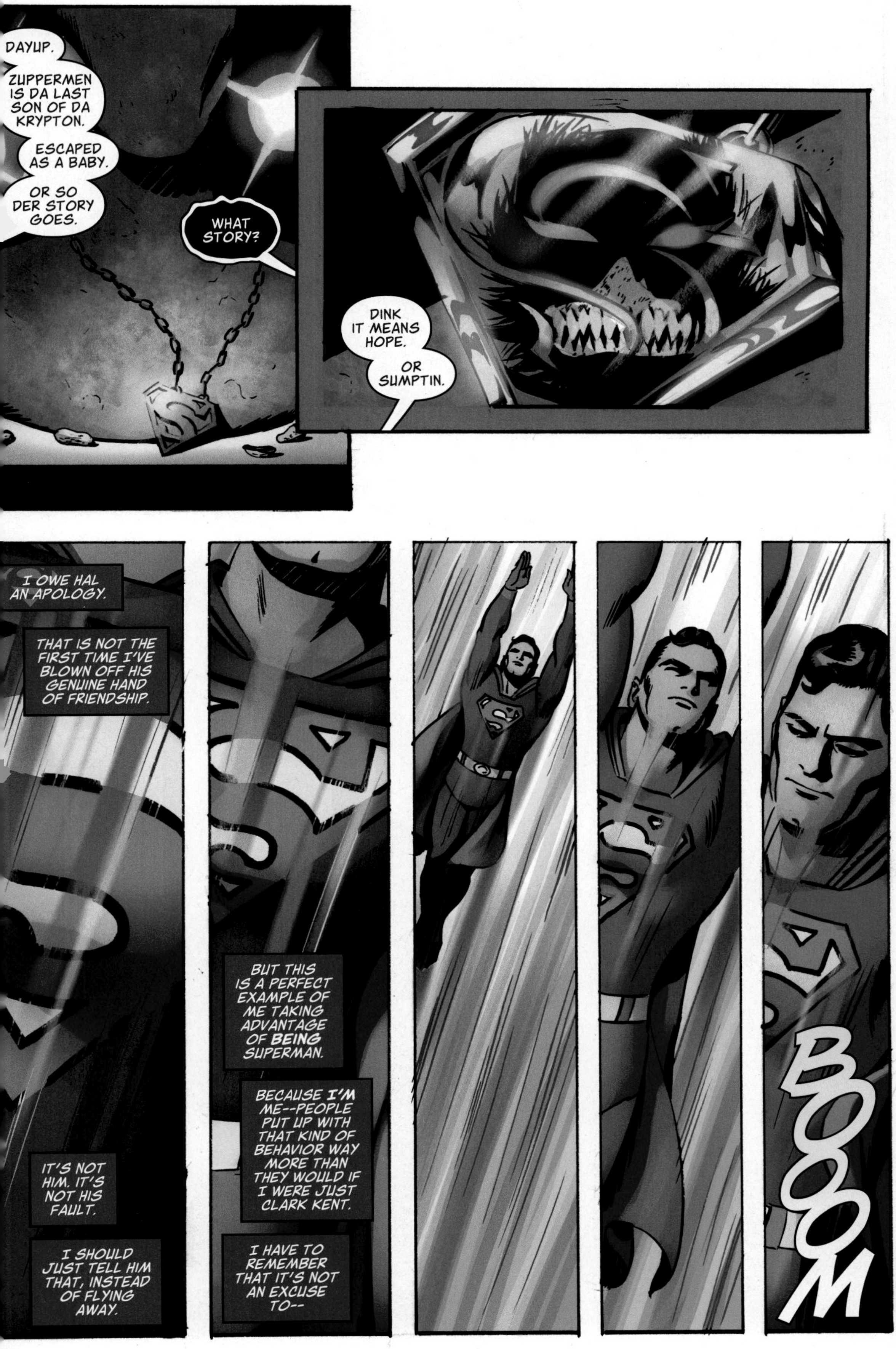
DAYUP.
ZUPPERMEN IS DA LAST SON OF DA KRYPTON.
ESCAPED AS A BABY.
OR SO DER STORY GOES.
WHAT STORY?
DINK IT MEANS HOPE.
OR SUMPTIN.
I OWE HAL AN APOLOGY.
THAT IS NOT THE FIRST TIME I'VE BLOWN OFF HIS GENUINE HAND OF FRIENDSHIP.
IT'S NOT HIM. IT'S NOT HIS FAULT.
I SHOULD JUST TELL HIM THAT, INSTEAD OF FLYING AWAY.
BUT THIS IS A PERFECT EXAMPLE OF ME TAKING ADVANTAGE OF BEING SUPERMAN.
BECAUSE I'M ME--PEOPLE PUT UP WITH THAT KIND OF BEHAVIOR WAY MORE THAN THEY WOULD IF I WERE JUST CLARK KENT.
I HAVE TO REMEMBER THAT IT'S NOT AN EXCUSE TO--
BOOOOM

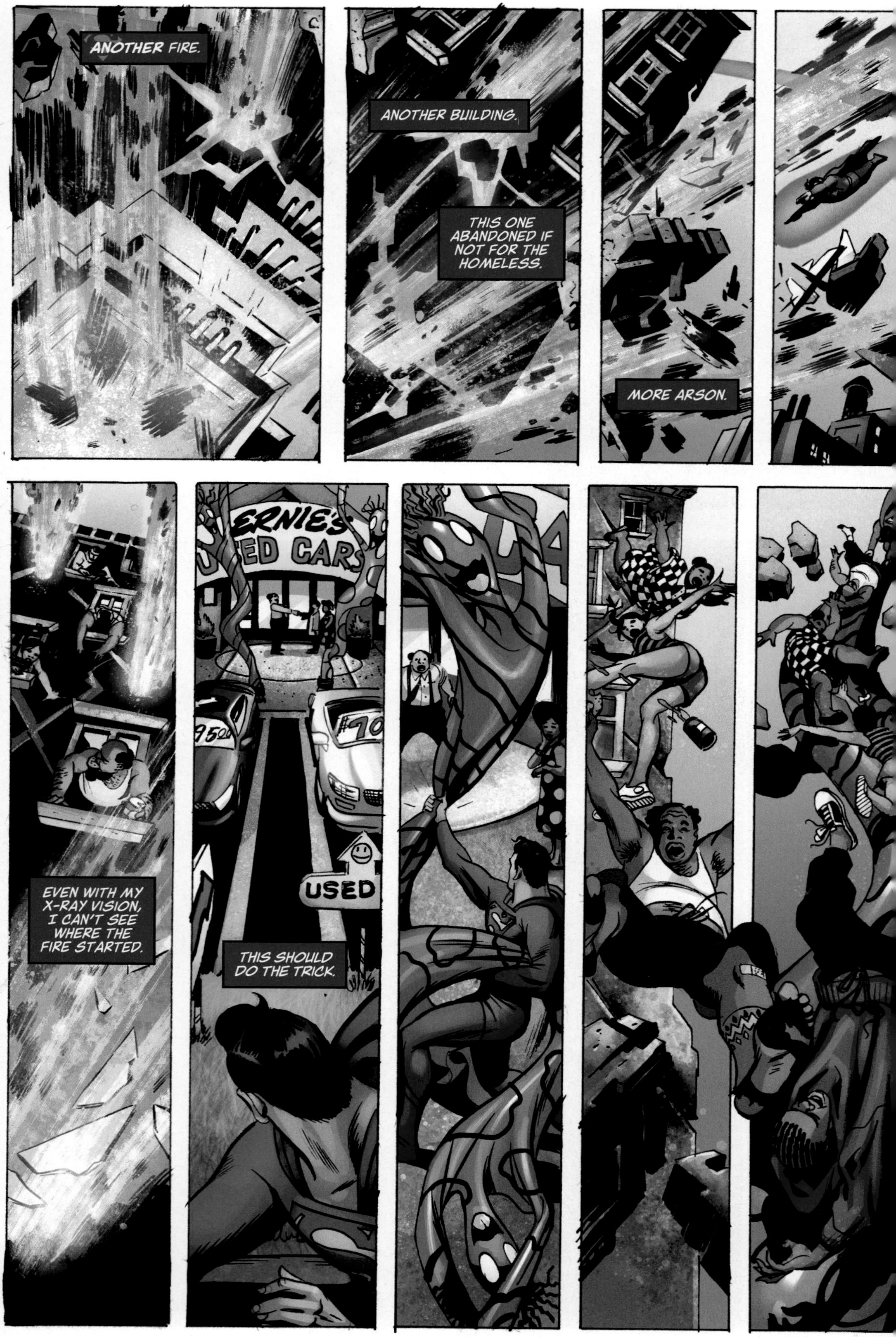
ANOTHER FIRE.
ANOTHER BUILDING.
THIS ONE ABANDONED IF NOT FOR THE HOMELESS.
MORE ARSON.
EVEN WITH MY X-RAY VISION, I CAN'T SEE WHERE THE FIRE STARTED.
ERNIE'S USED CARS
USED
THIS SHOULD DO THE TRICK.

SOMEONE IS BURNING DOWN METROPOLIS...

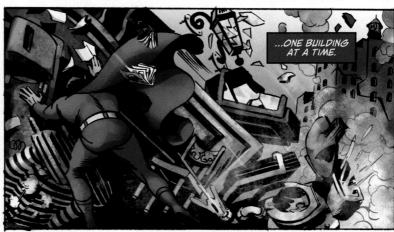

...ONE BUILDING AT A TIME.

AND THEY'RE TRYING TO DO IT RIGHT IN FRONT OF ME.

MISTER WHITE, I HAVE MORE ON THE ARSON STUFF.

OH, AND I GOT A STORY ON TOYMAN SETTING UP SHOP IN COAST CITY, BUT--

YEAH, YEAH, BIG ROBOT, SUPERMAN AND GREEN LANTERN.

YEAH, UH, HOW'D YOU KNOW?

I'M BEING SLOWLY BLED TO DEATH, KENT.

SIR?

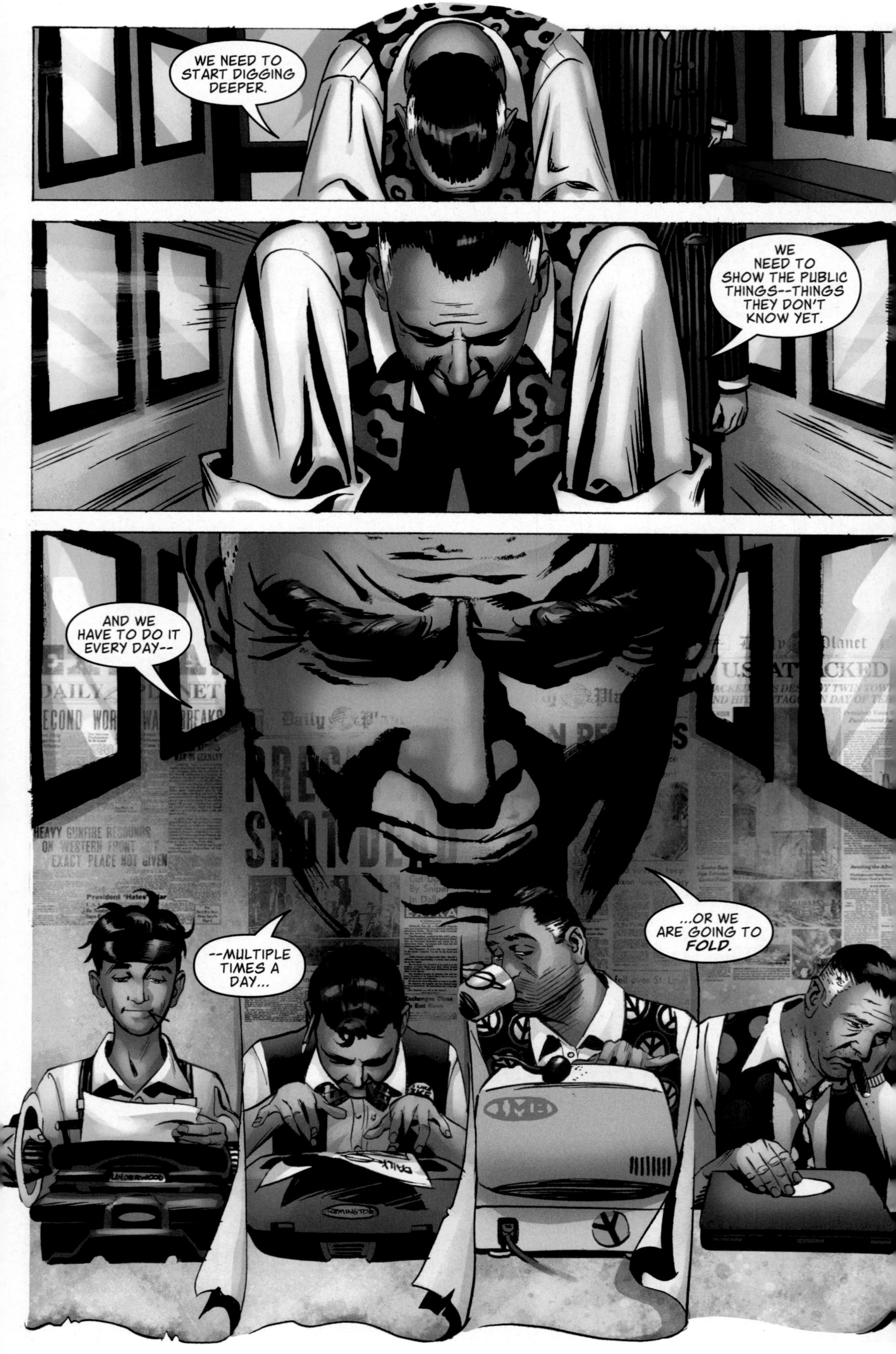
WE NEED TO START DIGGING DEEPER.
WE NEED TO SHOW THE PUBLIC THINGS--THINGS THEY DON'T KNOW YET.
AND WE HAVE TO DO IT EVERY DAY--
--MULTIPLE TIMES A DAY...
...OR WE ARE GOING TO FOLD.

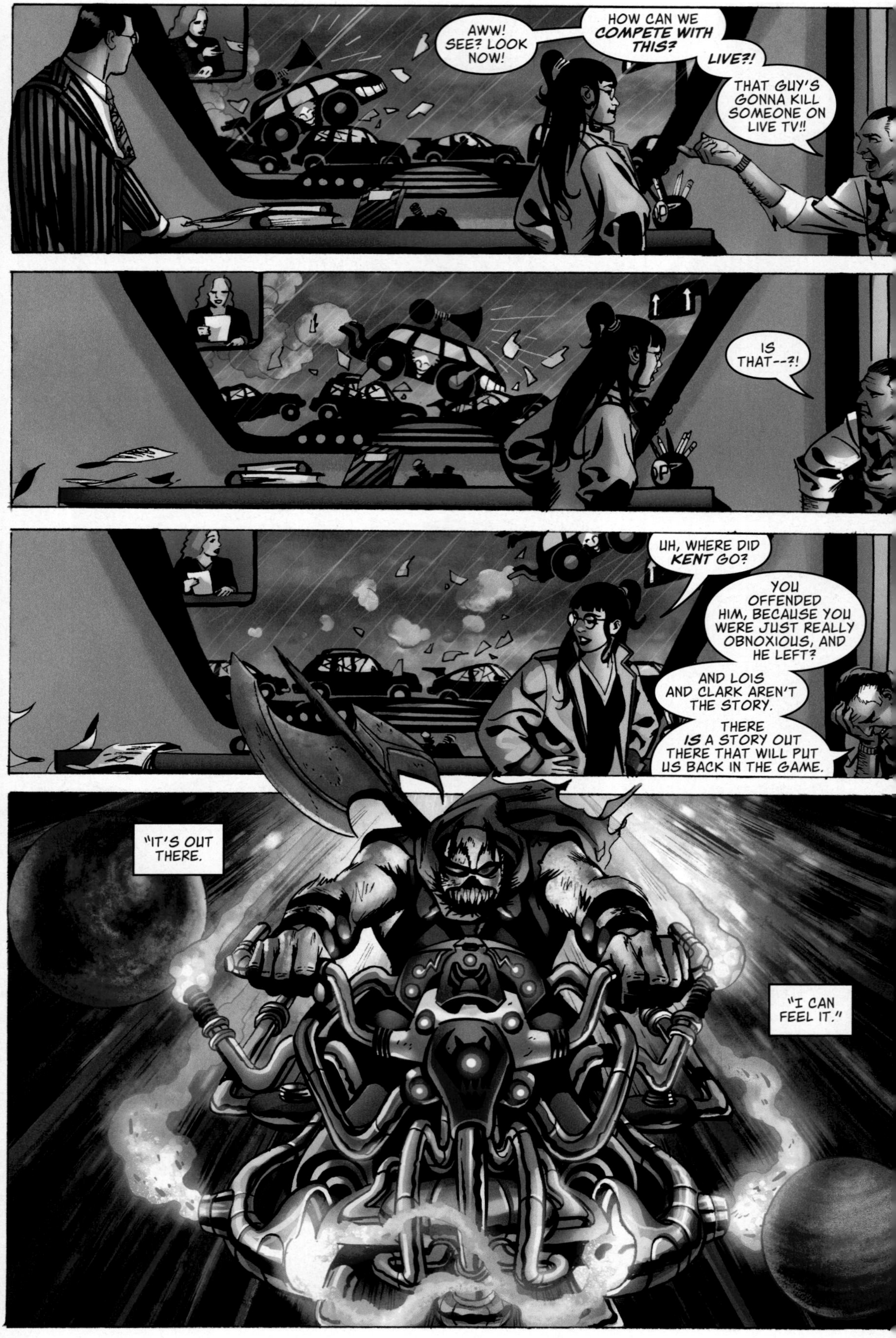
AWW! SEE? LOOK NOW!
HOW CAN WE COMPETE WITH THIS?
LIVE?!
THAT GUY'S GONNA KILL SOMEONE ON LIVE TV!!
IS THAT--?!
UH, WHERE DID KENT GO?
YOU OFFENDED HIM, BECAUSE YOU WERE JUST REALLY OBNOXIOUS, AND HE LEFT?
AND LOIS AND CLARK AREN'T THE STORY.
THERE IS A STORY OUT THERE THAT WILL PUT US BACK IN THE GAME.
"IT'S OUT THERE.
"I CAN FEEL IT."

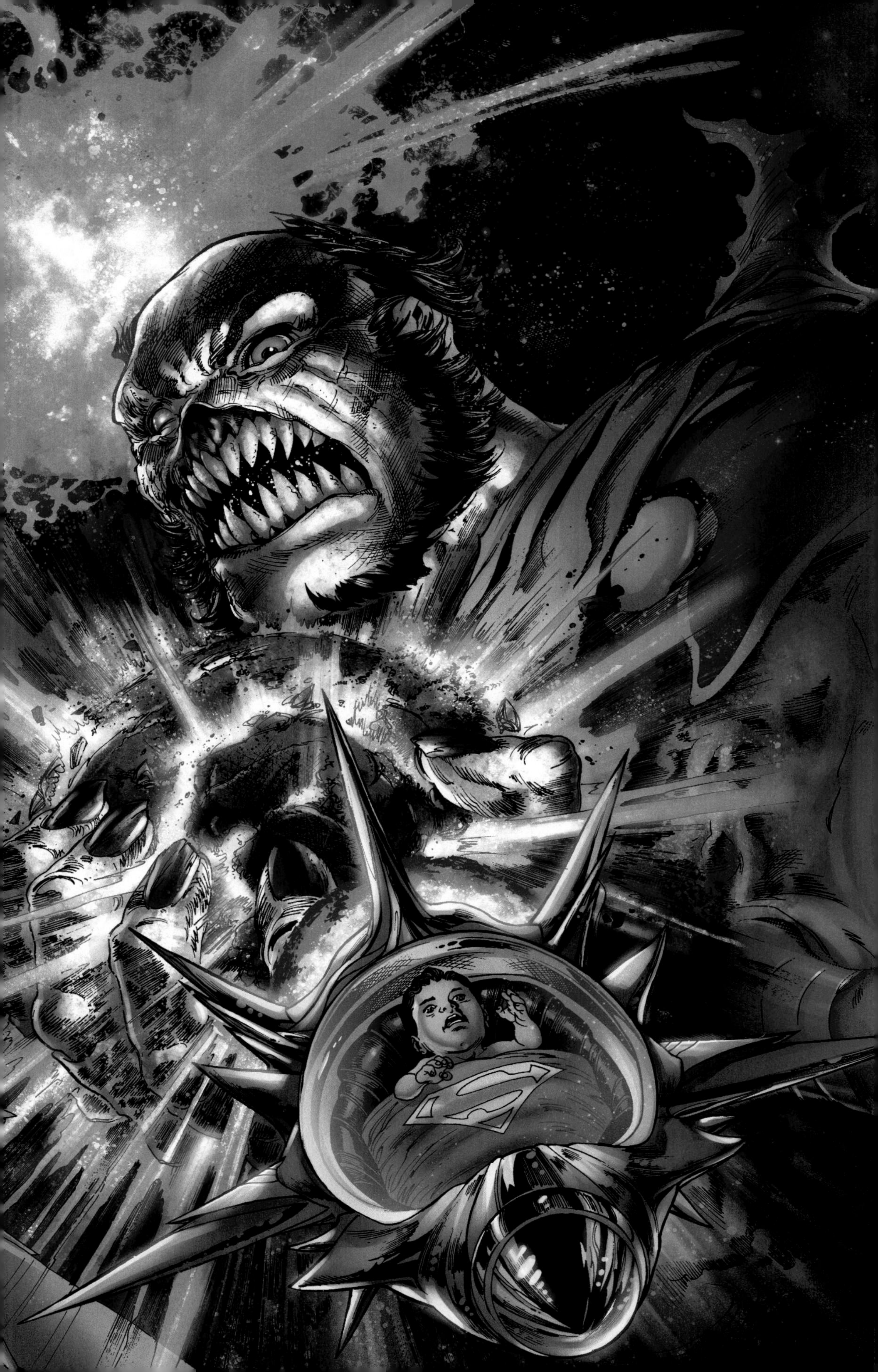

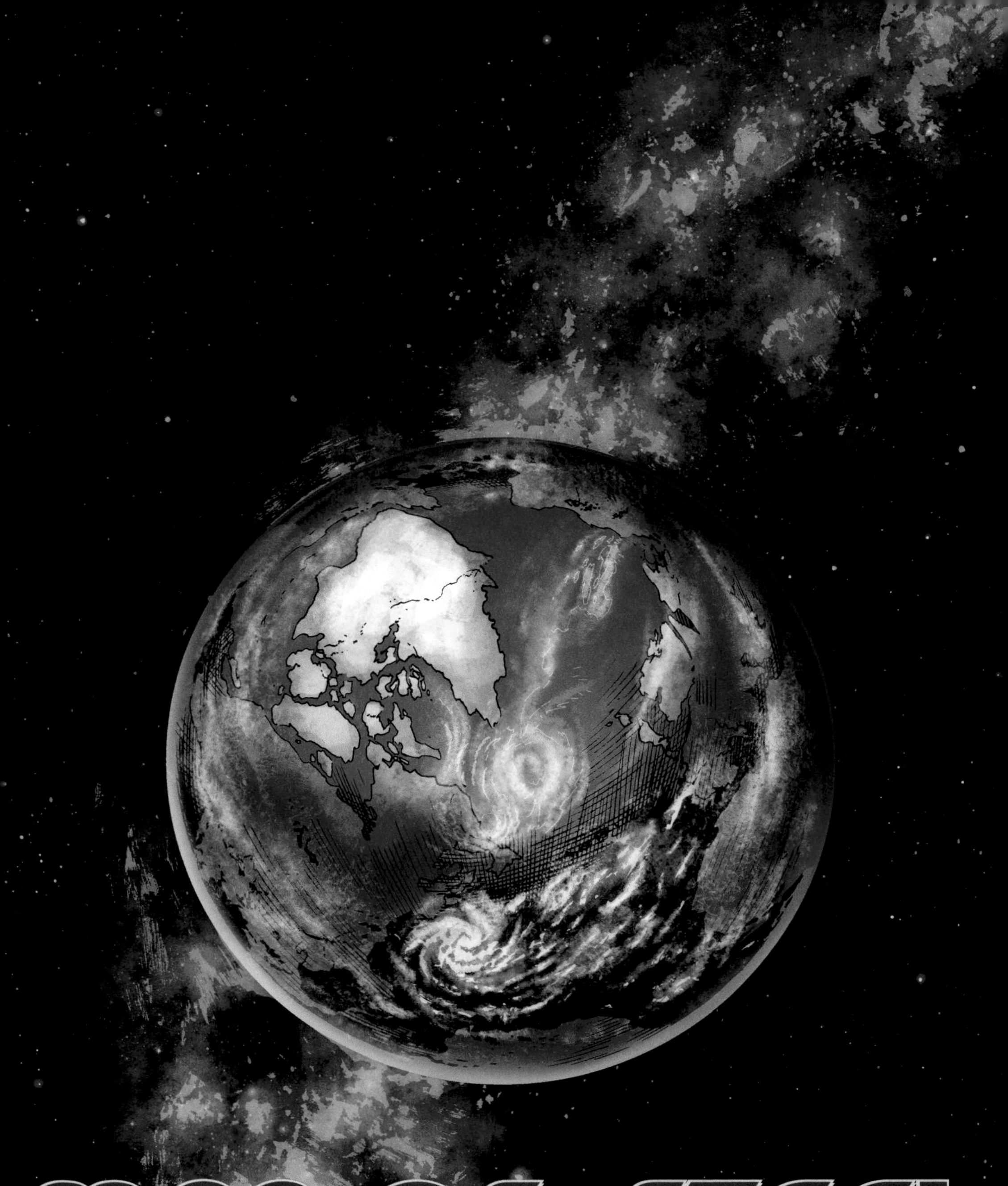

MAN OF STEEL
PART 3

BRIAN MICHAEL BENDIS WRITER
YAN SOOK & JASON FABOK (PP16) ARTISTS WADE VON GRAWBADGER INKS (PP12-13,15
ALEX SINCLAIR COLORS JOSH REED LETTERS IVAN REIS, JOE PRADO, SINCLAIR COVE
JESSICA CHEN ASSOCIATE EDITOR MICHAEL COTTON EDITOR BRIAN CUNNINGHAM GROUP EDITOR

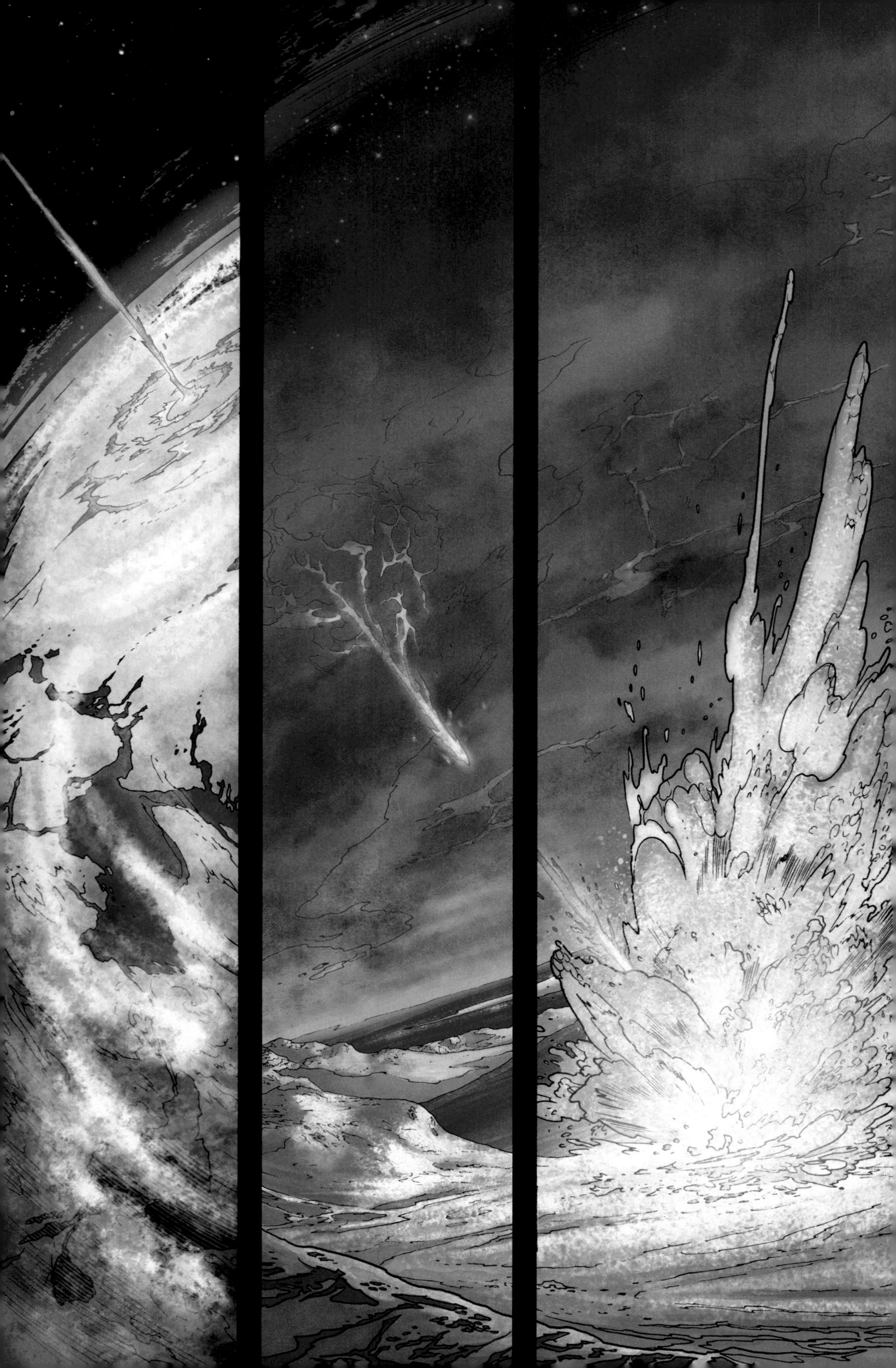

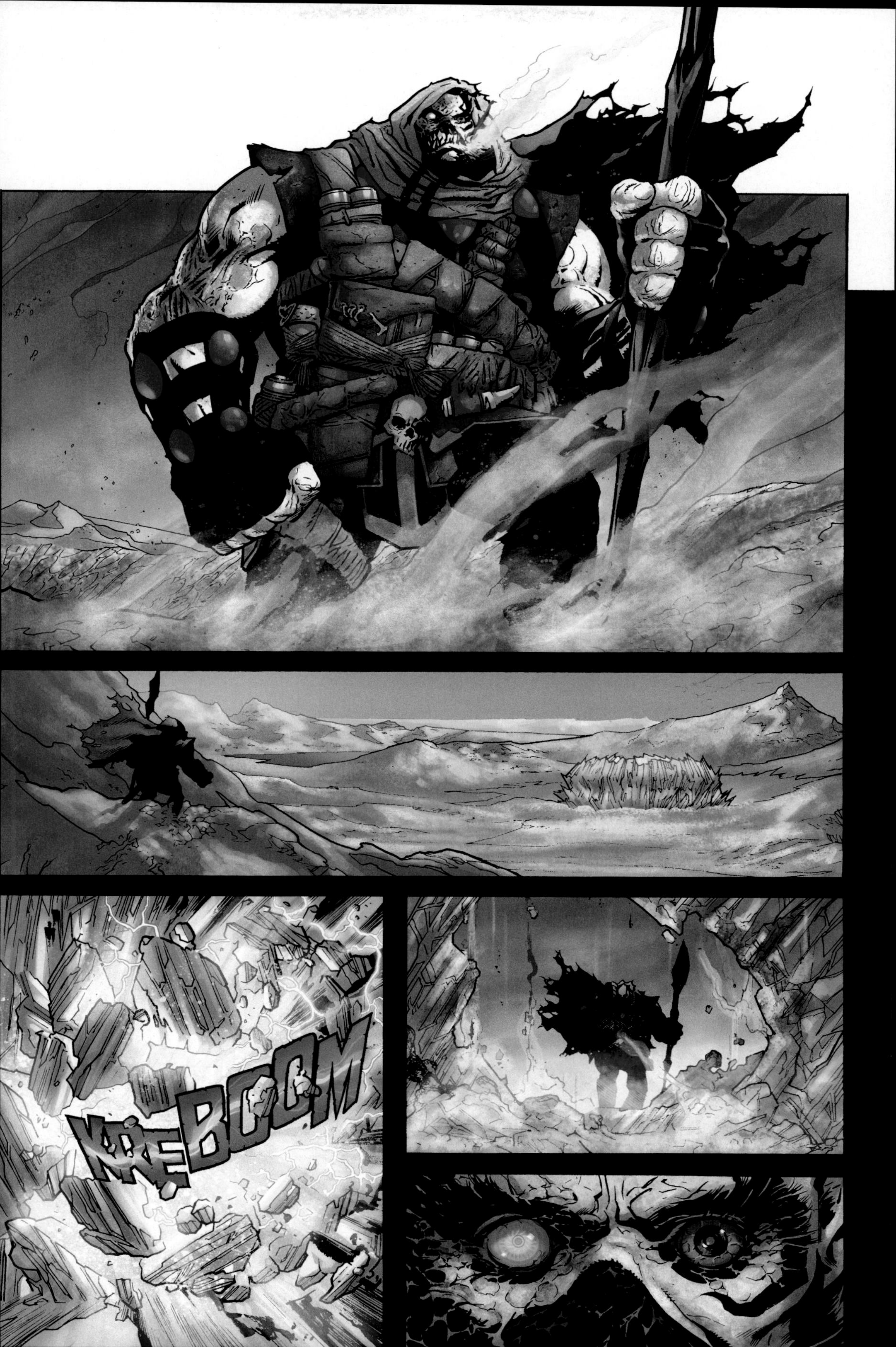
KRE-BOOM

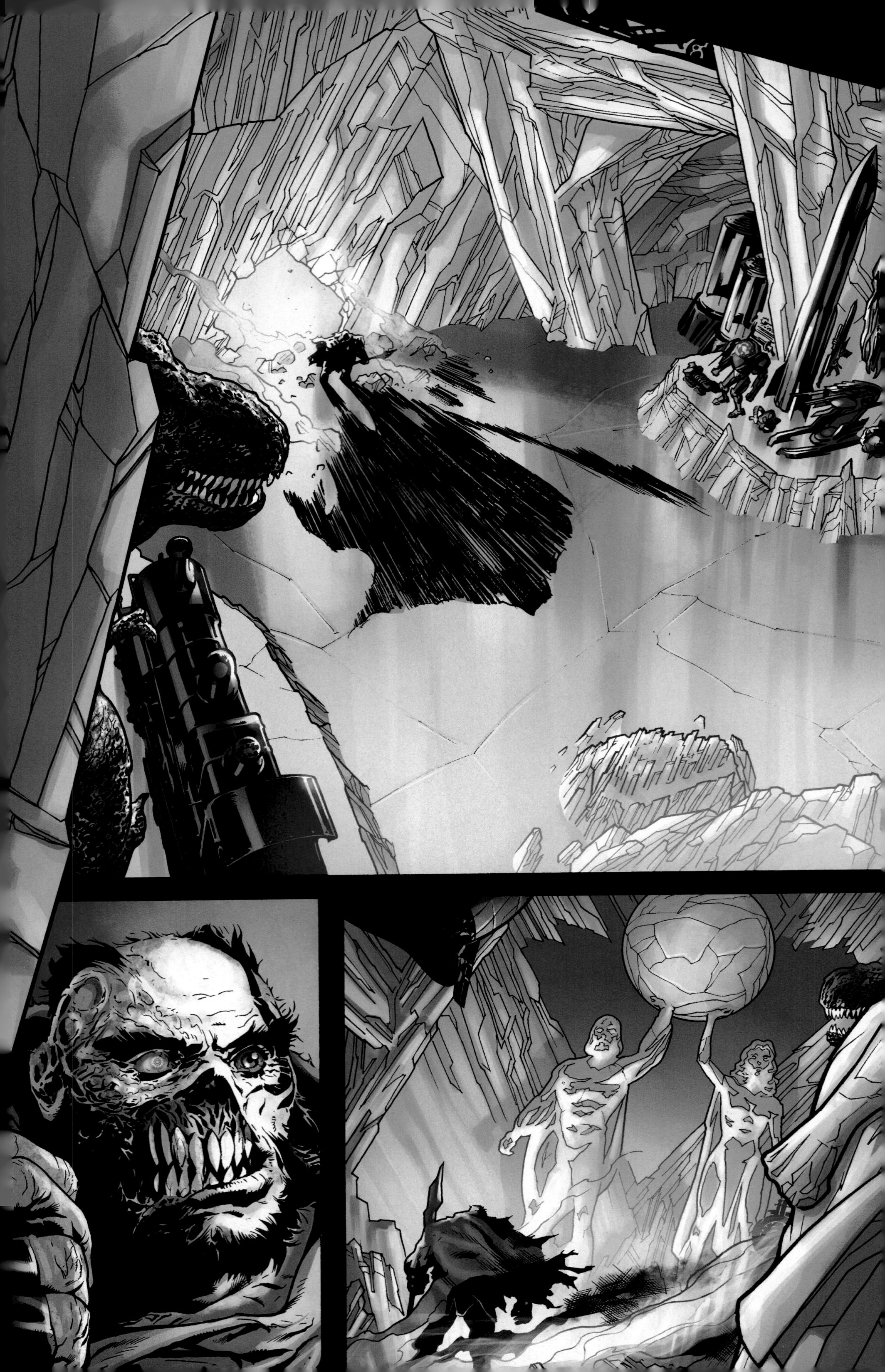

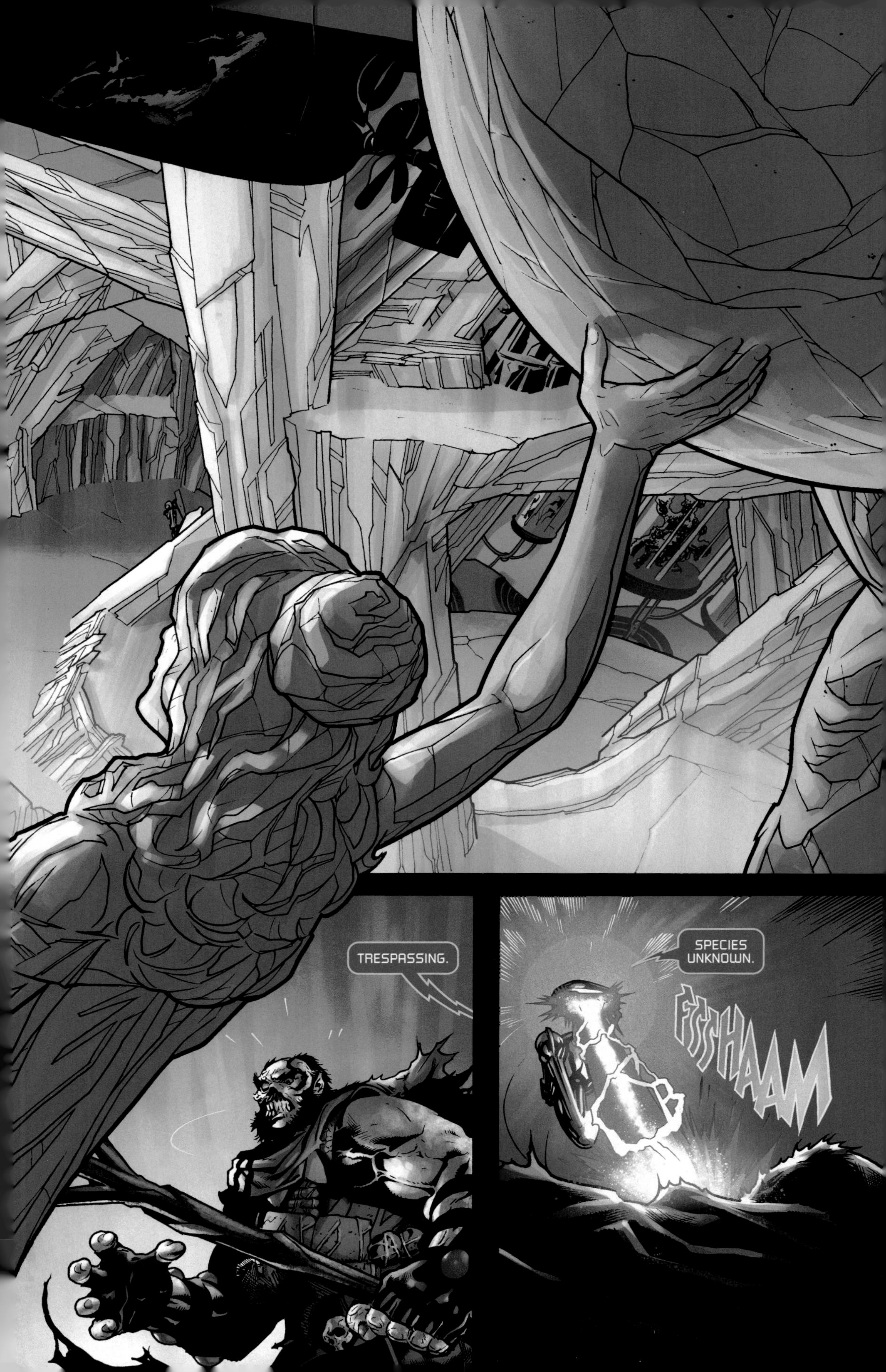
TRESPASSING.
SPECIES UNKNOWN.
FSSHAAM

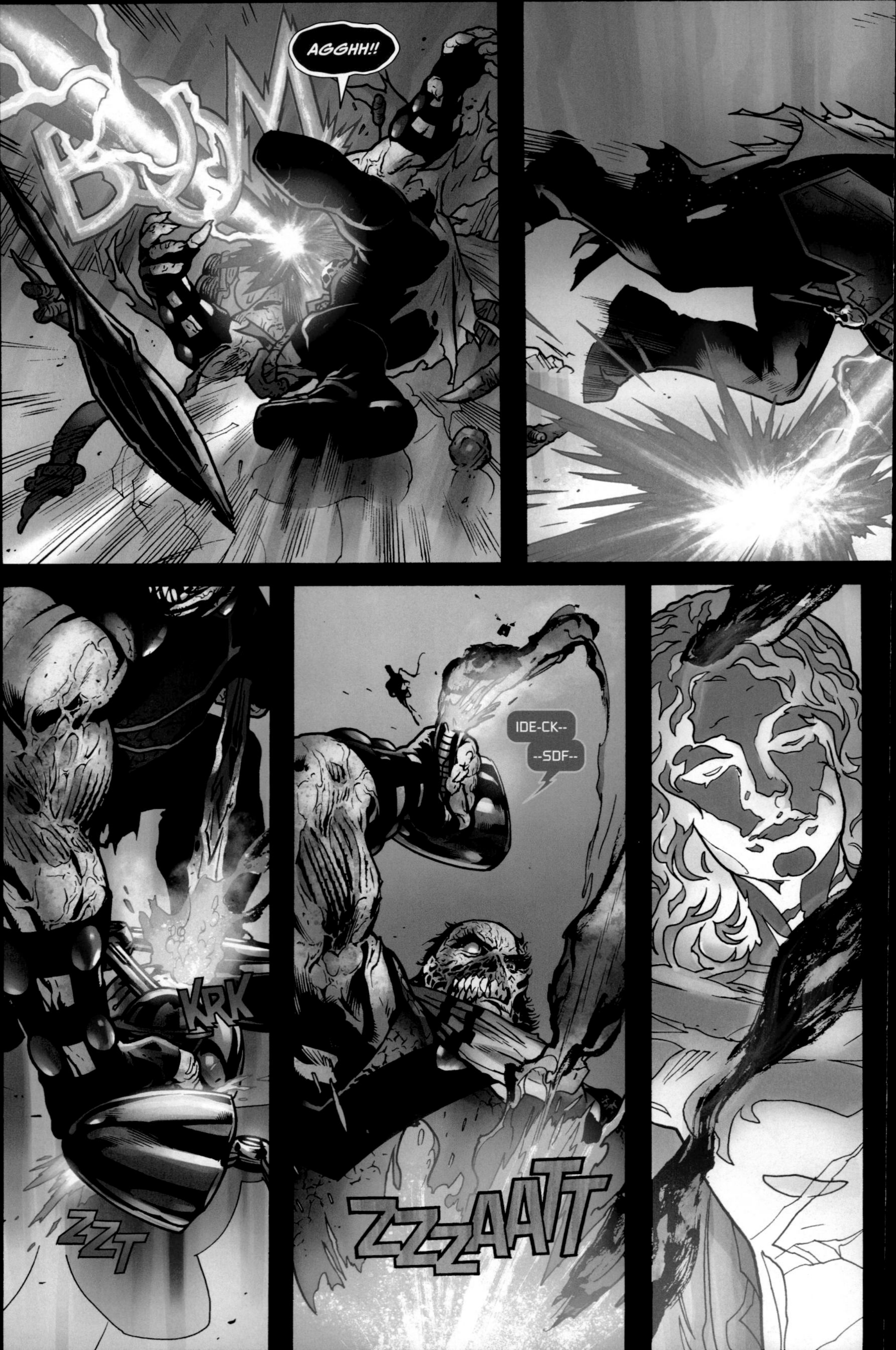
BOOM
AGGHH!!
KRK
ZZT
IDE-CK--
--SDF--
ZZZAATT

FSSHAM

IDENTIFY YOURSELF.

KRA--KOOM

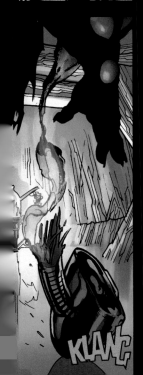

KAN--

--DOR!

IT'S REALLY BOTHERING ME...

KLANG

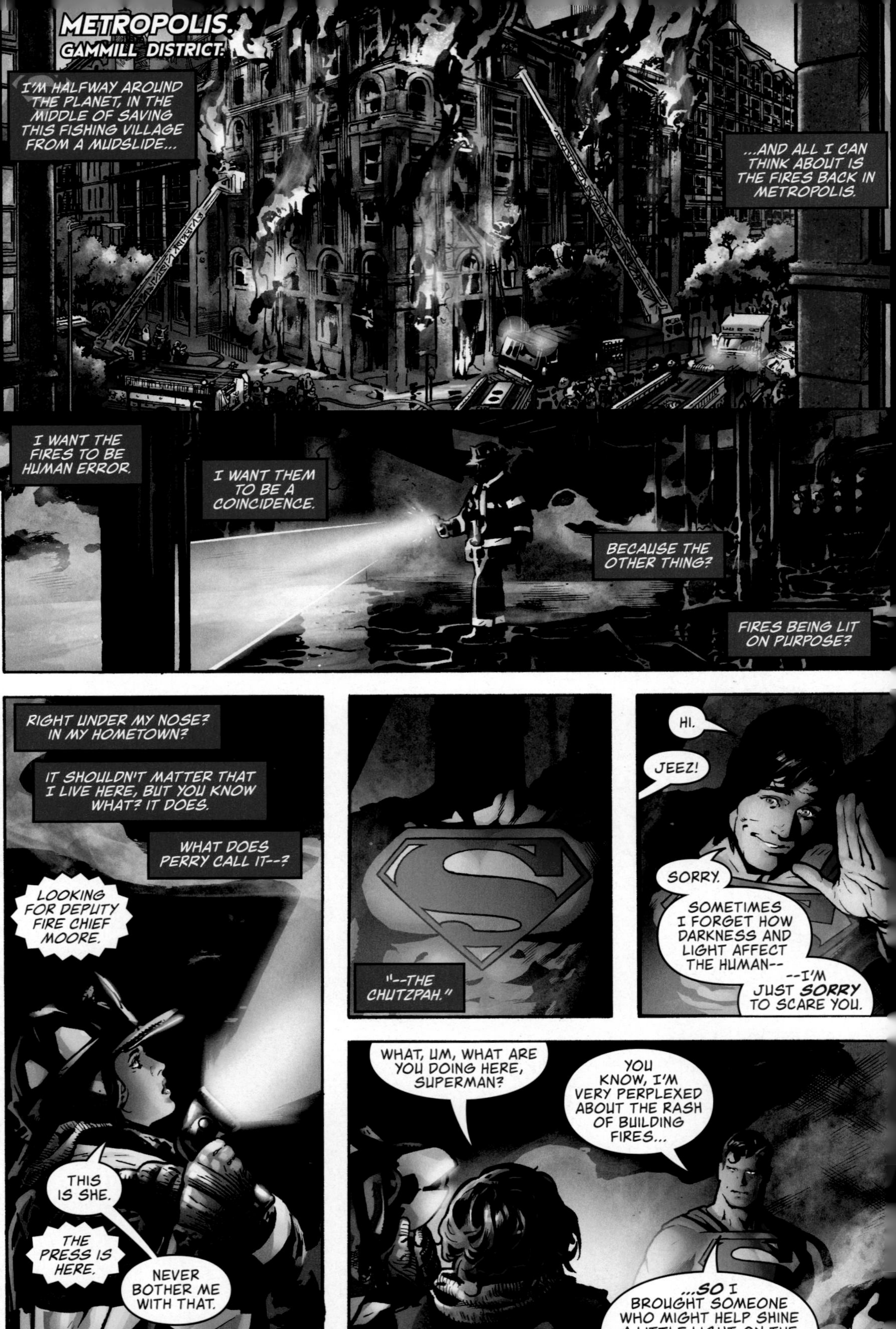
METROPOLIS.
GAMMILL DISTRICT.
I'M HALFWAY AROUND THE PLANET, IN THE MIDDLE OF SAVING THIS FISHING VILLAGE FROM A MUDSLIDE...
...AND ALL I CAN THINK ABOUT IS THE FIRES BACK IN METROPOLIS.
I WANT THE FIRES TO BE HUMAN ERROR.
I WANT THEM TO BE A COINCIDENCE.
BECAUSE THE OTHER THING?
FIRES BEING LIT ON PURPOSE?
RIGHT UNDER MY NOSE? IN MY HOMETOWN?
IT SHOULDN'T MATTER THAT I LIVE HERE, BUT YOU KNOW WHAT? IT DOES.
WHAT DOES PERRY CALL IT--?
LOOKING FOR DEPUTY FIRE CHIEF MOORE.
THIS IS SHE.
THE PRESS IS HERE.
NEVER BOTHER ME WITH THAT.
"--THE CHUTZPAH."
HI.
JEEZ!
SORRY.
SOMETIMES I FORGET HOW DARKNESS AND LIGHT AFFECT THE HUMAN--
--I'M JUST SORRY TO SCARE YOU.
WHAT, UM, WHAT ARE YOU DOING HERE, SUPERMAN?
YOU KNOW, I'M VERY PERPLEXED ABOUT THE RASH OF BUILDING FIRES...
...SO I BROUGHT SOMEONE WHO MIGHT HELP SHINE A LITTLE LIGHT ON THE INVESTIGATION FOR US--

OH !#$!@!

OKAY, I SCARED HER BY ACCIDENT.

YOU DID THAT ON PURPOSE.

I'M BATMAN.

YOU JUST COULDN'T HAVE HER NOT--

HOW MANY FIRES?

NINE.

NINE? I THOUGHT IT WAS SEVEN.

I'M INCLUDING A COUPLE FROM BEFORE I JOINED METRO FIRE.

BEFORE ANYONE EVEN CONSIDERED THESE MIGHT BE A PART OF AN ACTUAL RASH OF SUSPICIOUS FIRES.

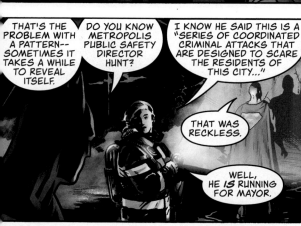

THAT'S THE PROBLEM WITH A PATTERN-- SOMETIMES IT TAKES A WHILE TO REVEAL ITSELF.

DO YOU KNOW METROPOLIS PUBLIC SAFETY DIRECTOR HUNT?

I KNOW HE SAID THIS IS A "SERIES OF COORDINATED CRIMINAL ATTACKS THAT ARE DESIGNED TO SCARE THE RESIDENTS OF THIS CITY..."

THAT WAS RECKLESS.

WELL, HE IS RUNNING FOR MAYOR.

PRACTICALLY ANYTHING THAT COULD ESTABLISH OR ARGUE HIS POINT WAS DESTROYED BY THE FIRE.

PLUS, THERE ARE SEVERAL POSSIBLE IGNITION POINTS AND SOURCES.

ANYTHING ON YOUR X-RAY OR OTHER ASSORTED SUPER-SENSES?

AN ALARM.

A SOUND ONLY SOMEONE LIKE ME CAN HEAR.

HAVE YOU MADE A LOCATION MAP OF THE FIRES? PINNED THEM?

OF COURSE.

SOMETIMES THEY MAKE A SHAPE.

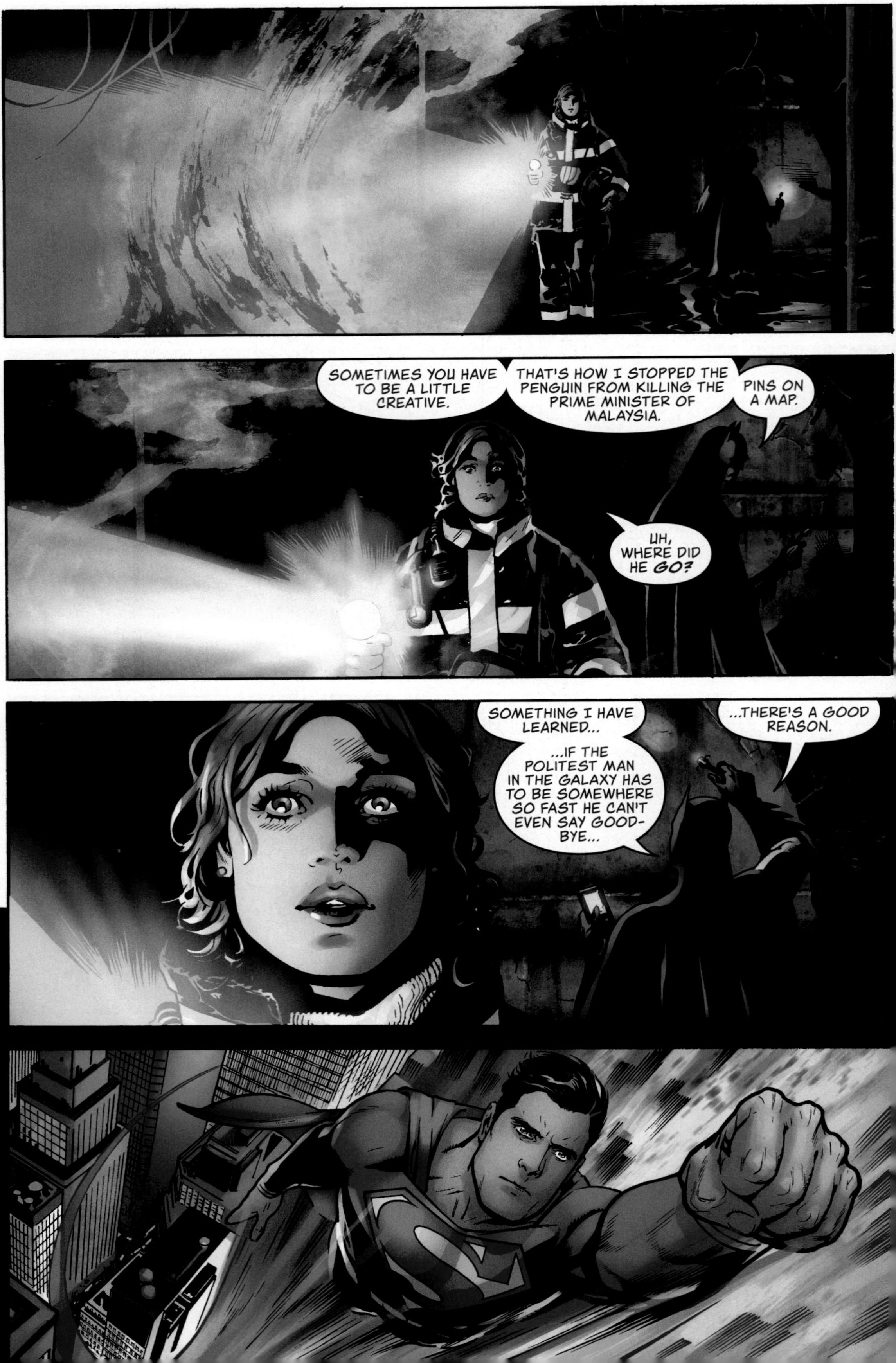
SOMETIMES YOU HAVE TO BE A LITTLE CREATIVE.
THAT'S HOW I STOPPED THE PENGUIN FROM KILLING THE PRIME MINISTER OF MALAYSIA.
PINS ON A MAP.
UH, WHERE DID HE GO?
SOMETHING I HAVE LEARNED...
...IF THE POLITEST MAN IN THE GALAXY HAS TO BE SOMEWHERE SO FAST HE CAN'T EVEN SAY GOOD-BYE...
...THERE'S A GOOD REASON.

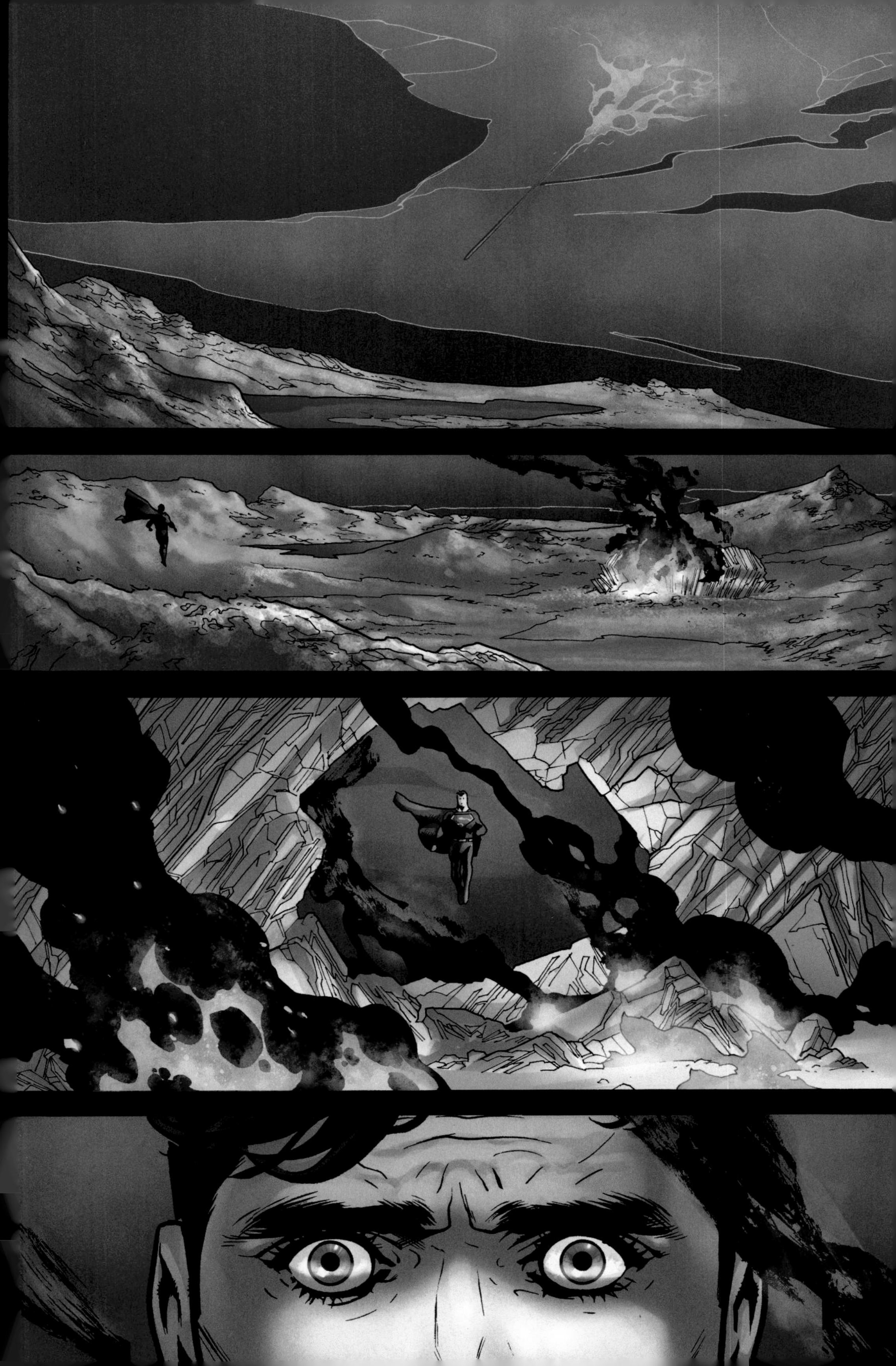

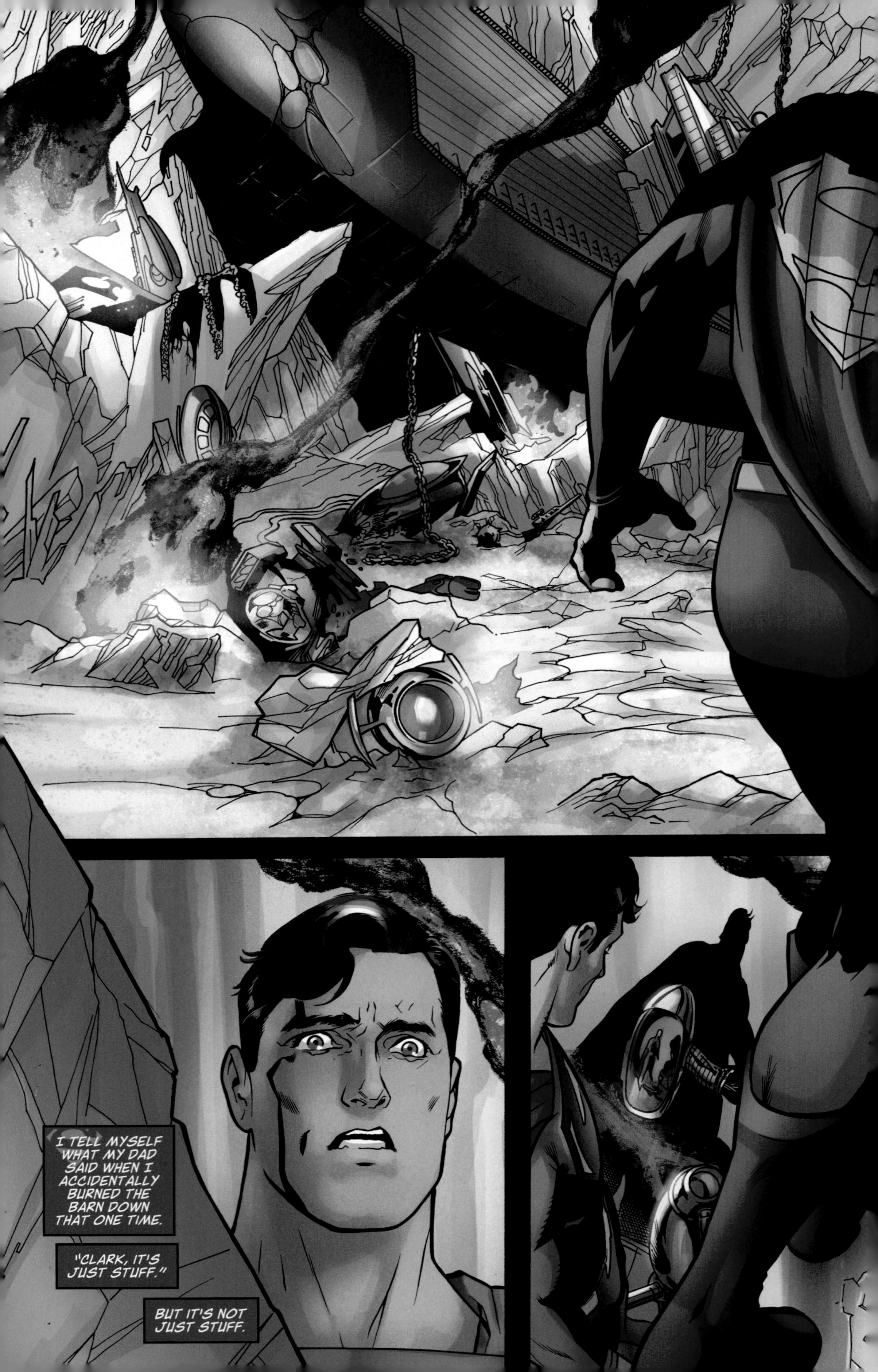
I TELL MYSELF WHAT MY DAD SAID WHEN I ACCIDENTALLY BURNED THE BARN DOWN THAT ONE TIME.
"CLARK, IT'S JUST STUFF."
BUT IT'S NOT JUST STUFF.

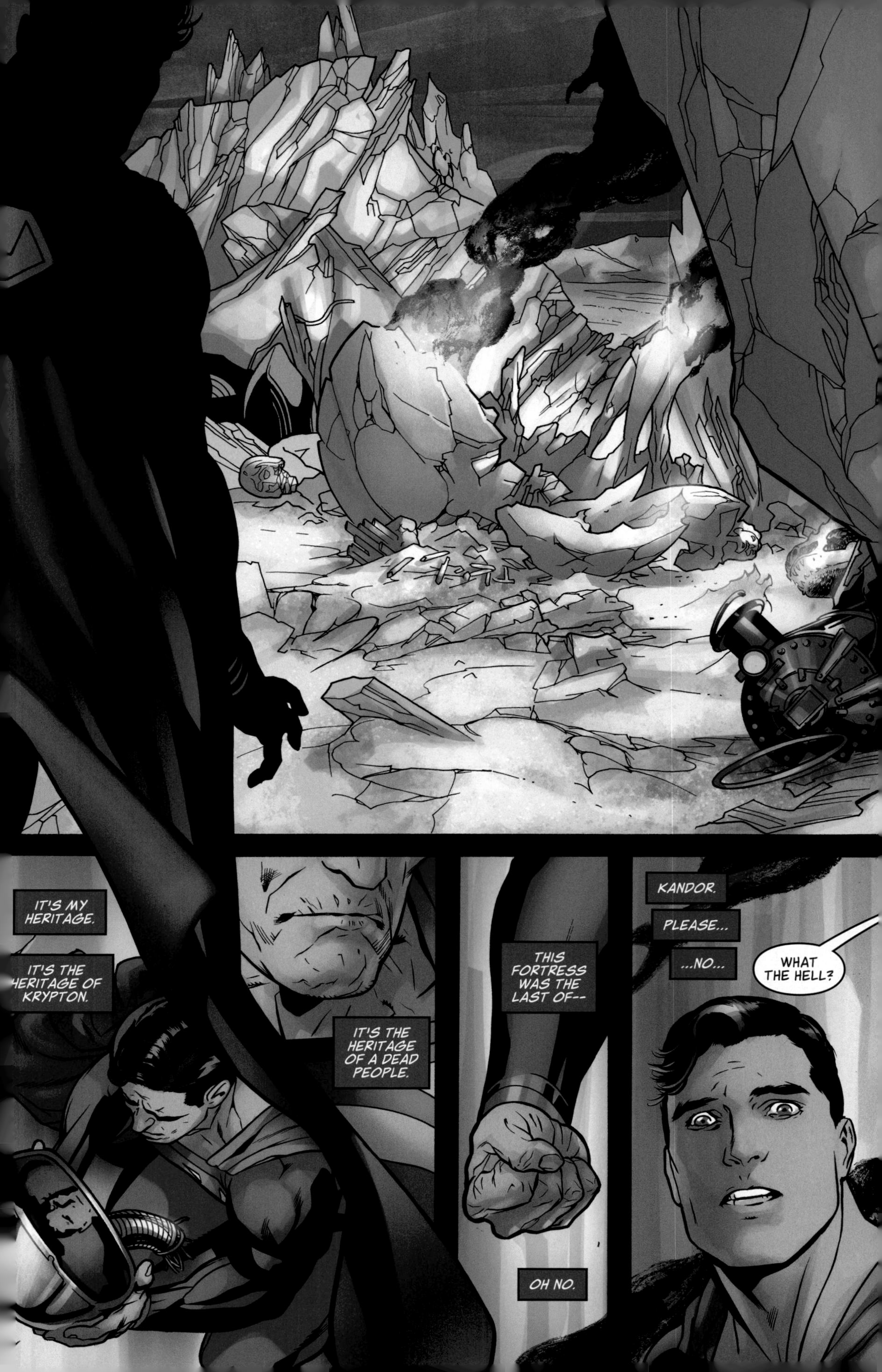
IT'S MY HERITAGE.
IT'S THE HERITAGE OF KRYPTON.
IT'S THE HERITAGE OF A DEAD PEOPLE.
THIS FORTRESS WAS THE LAST OF--
OH NO.
KANDOR.
PLEASE...
...NO...
WHAT THE HELL?

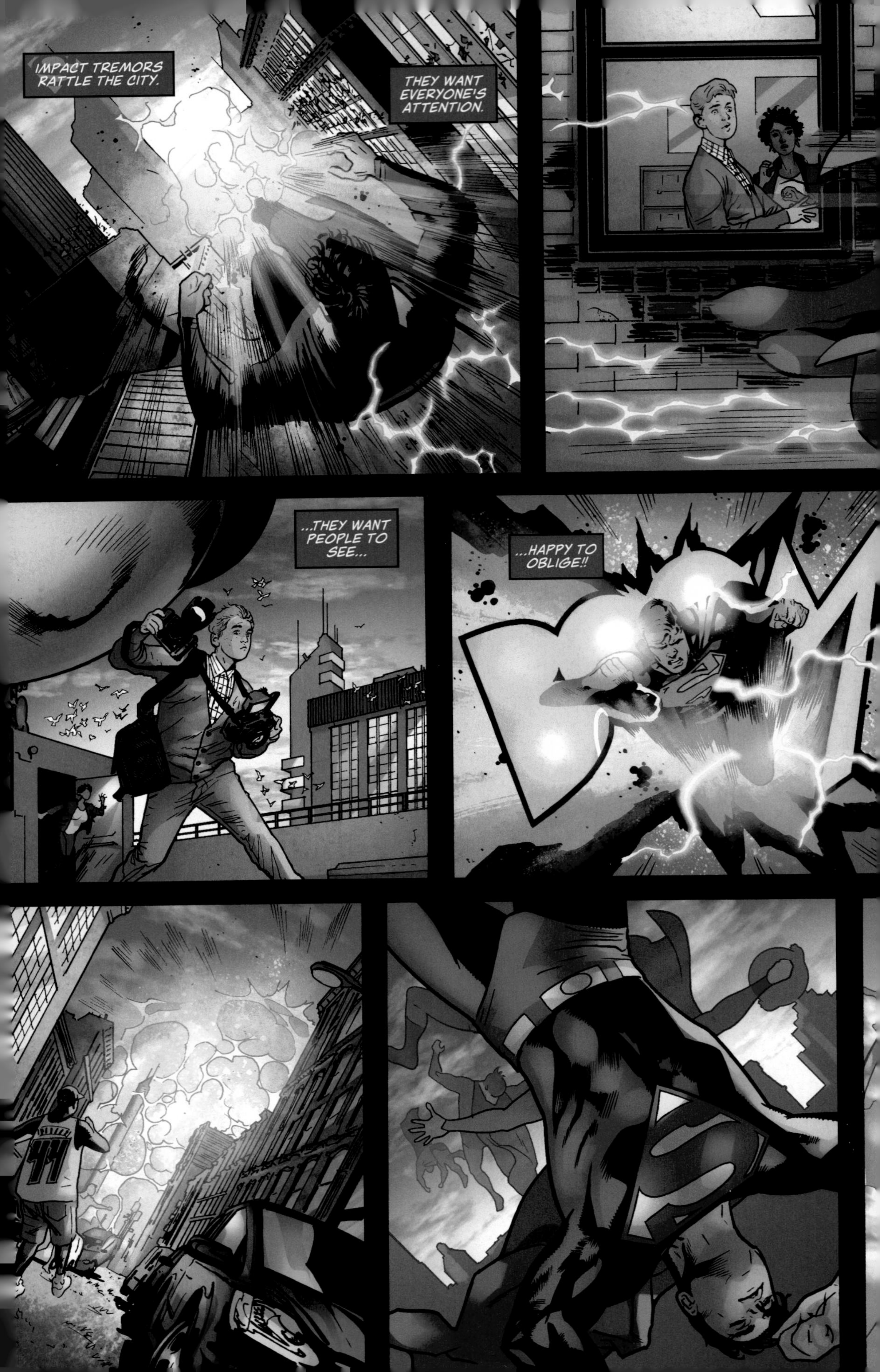
IMPACT TREMORS RATTLE THE CITY.
THEY WANT EVERYONE'S ATTENTION.
...THEY WANT PEOPLE TO SEE...
...HAPPY TO OBLIGE!!

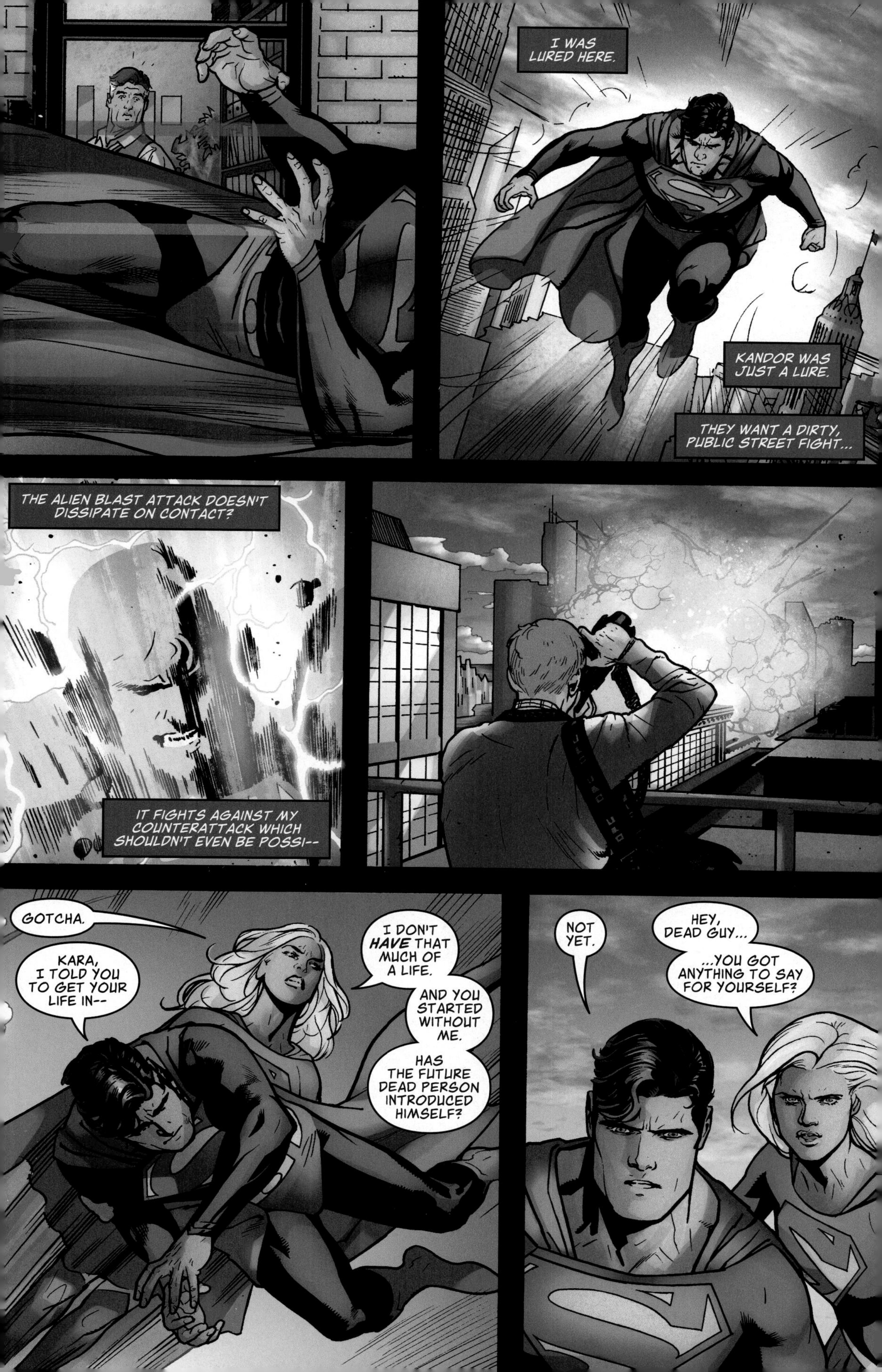
I WAS LURED HERE.
KANDOR WAS JUST A LURE.
THEY WANT A DIRTY, PUBLIC STREET FIGHT...
THE ALIEN BLAST ATTACK DOESN'T DISSIPATE ON CONTACT?
IT FIGHTS AGAINST MY COUNTERATTACK WHICH SHOULDN'T EVEN BE POSSI--
GOTCHA.
KARA, I TOLD YOU TO GET YOUR LIFE IN--
I DON'T HAVE THAT MUCH OF A LIFE.
AND YOU STARTED WITHOUT ME.
HAS THE FUTURE DEAD PERSON INTRODUCED HIMSELF?
NOT YET.
HEY, DEAD GUY...
...YOU GOT ANYTHING TO SAY FOR YOURSELF?

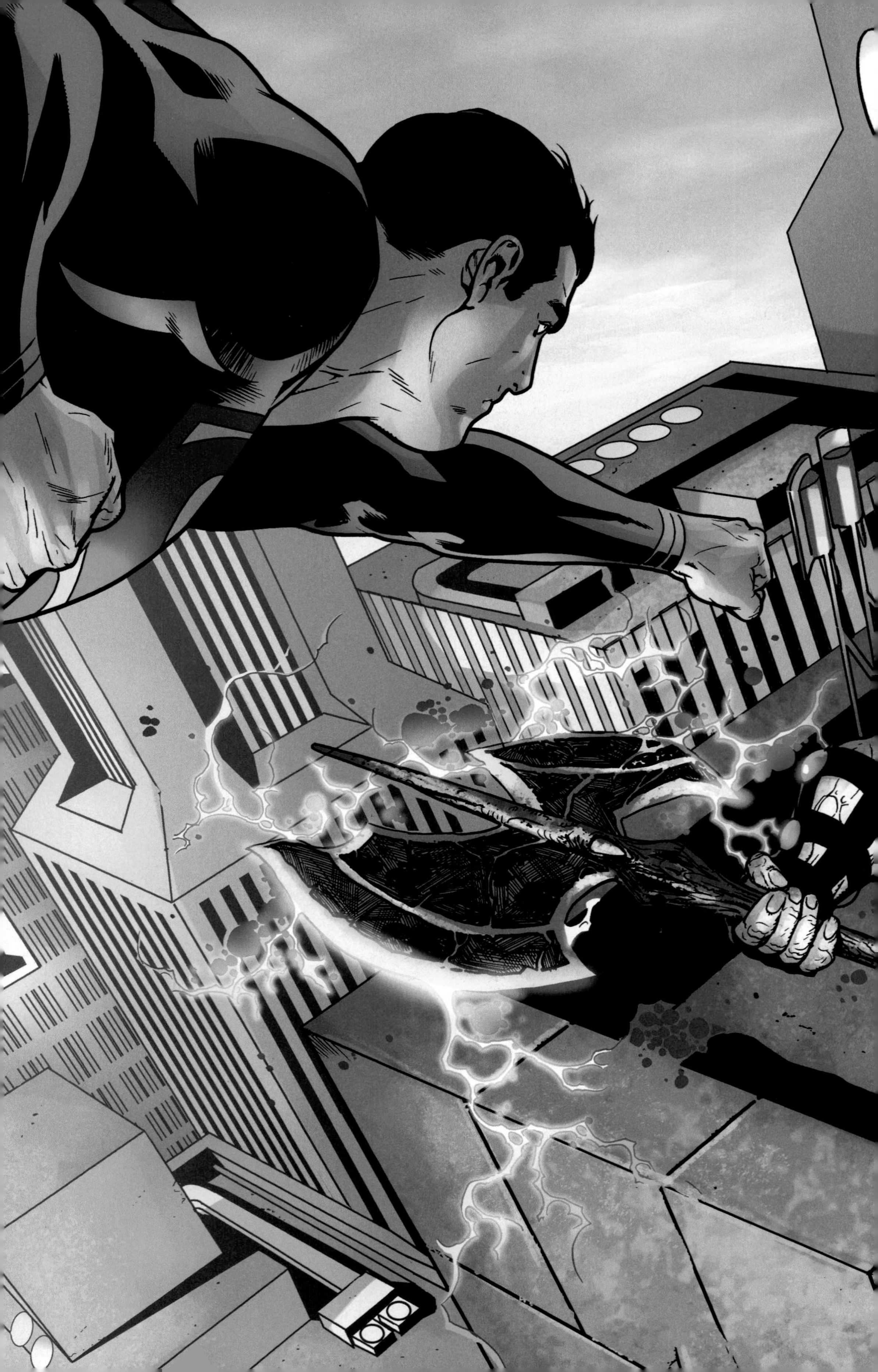

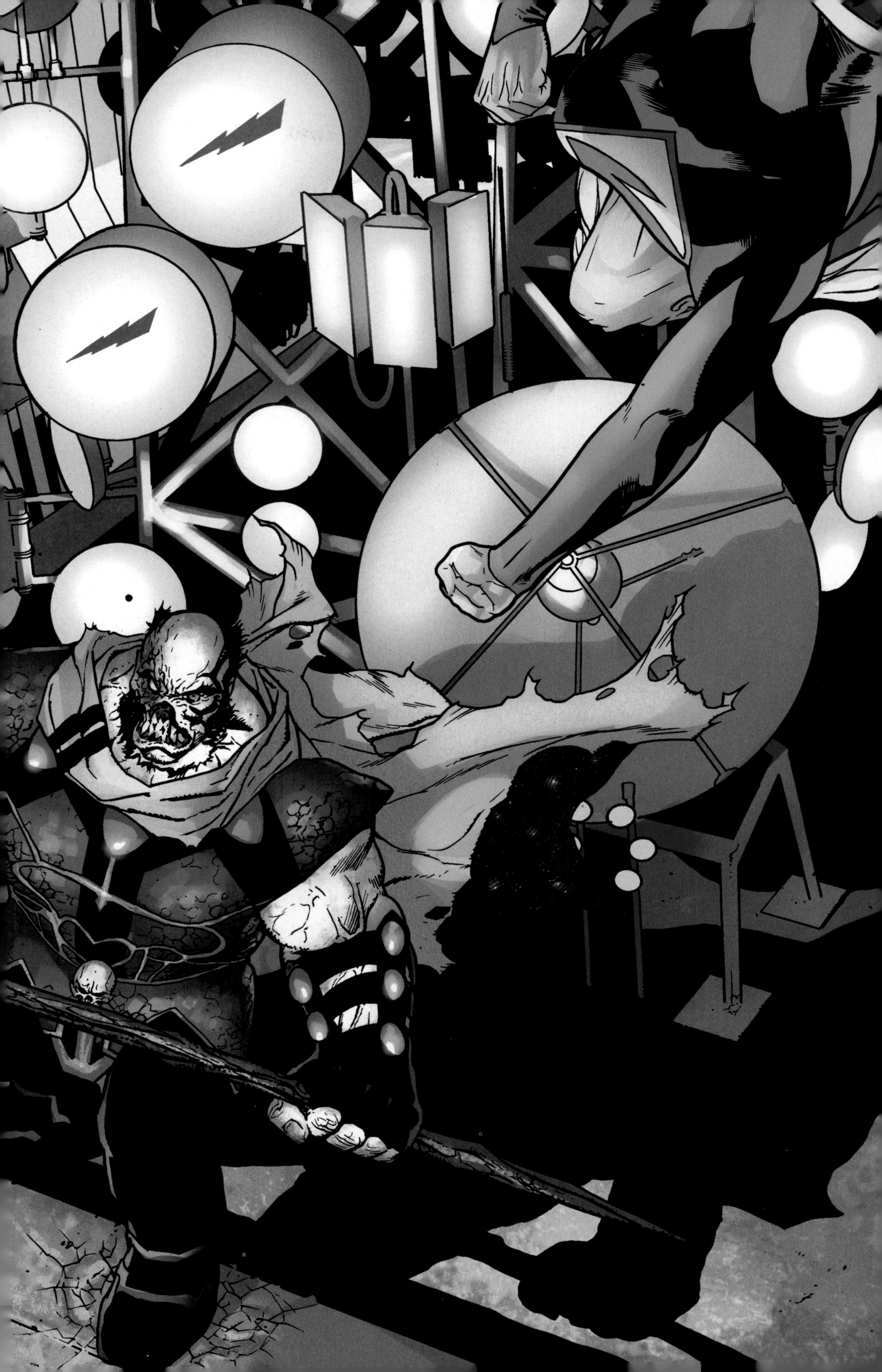

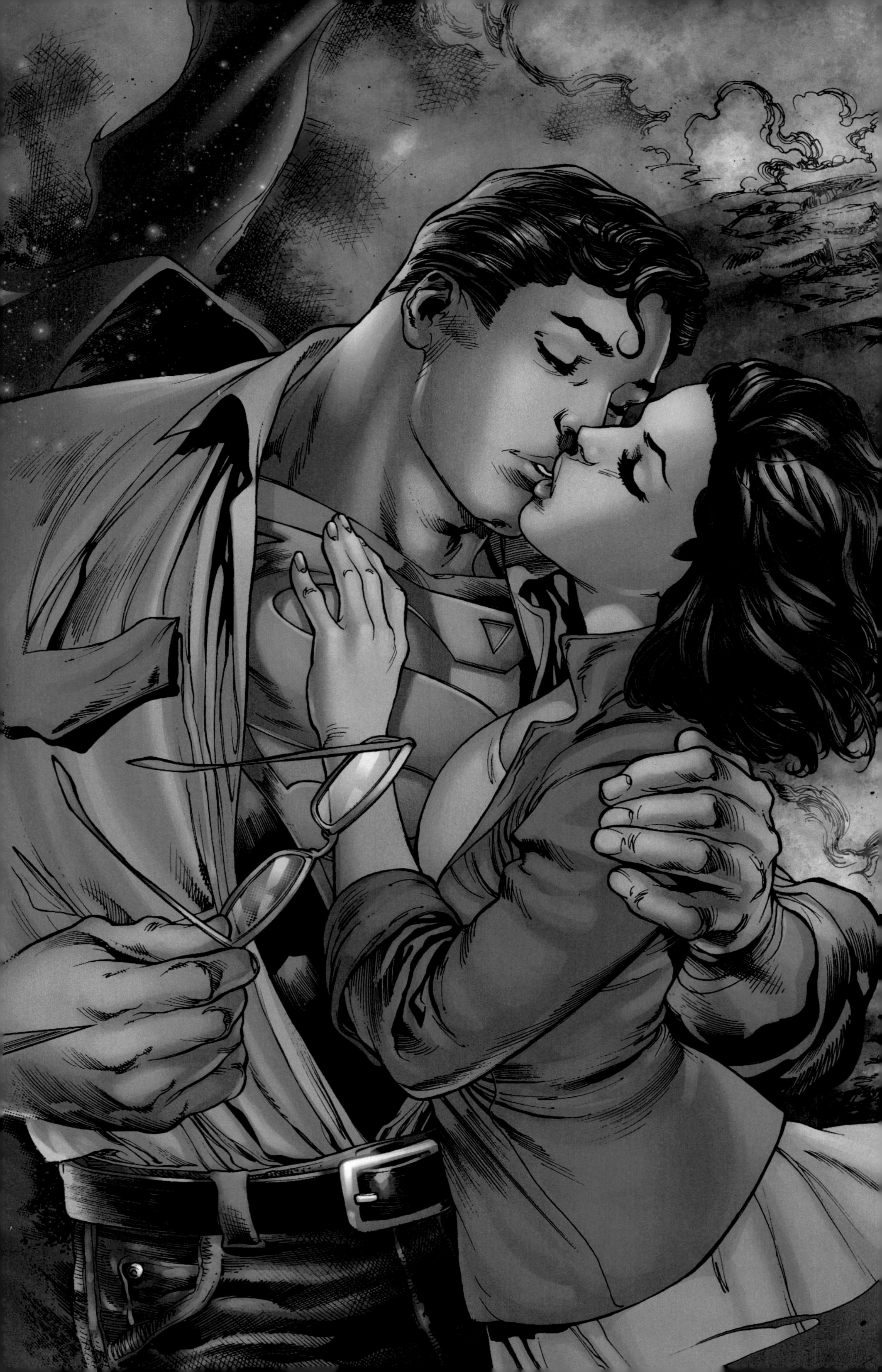

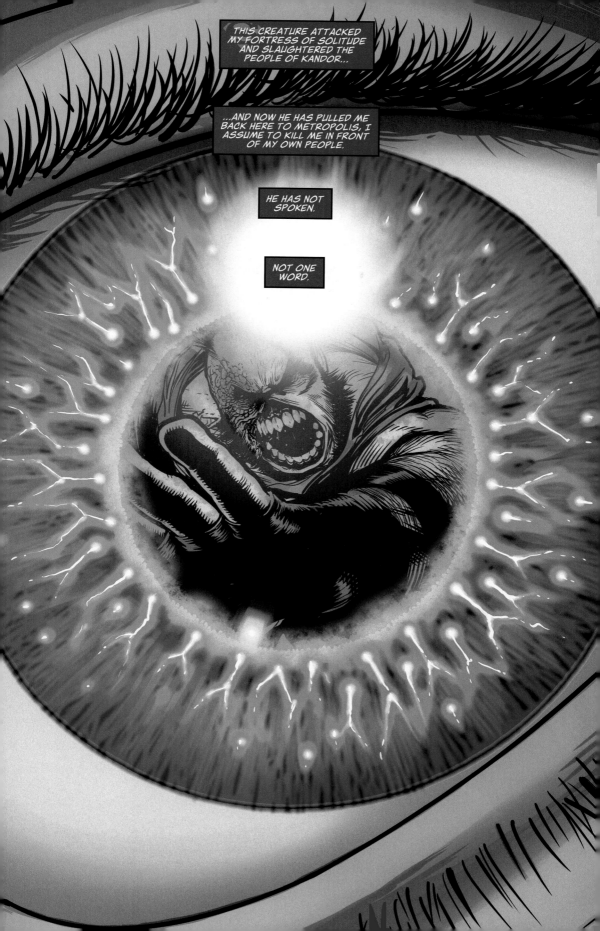

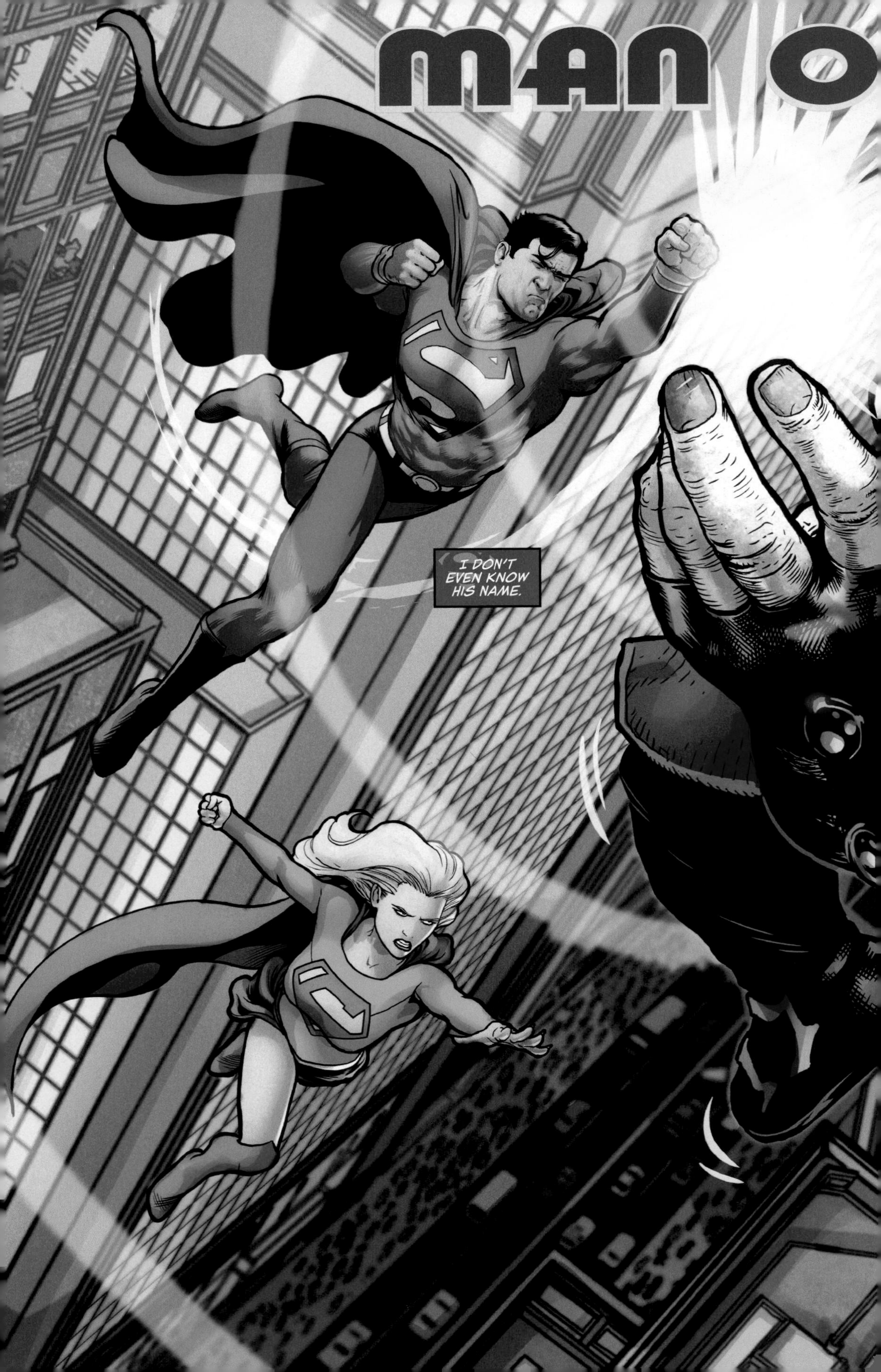
MAN O
I DON'T EVEN KNOW HIS NAME.

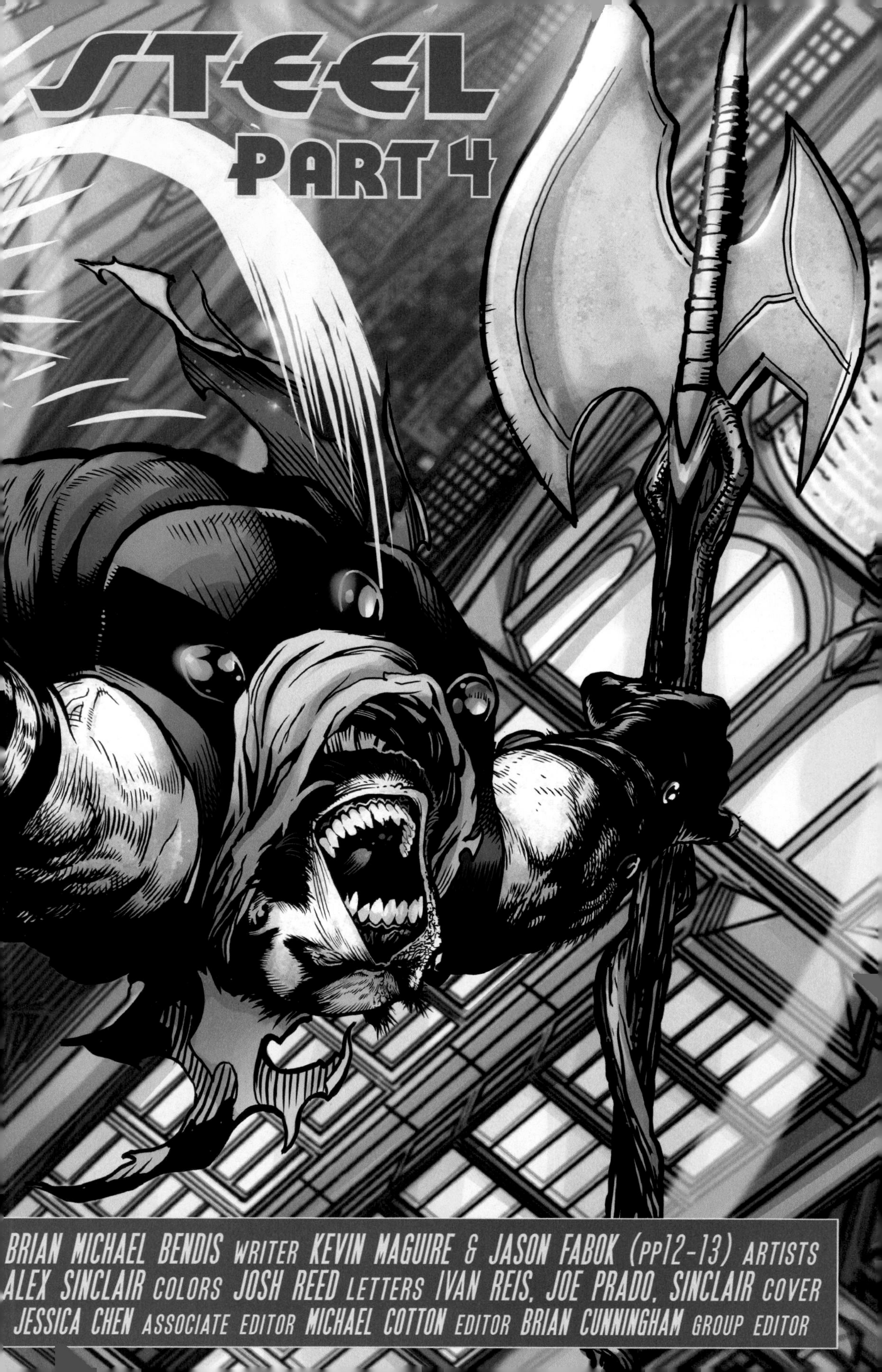
STEEL
PART 4
BRIAN MICHAEL BENDIS WRITER KEVIN MAGUIRE & JASON FABOK (PP12-13) ARTISTS
ALEX SINCLAIR COLORS JOSH REED LETTERS IVAN REIS, JOE PRADO, SINCLAIR COVER
JESSICA CHEN ASSOCIATE EDITOR MICHAEL COTTON EDITOR BRIAN CUNNINGHAM GROUP EDITOR

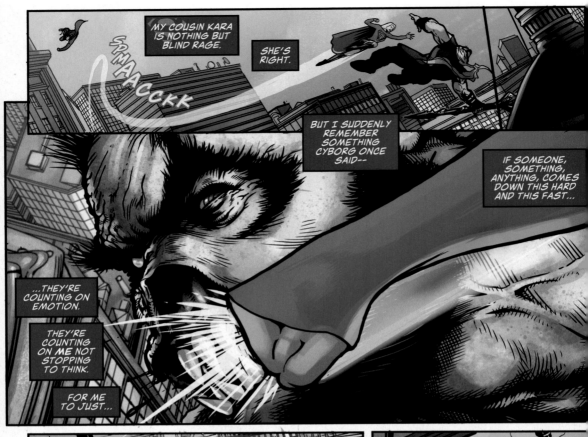

MY COUSIN KARA IS NOTHING BUT BLIND RAGE.

SHE'S RIGHT.

BUT I SUDDENLY REMEMBER SOMETHING CYBORG ONCE SAID--

IF SOMEONE, SOMETHING, ANYTHING, COMES DOWN THIS HARD AND THIS FAST...

...THEY'RE COUNTING ON EMOTION.

THEY'RE COUNTING ON ME NOT STOPPING TO THINK.

FOR ME TO JUST...

SMACK

...REACT.

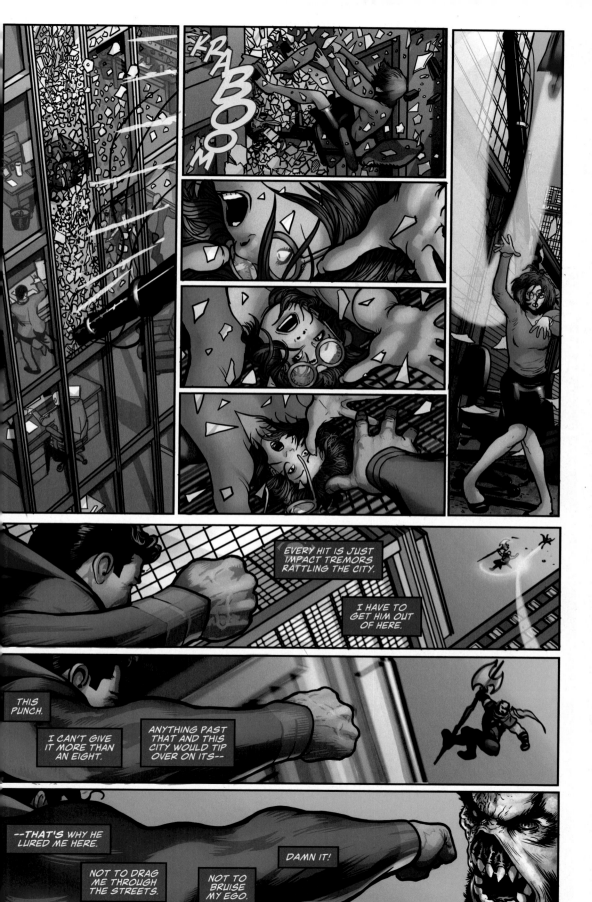

SMART.

FAST.

IT'S HIS POWER SOURCE.

IT HAS TO BE.

IT HAS TO BE COMING FROM-- HIS STAFF?

OKAY, LET'S PLAY BATMAN...

...OBVIOUS ALIEN TECH, ALIEN GARB, ALIEN TEXTILES.

HE KNOWS A LOT MORE ABOUT ME THAN I DO ABOUT HIM.

HE DEFIES THE LAWS OF PHYSICS.

AND HE CERTAINLY DOES HATE MY-- I SEE IT.

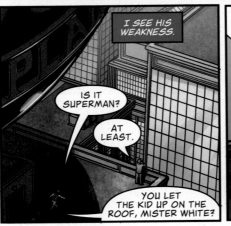

I SEE HIS WEAKNESS.

IS IT SUPERMAN?

AT LEAST.

YOU LET THE KID UP ON THE ROOF, MISTER WHITE?

THIS "KID" IS JIMMY OLSEN.

HE'S BOTH.

THIS IS JIMMY OLSEN?

MAN, THEY ARE MOVING FAST.

I THOUGHT HE WAS THE COFFEE BOY.

WHAT ARE? I DON'T SEE ANY--

KATOOOMM

EITHER WAY...

...I HAVE TO GET HIM OFF EARTH.

"CLARK??"

"DAD, WHAT IS THAT?"

"CLARK??"

SKATOOM

HAVE TO GET HIM OUT OF THE CITY--

BENDIS

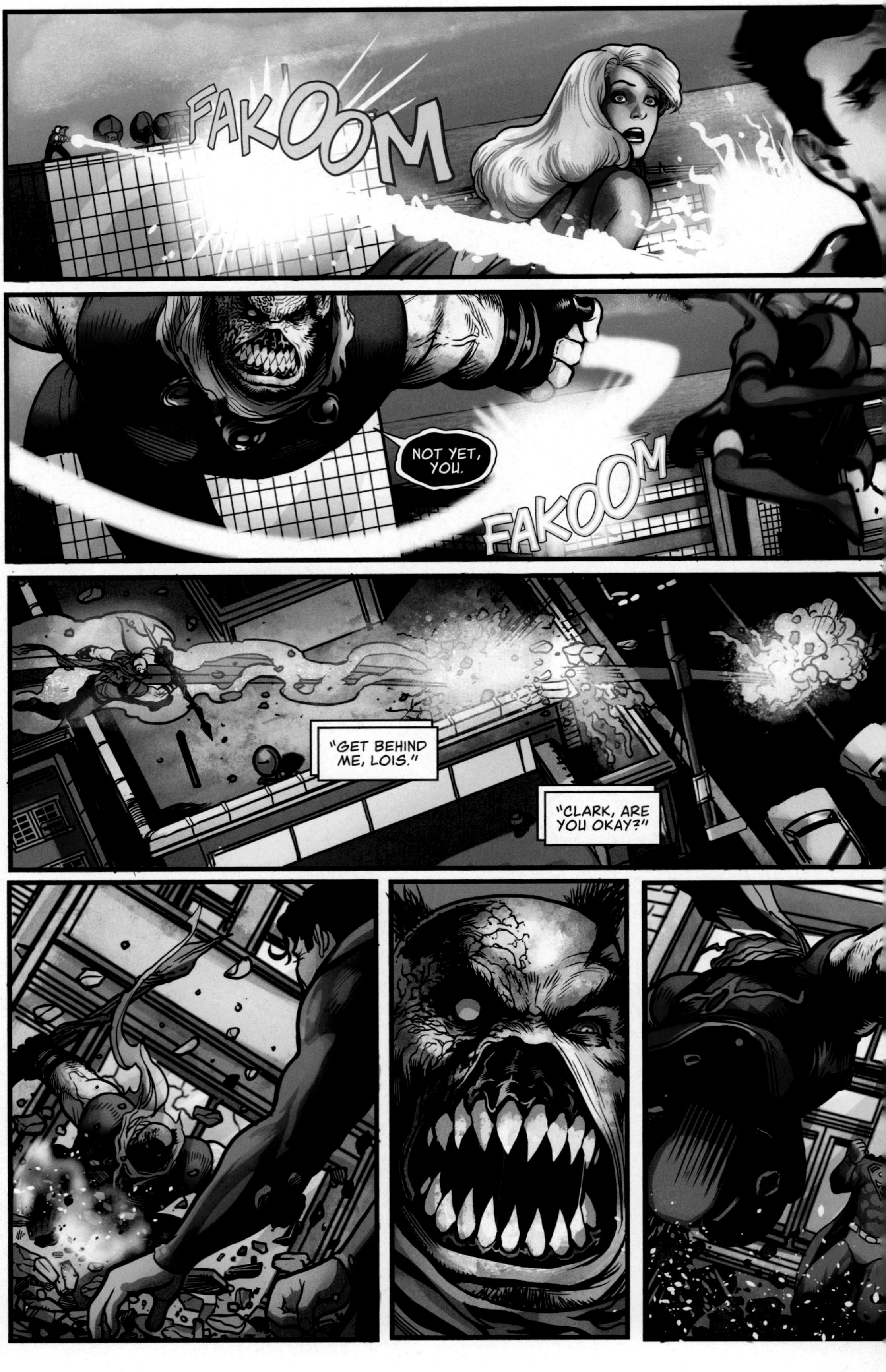
FAKOOM
NOT YET, YOU.
FAKOOM
"GET BEHIND ME, LOIS."
"CLARK, ARE YOU OKAY?"

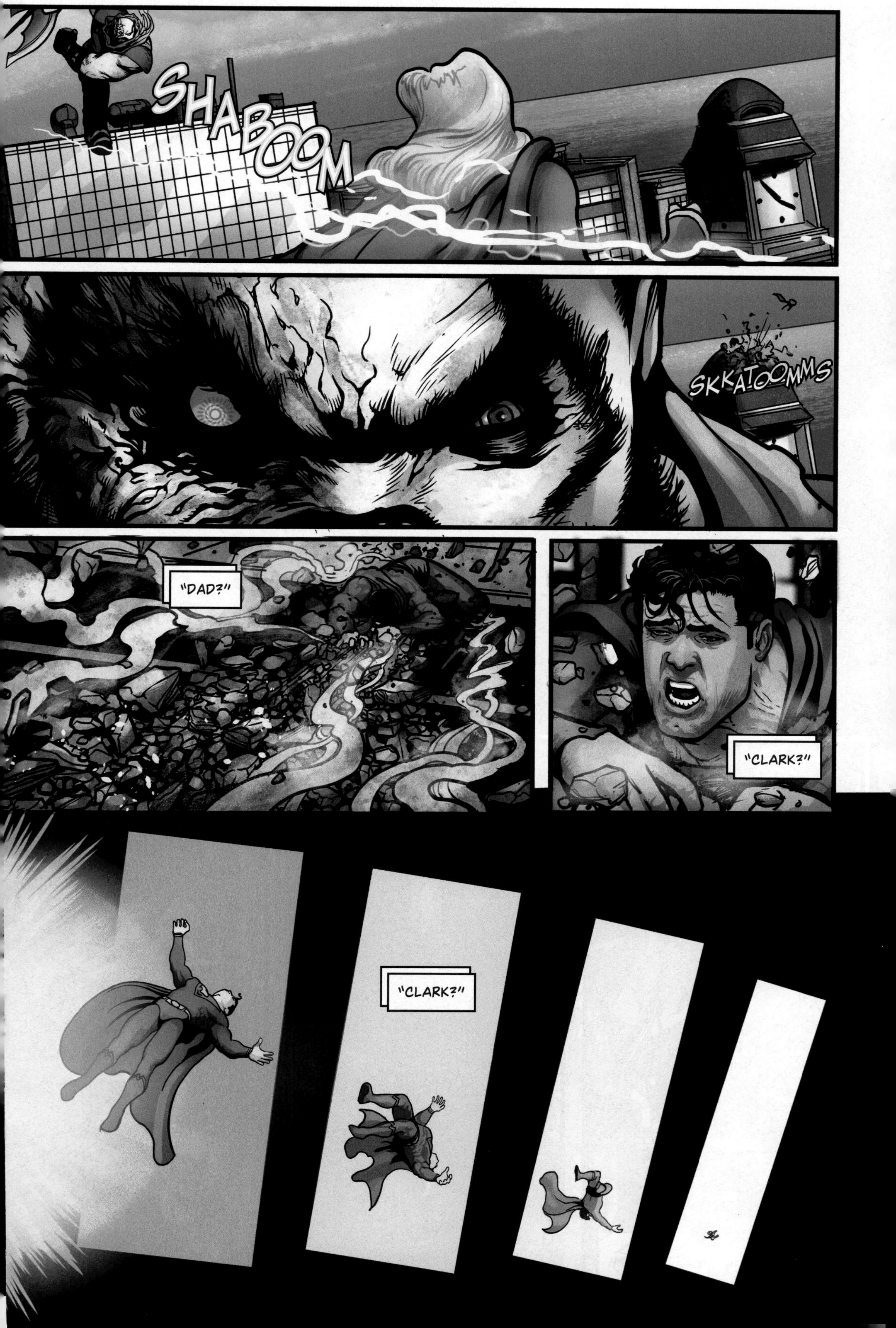
SHABOOM
SKKATOOMMS
"DAD?"
"CLARK?"
"CLARK?"

HI, I'M THE GREEN LANTERN OF THIS SECTOR.

CAN YOU TELL ME EXACTLY WHAT YOU'VE SEEN AND HEARD?

SUPERMAN CAME CRASHING RIGHT INTO MY DELI!!

I HAVE INSURANCE. I'M NOT INSANE, BUT, STILL--

DID YOU KNOW HE WENT BACK TO WEARING THE RED SHORTS?

HEY! I'M CAPTAIN MAGGIE SAWYER, METROPOLIS SPECIAL CRIMES UNIT.

THE BIG ALIEN PERP ACCUSED SUPERMAN OF STALLING.

WHICH WAS RUDE.

AND THEN THE FIGHT HEADED DOWN PUZO PLAZA THAT WAY.

BUT I DID HEAR HIM SAY--

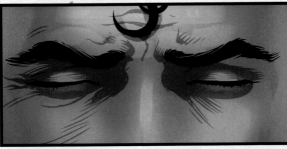

IT'S A CLEANSING

THIS IS NOT A FIGHT.

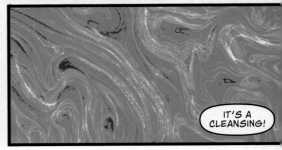

IT'S A CLEANSING!

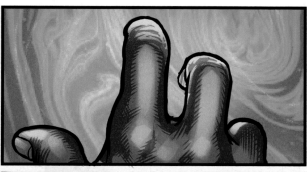

A CLEANSING?

UH, THE BIG GUY'S AWAKE.

OH.

HEY HAL...

...WHERE'S SUPERGIRL?

I JUST GOT HERE.

HEY, THANKS FOR THE ASSIST...

ARE YOU OKAY?

DID YOU SEE HIM?

NO.

THE CIVILIANS SAID HE WENT THAT WAY THE SECOND BEFORE I SHOWED UP.

MAYBE HE KNEW I WAS COMING.

I WAS IN PURSUIT BUT--

'S OUT HERE.

I SCANNED THE AREA.

HE'S USING TECH AND TECHNIQUES I HAVEN'T FELT OR SEEN BEFORE.

HE SAID "CLEANSING"?

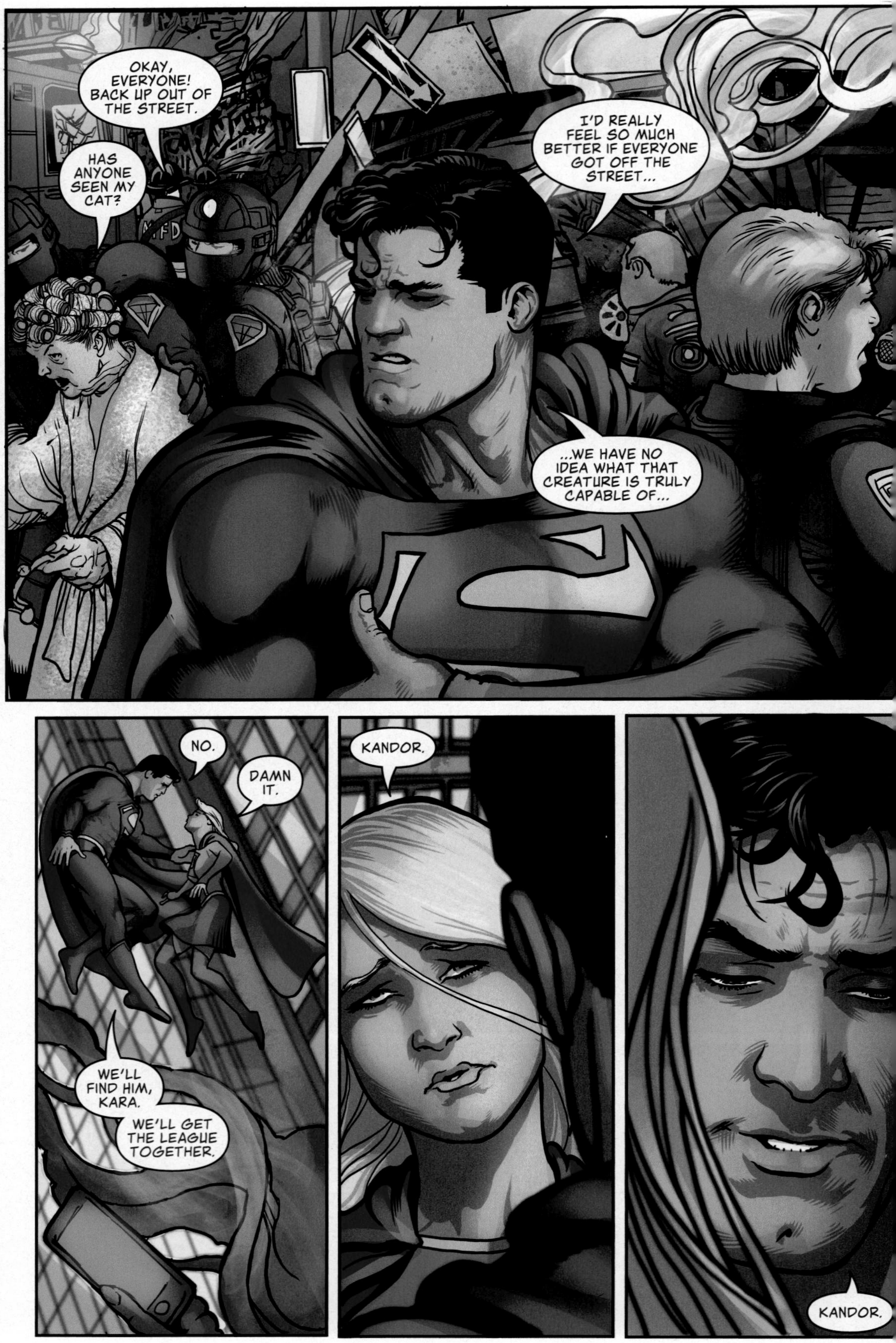
OKAY, EVERYONE! BACK UP OUT OF THE STREET.
HAS ANYONE SEEN MY CAT?
I'D REALLY FEEL SO MUCH BETTER IF EVERYONE GOT OFF THE STREET...
...WE HAVE NO IDEA WHAT THAT CREATURE IS TRULY CAPABLE OF...
NO.
DAMN IT.
WE'LL FIND HIM, KARA.
WE'LL GET THE LEAGUE TOGETHER.
KANDOR.
KANDOR.

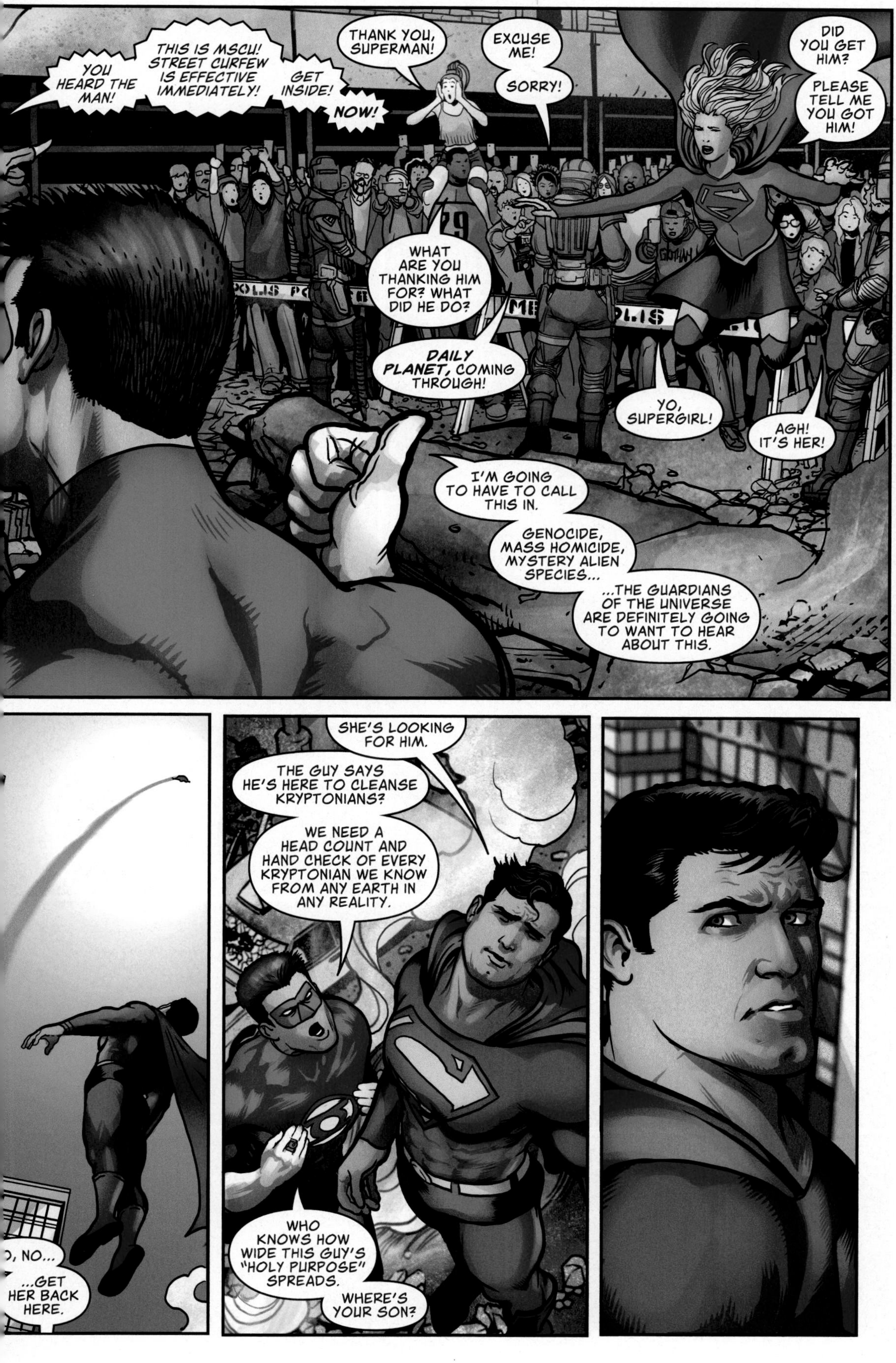
YOU HEARD THE MAN!
THIS IS MSCU! STREET CURFEW IS EFFECTIVE IMMEDIATELY!
GET INSIDE!
NOW!
THANK YOU, SUPERMAN!
EXCUSE ME!
SORRY!
DID YOU GET HIM?
PLEASE TELL ME YOU GOT HIM!
WHAT ARE YOU THANKING HIM FOR? WHAT DID HE DO?
DAILY PLANET, COMING THROUGH!
YO, SUPERGIRL!
AGH! IT'S HER!
I'M GOING TO HAVE TO CALL THIS IN.
GENOCIDE, MASS HOMICIDE, MYSTERY ALIEN SPECIES...
...THE GUARDIANS OF THE UNIVERSE ARE DEFINITELY GOING TO WANT TO HEAR ABOUT THIS.
...GET HER BACK HERE.
SHE'S LOOKING FOR HIM.
THE GUY SAYS HE'S HERE TO CLEANSE KRYPTONIANS?
WE NEED A HEAD COUNT AND HAND CHECK OF EVERY KRYPTONIAN WE KNOW FROM ANY EARTH IN ANY REALITY.
WHO KNOWS HOW WIDE THIS GUY'S "HOLY PURPOSE" SPREADS.
WHERE'S YOUR SON?

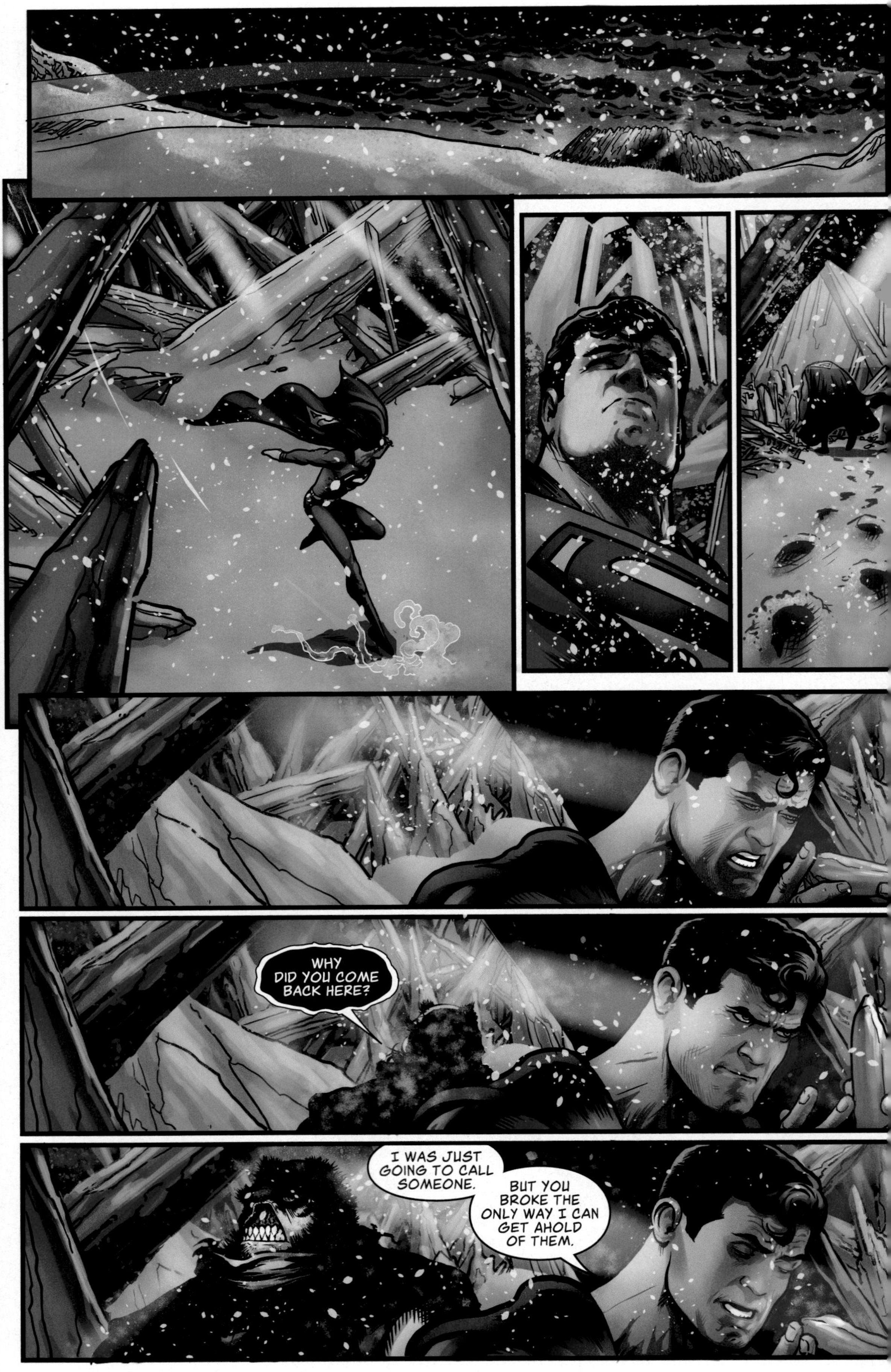
WHY DID YOU COME BACK HERE?
I WAS JUST GOING TO CALL SOMEONE.
BUT YOU BROKE THE ONLY WAY I CAN GET AHOLD OF THEM.

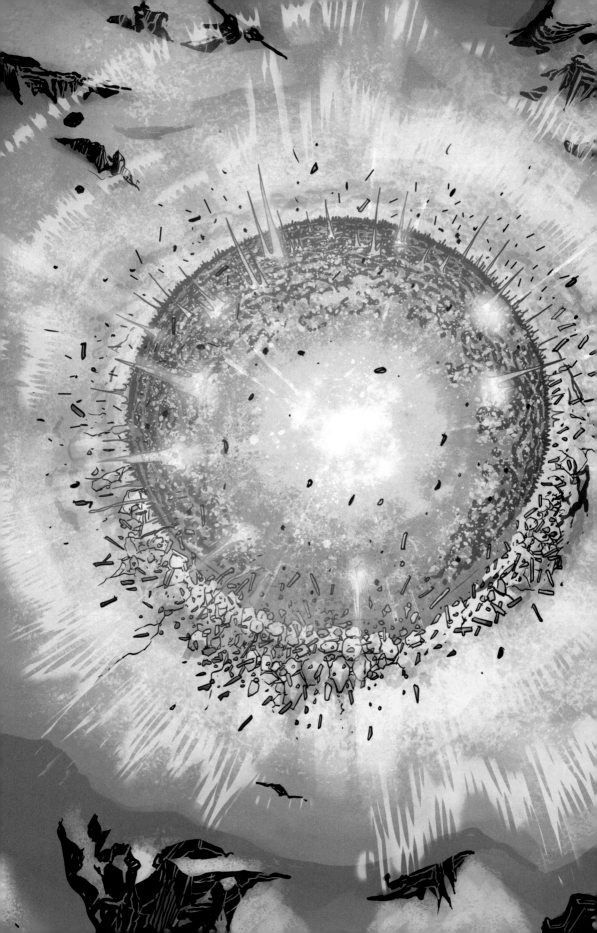

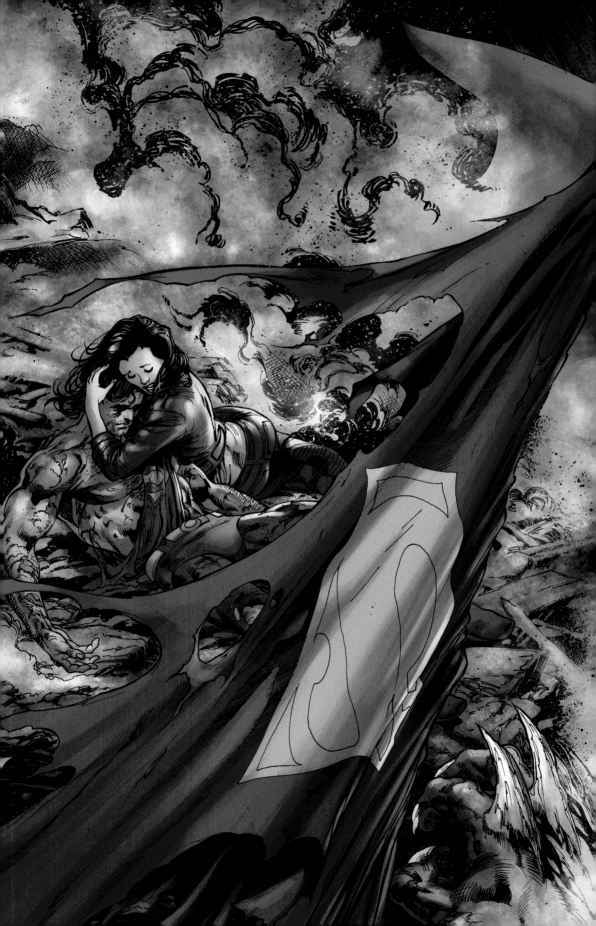

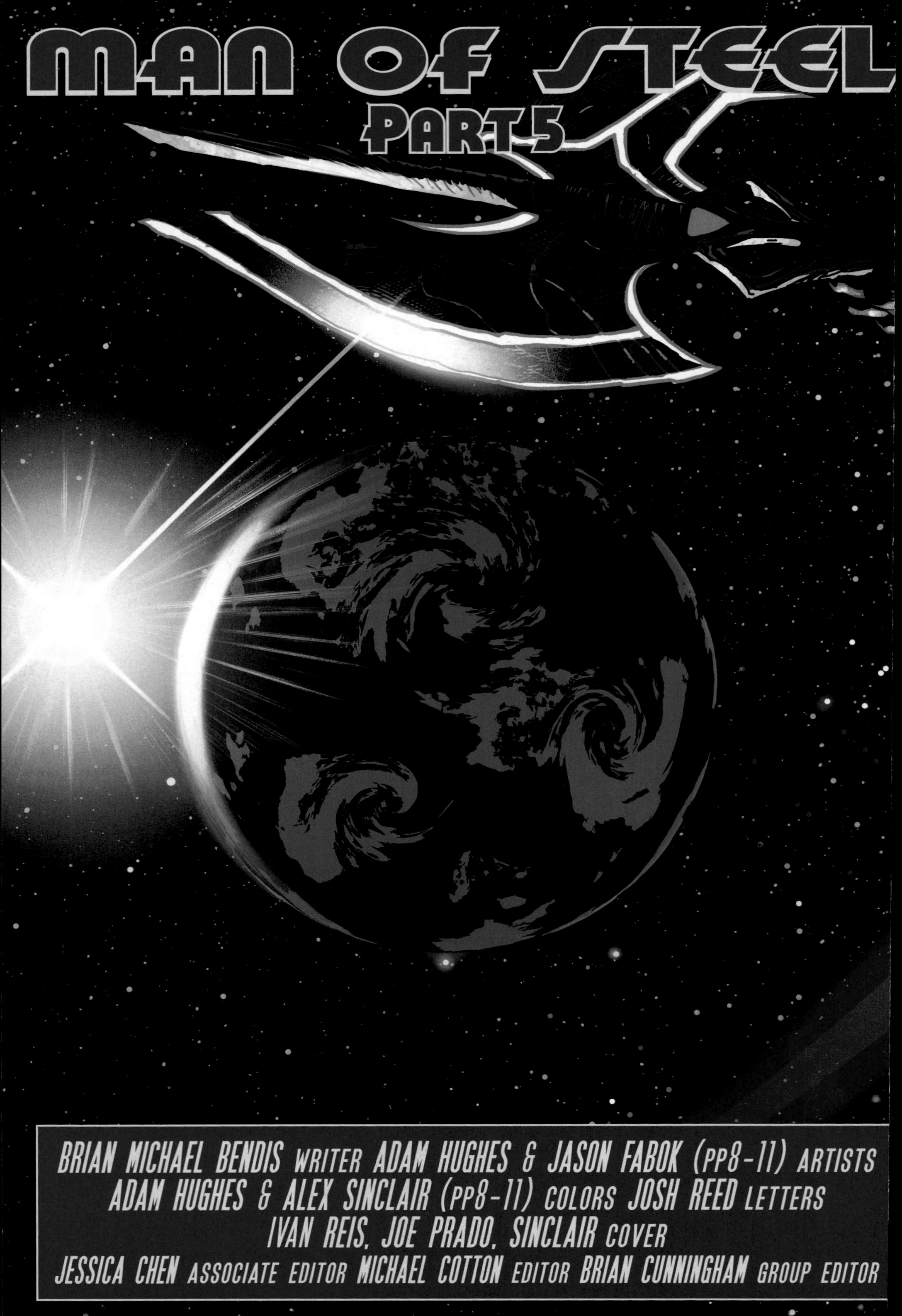
MAN OF STEEL
PART 5
BRIAN MICHAEL BENDIS WRITER ADAM HUGHES & JASON FABOK (PP8-11) ARTISTS
ADAM HUGHES & ALEX SINCLAIR (PP8-11) COLORS JOSH REED LETTERS
IVAN REIS, JOE PRADO, SINCLAIR COVER
JESSICA CHEN ASSOCIATE EDITOR MICHAEL COTTON EDITOR BRIAN CUNNINGHAM GROUP EDITOR

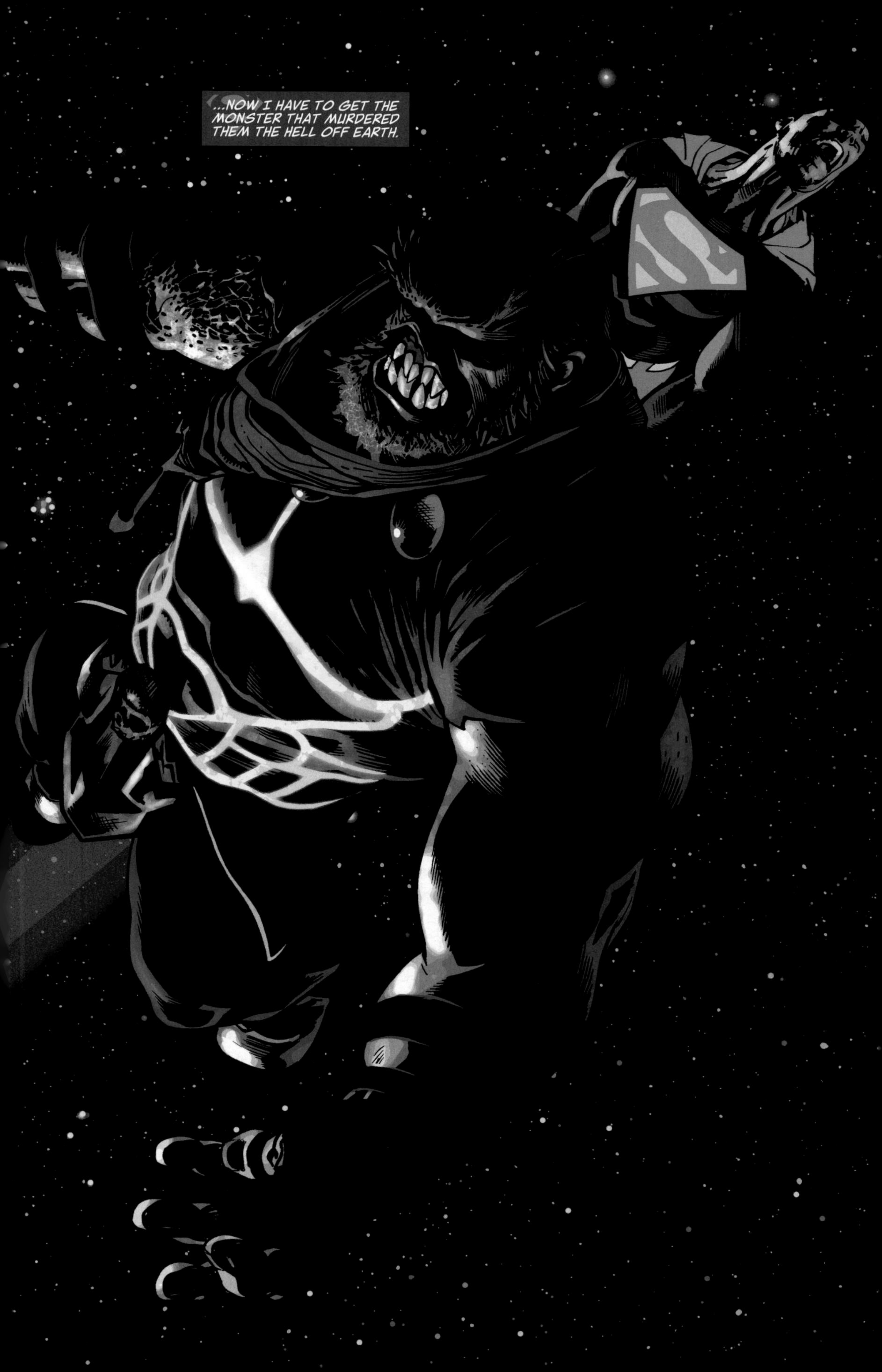
...NOW I HAVE TO GET THE MONSTER THAT MURDERED THEM THE HELL OFF EARTH.

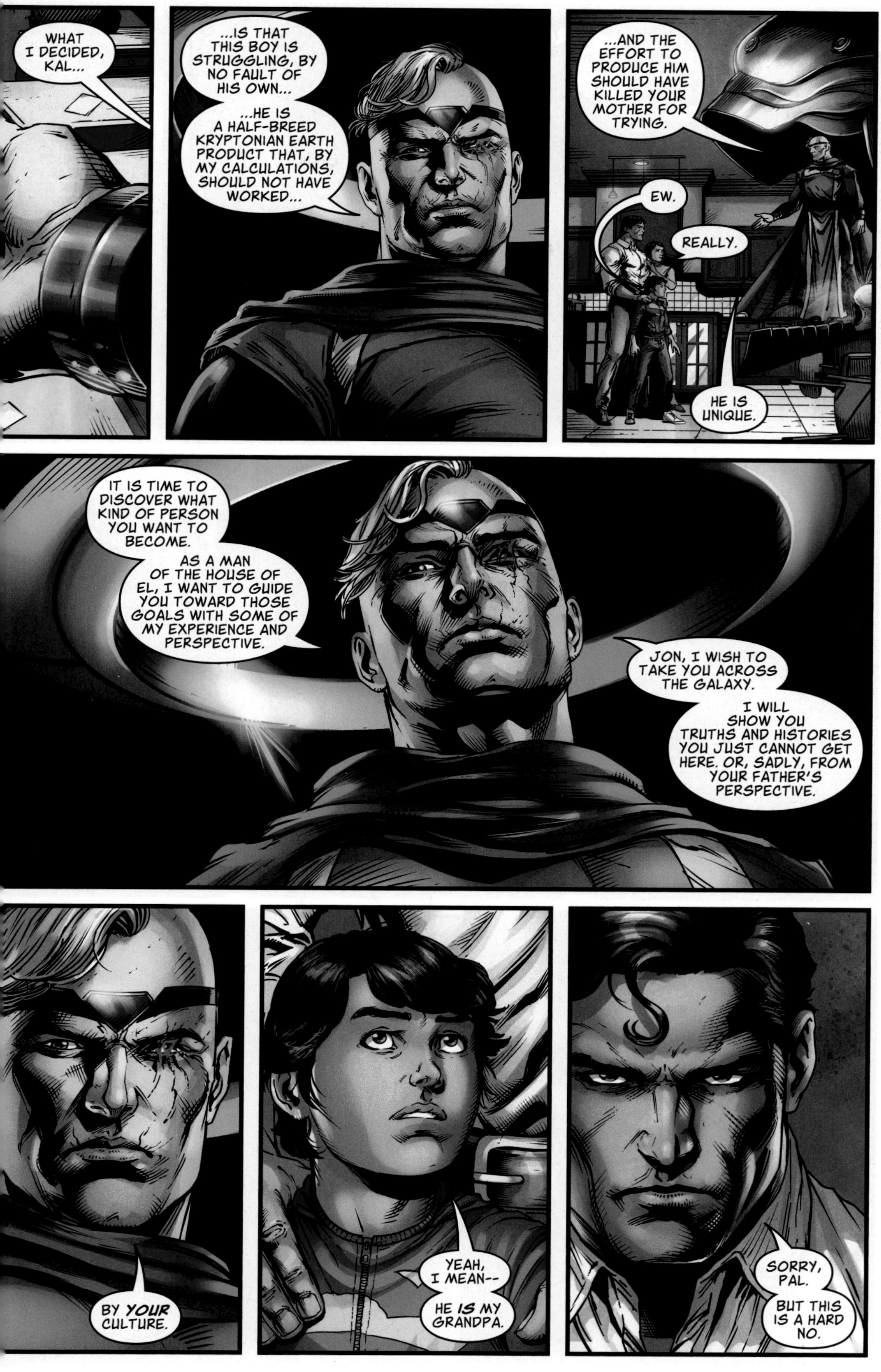
WHAT I DECIDED, KAL...
...IS THAT THIS BOY IS STRUGGLING, BY NO FAULT OF HIS OWN...
...HE IS A HALF-BREED KRYPTONIAN EARTH PRODUCT THAT, BY MY CALCULATIONS, SHOULD NOT HAVE WORKED...
...AND THE EFFORT TO PRODUCE HIM SHOULD HAVE KILLED YOUR MOTHER FOR TRYING.
EW.
REALLY.
HE IS UNIQUE.
IT IS TIME TO DISCOVER WHAT KIND OF PERSON YOU WANT TO BECOME.
AS A MAN OF THE HOUSE OF EL, I WANT TO GUIDE YOU TOWARD THOSE GOALS WITH SOME OF MY EXPERIENCE AND PERSPECTIVE.
JON, I WISH TO TAKE YOU ACROSS THE GALAXY.
I WILL SHOW YOU TRUTHS AND HISTORIES YOU JUST CANNOT GET HERE. OR, SADLY, FROM YOUR FATHER'S PERSPECTIVE.
BY YOUR CULTURE.
YEAH, I MEAN--
HE IS MY GRANDPA.
SORRY, PAL.
BUT THIS IS A HARD NO.

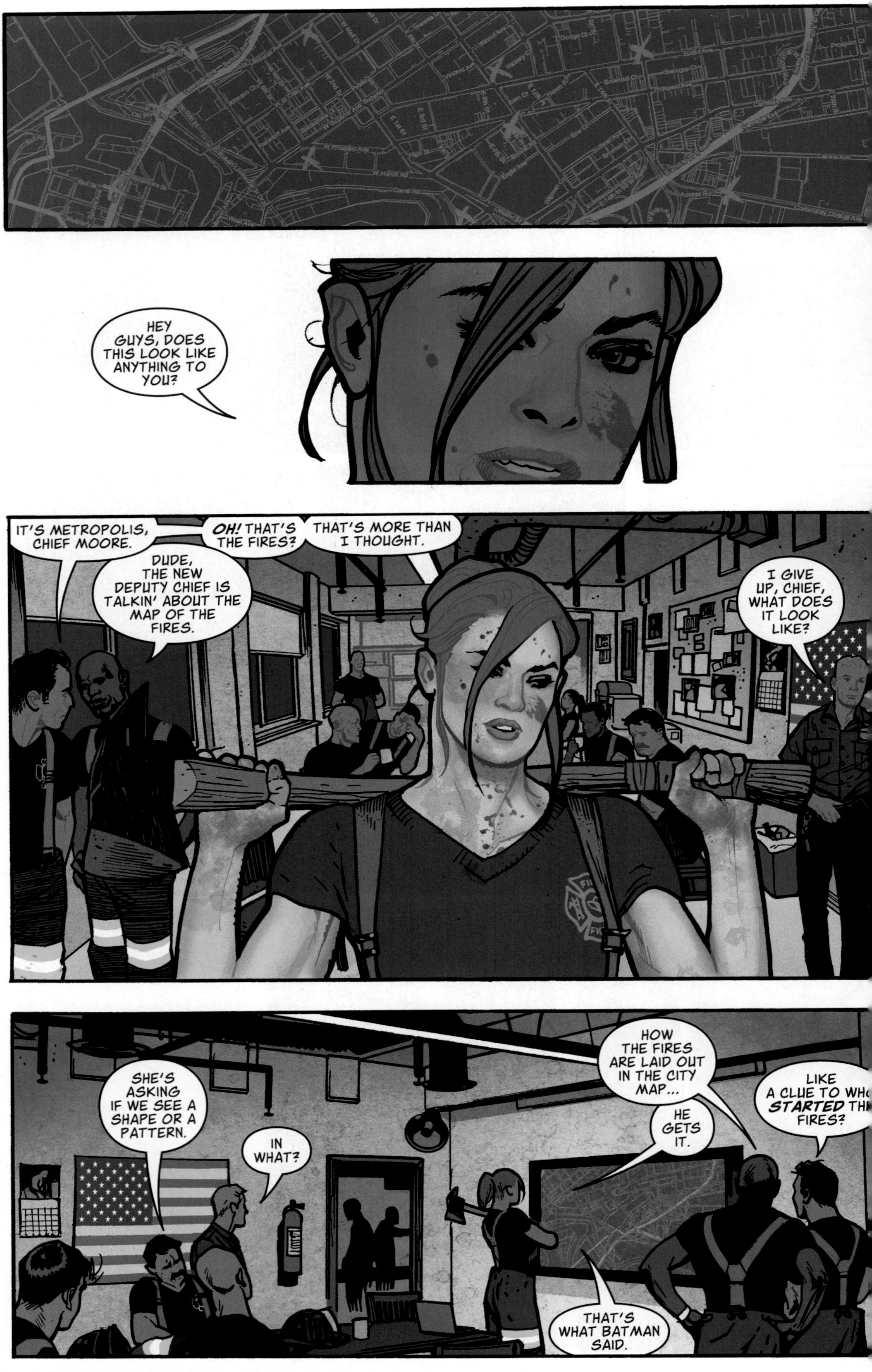
HEY GUYS, DOES THIS LOOK LIKE ANYTHING TO YOU?
IT'S METROPOLIS, CHIEF MOORE.
DUDE, THE NEW DEPUTY CHIEF IS TALKIN' ABOUT THE MAP OF THE FIRES.
OH! THAT'S THE FIRES?
THAT'S MORE THAN I THOUGHT.
I GIVE UP, CHIEF, WHAT DOES IT LOOK LIKE?
SHE'S ASKING IF WE SEE A SHAPE OR A PATTERN.
IN WHAT?
HOW THE FIRES ARE LAID OUT IN THE CITY MAP...
HE GETS IT.
LIKE A CLUE TO WH
STARTED TH
FIRES?
THAT'S WHAT BATMAN SAID.

YOU TALKED TO *BATMAN*?

YOU'VE BEEN HERE *TWO DAYS*, CHIEF.

YA PALLIN' UP TO SUPERMAN, BATMAN--WHO'S NEXT?

IF I HAVE A SAY...THE GUY WHO'S LIGHTING THESE DAMN FIRES--

WHAT IF IT'S--?

WHAT IF THE FIRES IS JUST A BUNCH OF RANDOS?

WE HAVE A STRUCTURE FIRE AT 101 FOX AND GARDNER!

FULLY ENGULFED!

ATTENTION ENGINE FIVE, ENGINE TWO, LADDER ONE, RESCUE ONE.

TIME IS 18:56. USE CHANNEL ONE. PATH ONE.

♪ HERE WE GO, HERE WE GO AGAIN! ♪

WEEEOOOOOO

BLANH

BLANHHB

WOOP!

HEY!

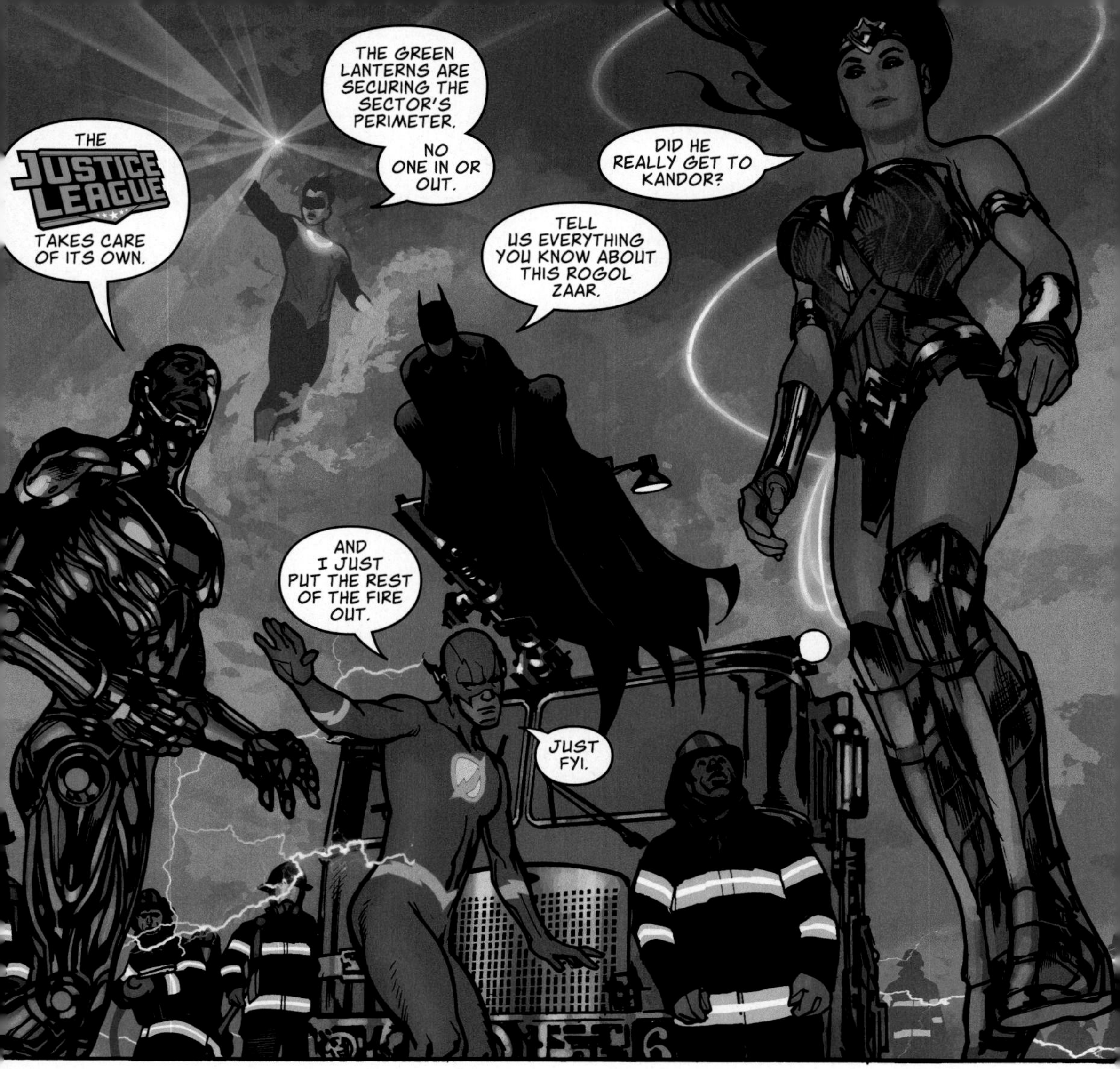
THE JUSTICE LEAGUE TAKES CARE OF ITS OWN.
THE GREEN LANTERNS ARE SECURING THE SECTOR'S PERIMETER.
NO ONE IN OR OUT.
DID HE REALLY GET TO KANDOR?
TELL US EVERYTHING YOU KNOW ABOUT THIS ROGOL ZAAR.
AND I JUST PUT THE REST OF THE FIRE OUT.
JUST FYI.

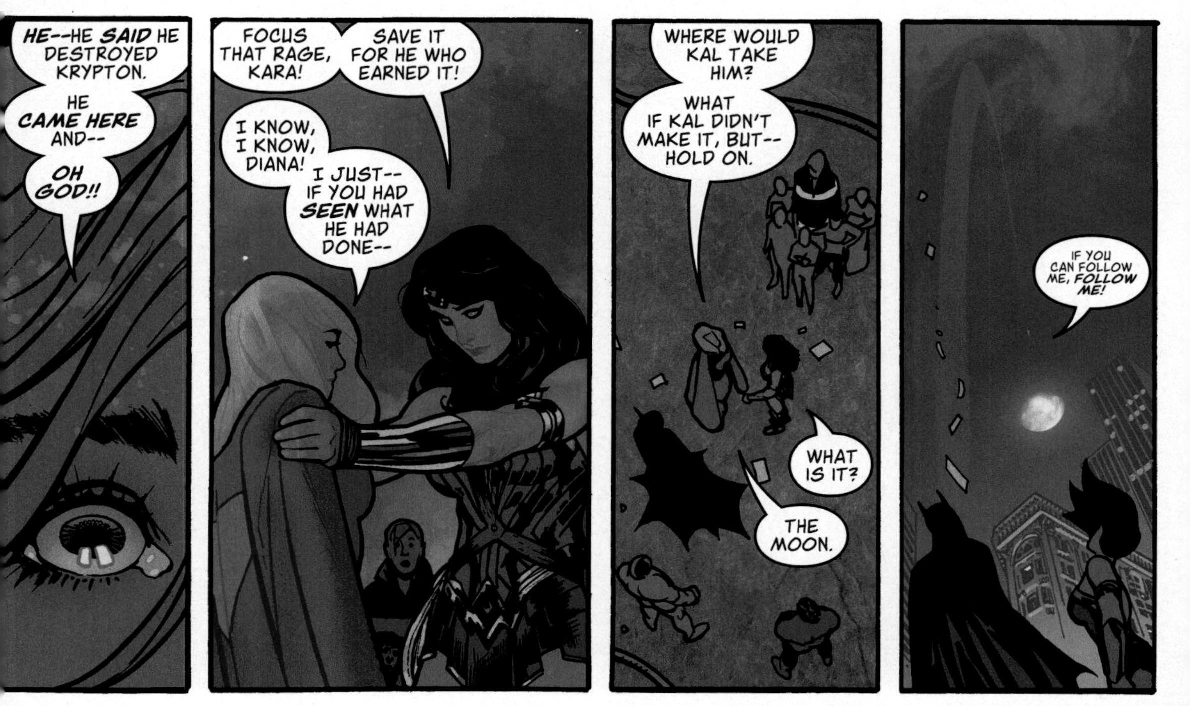
HE--HE SAID HE DESTROYED KRYPTON.
HE CAME HERE AND--
OH GOD!!
FOCUS THAT RAGE, KARA!
SAVE IT FOR HE WHO EARNED IT!
I KNOW, I KNOW, DIANA!
I JUST-- IF YOU HAD SEEN WHAT HE HAD DONE--
WHERE WOULD KAL TAKE HIM?
WHAT IF KAL DIDN'T MAKE IT, BUT-- HOLD ON.
WHAT IS IT?
THE MOON.
IF YOU CAN FOLLOW ME, FOLLOW ME!

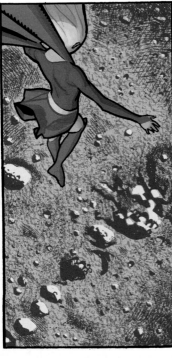

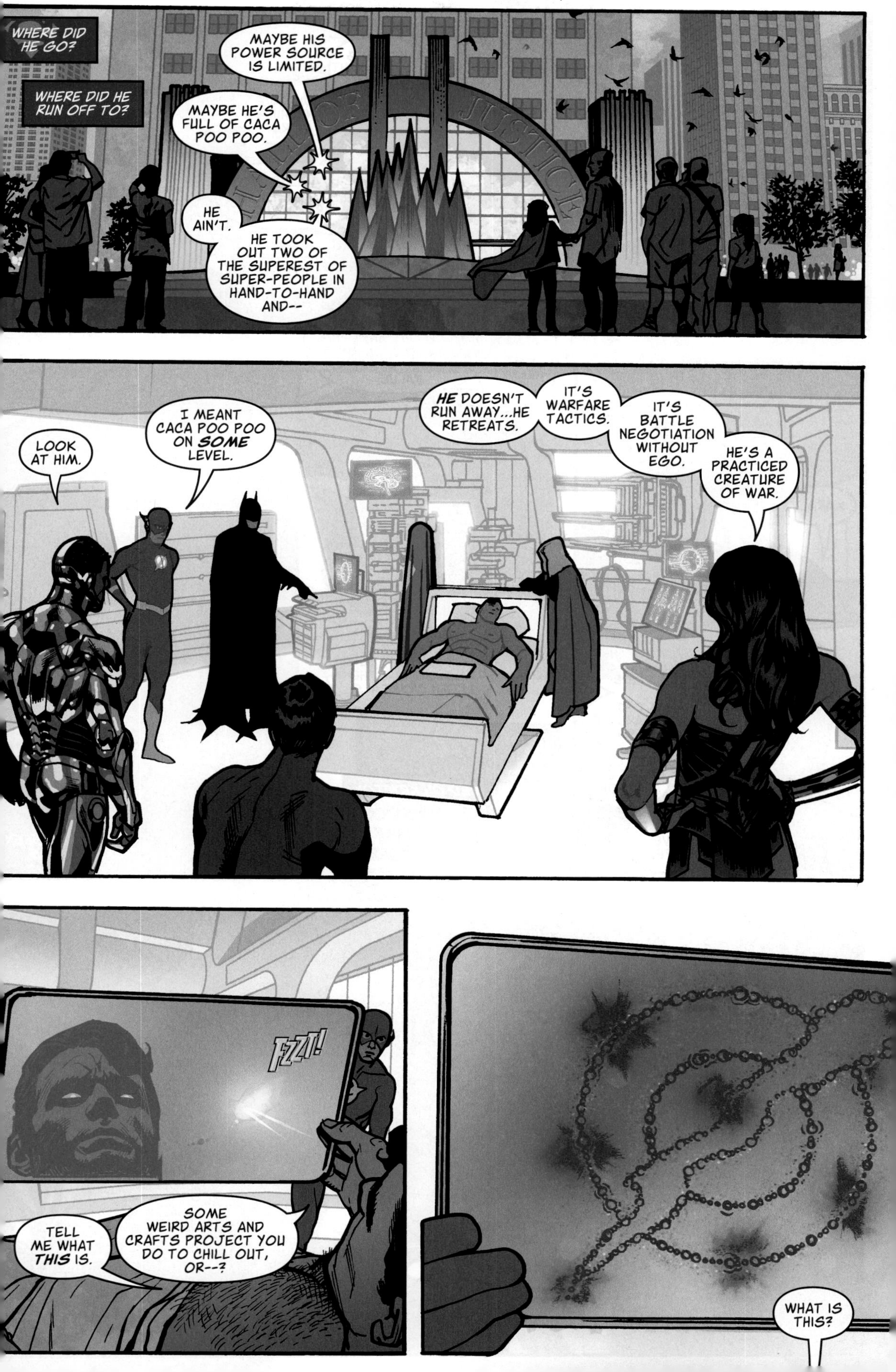
WHERE DID HE GO?
WHERE DID HE RUN OFF TO?
MAYBE HIS POWER SOURCE IS LIMITED.
MAYBE HE'S FULL OF CACA POO POO.
HE AIN'T.
HE TOOK OUT TWO OF THE SUPEREST OF SUPER-PEOPLE IN HAND-TO-HAND AND--
LOOK AT HIM.
I MEANT CACA POO POO ON SOME LEVEL.
HE DOESN'T RUN AWAY...HE RETREATS.
IT'S WARFARE TACTICS.
IT'S BATTLE NEGOTIATION WITHOUT EGO.
HE'S A PRACTICED CREATURE OF WAR.
FZZT!
TELL ME WHAT THIS IS.
SOME WEIRD ARTS AND CRAFTS PROJECT YOU DO TO CHILL OUT, OR--?
WHAT IS THIS?

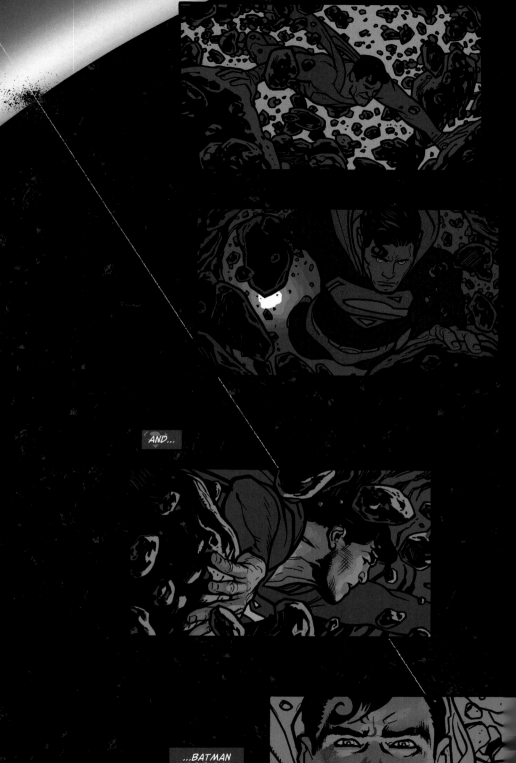

AND...

...BATMAN
WAS RIGHT...

...CLEANSING.

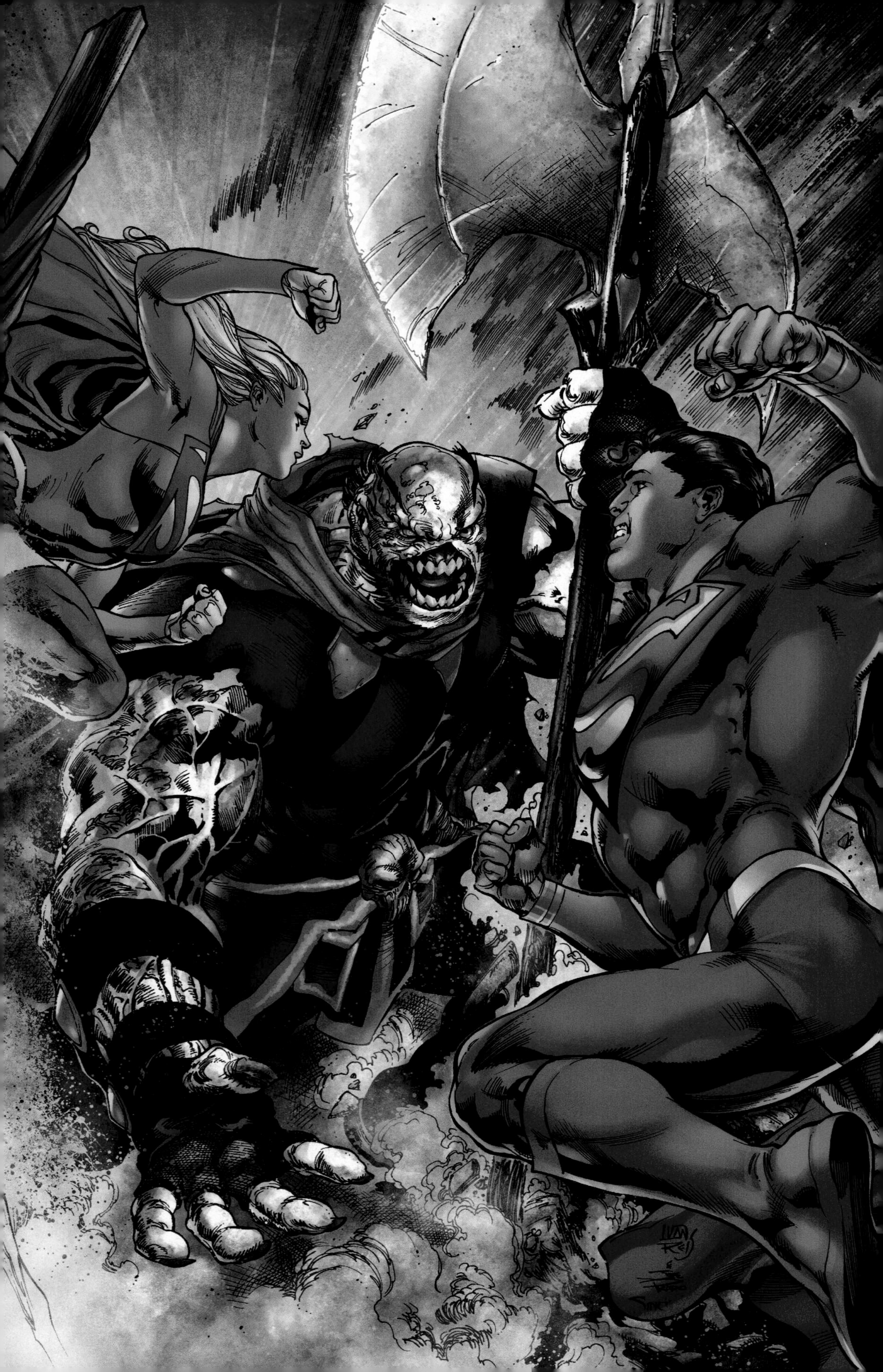

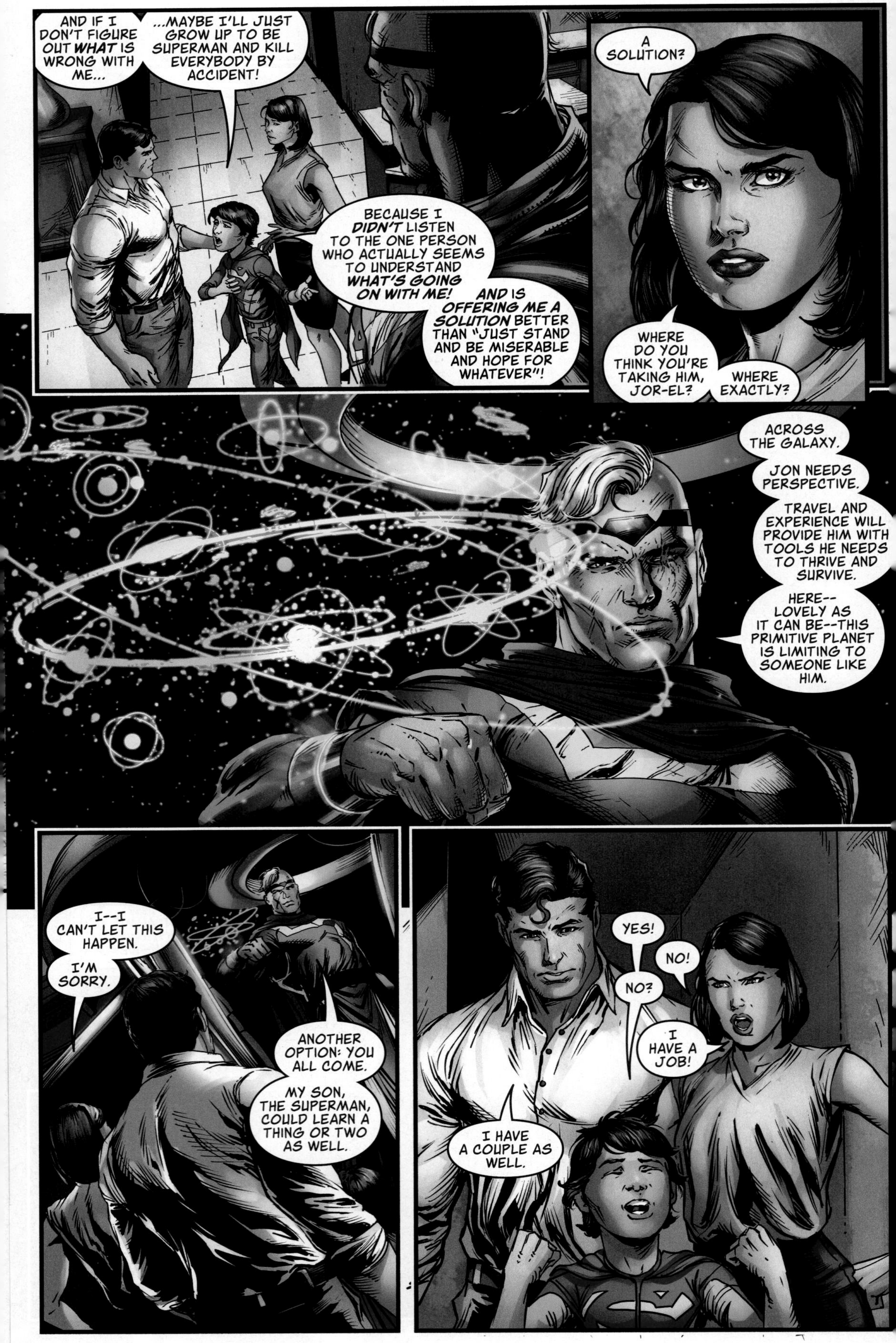
AND IF I DON'T FIGURE OUT WHAT IS WRONG WITH ME...
...MAYBE I'LL JUST GROW UP TO BE SUPERMAN AND KILL EVERYBODY BY ACCIDENT!
BECAUSE I DIDN'T LISTEN TO THE ONE PERSON WHO ACTUALLY SEEMS TO UNDERSTAND WHAT'S GOING ON WITH ME!
AND IS OFFERING ME A SOLUTION BETTER THAN "JUST STAND AND BE MISERABLE AND HOPE FOR WHATEVER"!
A SOLUTION?
WHERE DO YOU THINK YOU'RE TAKING HIM, JOR-EL?
WHERE EXACTLY?
ACROSS THE GALAXY.
JON NEEDS PERSPECTIVE.
TRAVEL AND EXPERIENCE WILL PROVIDE HIM WITH TOOLS HE NEEDS TO THRIVE AND SURVIVE.
HERE-- LOVELY AS IT CAN BE--THIS PRIMITIVE PLANET IS LIMITING TO SOMEONE LIKE HIM.
I--I CAN'T LET THIS HAPPEN.
I'M SORRY.
ANOTHER OPTION: YOU ALL COME.
MY SON, THE SUPERMAN, COULD LEARN A THING OR TWO AS WELL.
YES!
NO!
NO?
I HAVE A JOB!
I HAVE A COUPLE AS WELL.

WE *JUST* CLOSED A TWO-BOOK DEAL.

THE FIRST ONE IS A TELL-ALL ABOUT MY *DAILY PLANET* GREATEST BLAH BLAH BLAHS.

I GET TO CHOOSE THE SECOND.

THIS'LL BE THE SECOND.

WHAT?

WE'RE GOING?!

WELL, I *CAN'T* STOP YOU.

YOUR DAD CAN'T STOP YOU.

SO I GUESS I HAVE TO DROP EVERYTHING AND GO.

YOU'RE GOING TO WRITE A BOOK ABOUT IT?!

THAT'S GREAT!

KID, DON'T PUSH ME.

STOP!! EVERYBODY JUST-- STOP!

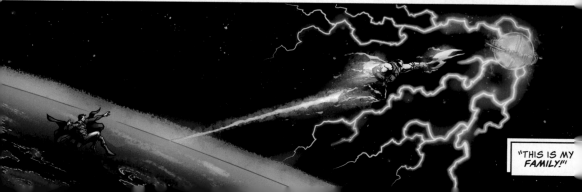

"THIS IS MY *FAMILY!*"

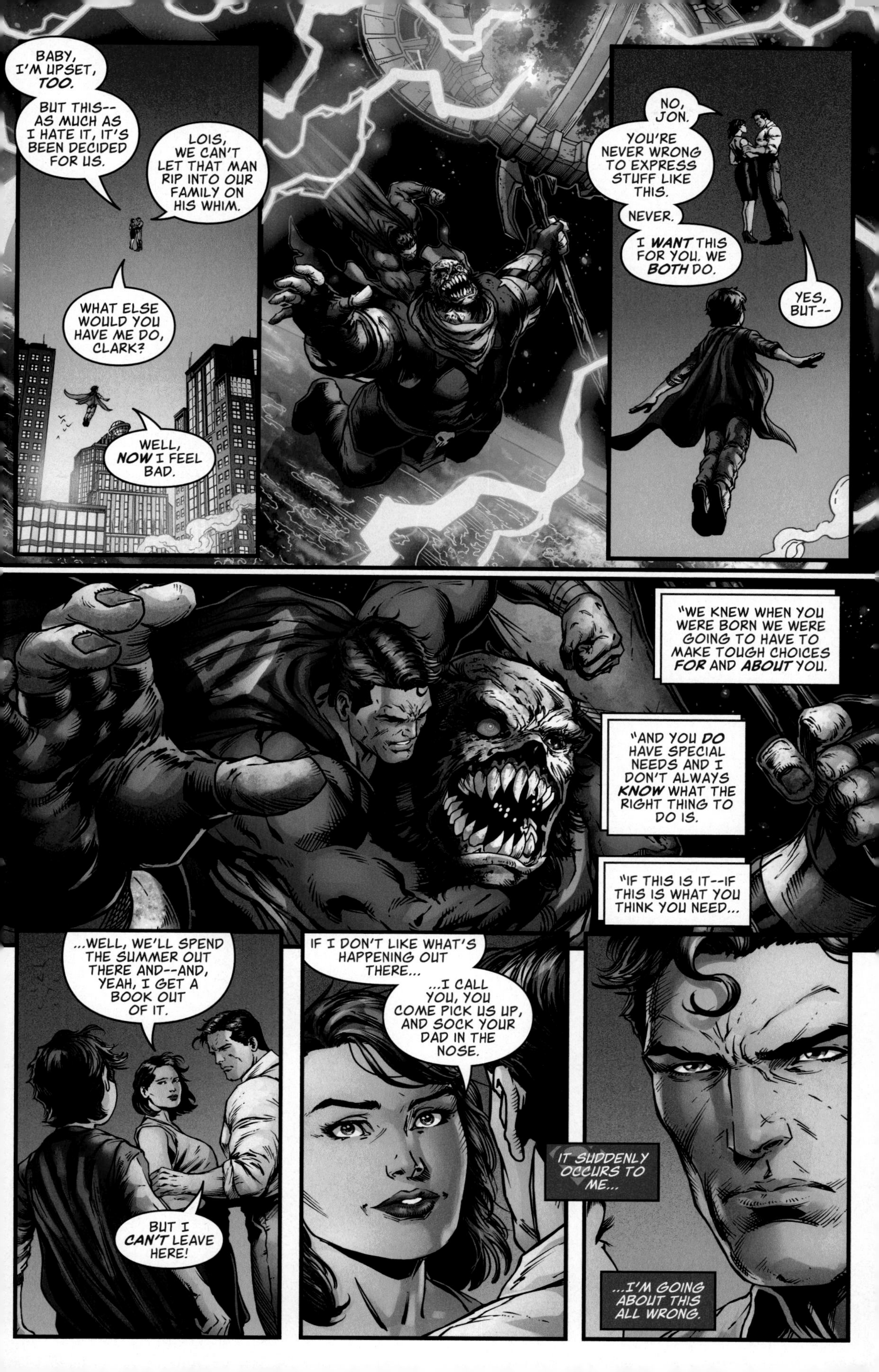
BABY, I'M UPSET, TOO.
BUT THIS-- AS MUCH AS I HATE IT, IT'S BEEN DECIDED FOR US.
LOIS, WE CAN'T LET THAT MAN RIP INTO OUR FAMILY ON HIS WHIM.
WHAT ELSE WOULD YOU HAVE ME DO, CLARK?
WELL, NOW I FEEL BAD.
NO, JON.
YOU'RE NEVER WRONG TO EXPRESS STUFF LIKE THIS.
NEVER.
I WANT THIS FOR YOU. WE BOTH DO.
YES, BUT--
"WE KNEW WHEN YOU WERE BORN WE WERE GOING TO HAVE TO MAKE TOUGH CHOICES FOR AND ABOUT YOU.
"AND YOU DO HAVE SPECIAL NEEDS AND I DON'T ALWAYS KNOW WHAT THE RIGHT THING TO DO IS.
"IF THIS IS IT--IF THIS IS WHAT YOU THINK YOU NEED...
...WELL, WE'LL SPEND THE SUMMER OUT THERE AND--AND, YEAH, I GET A BOOK OUT OF IT.
BUT I CAN'T LEAVE HERE!
IF I DON'T LIKE WHAT'S HAPPENING OUT THERE...
...I CALL YOU, YOU COME PICK US UP, AND SOCK YOUR DAD IN THE NOSE.
IT SUDDENLY OCCURS TO ME...
...I'M GOING ABOUT THIS ALL WRONG.

I WILL GIVE THEM BACK.

THIS IS--

THIS IS NOT *WHAT I WANT*.

AND HOPE-FULLY IN BETTER CONDITION.

BUT IT IS WHAT *HE* NEEDS.

THERE IS NOTHING MORE IMPORTANT TO ME THAN THE SAFETY AND VITALITY OF *THIS* FAMILY.

WE ARE KRYPTON'S *ONLY* HOPE FOR SURVIVAL.

JONATHAN NEEDS THIS.

HEY, IF DAMIAN COMES BY LOOKING FOR ME TELL HIM TO STAY OUT OF MY THIRD DRAWER.

IN FACT, *NO ONE* SHOULD GO INTO MY THIRD DRAWER.

IN FACT, HOLD ON.

I, UH, HAVE TO CHECK ON SOMETHING.

THAT IS A DEEP-SPACE COMMUNICATOR ATTACHED TO MY SHIP'S SPECIFIC SIGNAL.

FSSHHPOOO

I KNOW WHAT IT IS.

SPEAK YOUR MIND, SON.

YOUR HOUSE WAS *ALWAYS* IN DISARRAY.

I THINK YOU HANDLED THIS POORLY AND NOW MY HOUSE IS IN DISARRAY.

THIS JUST PROVES IT.

I TOOK CARE OF THE DRAWER SITUATION.

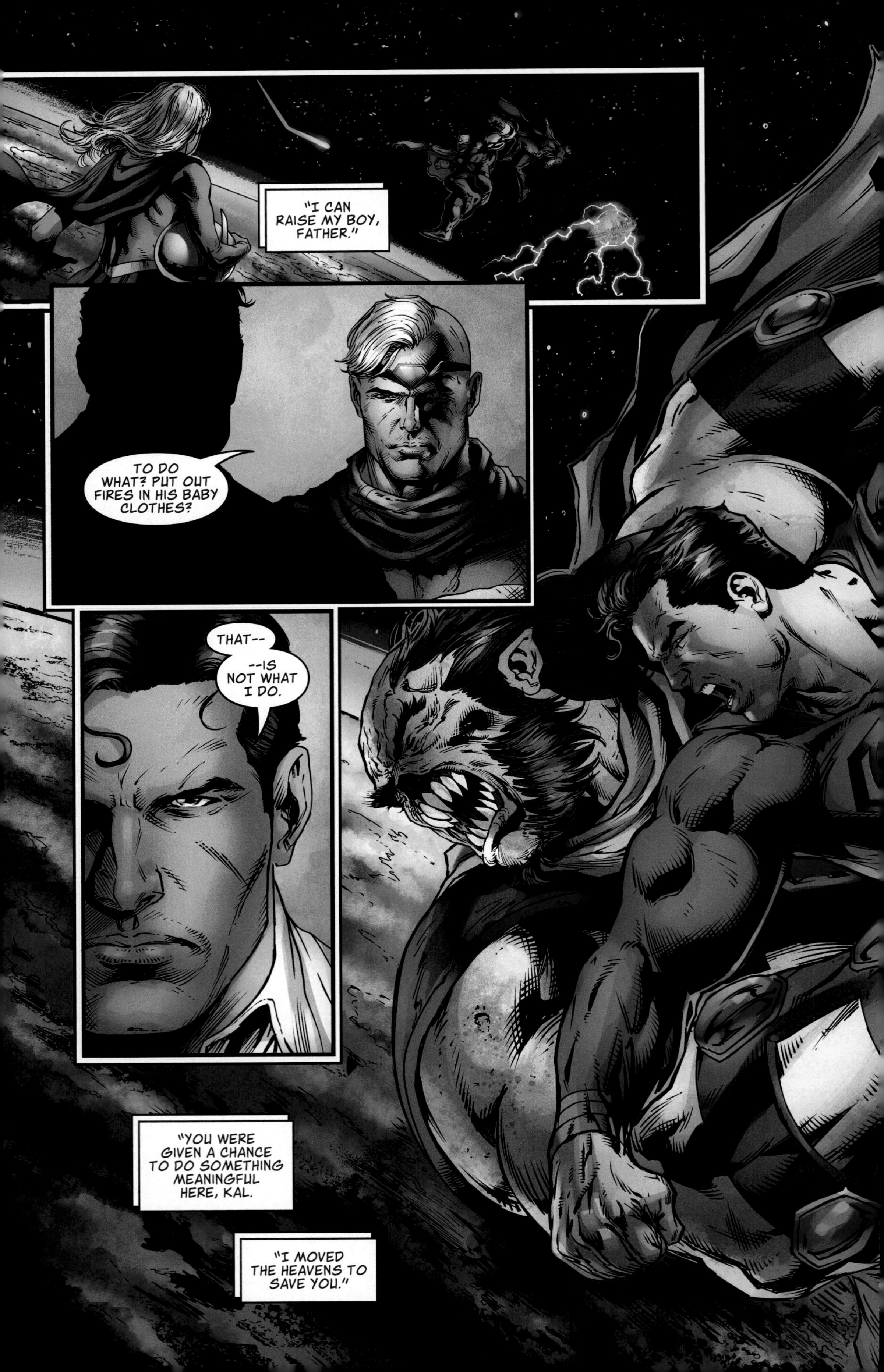
"I CAN RAISE MY BOY, FATHER."
TO DO WHAT? PUT OUT FIRES IN HIS BABY CLOTHES?
THAT--
--IS NOT WHAT I DO.
"YOU WERE GIVEN A CHANCE TO DO SOMETHING MEANINGFUL HERE, KAL.
"I MOVED THE HEAVENS TO SAVE YOU."

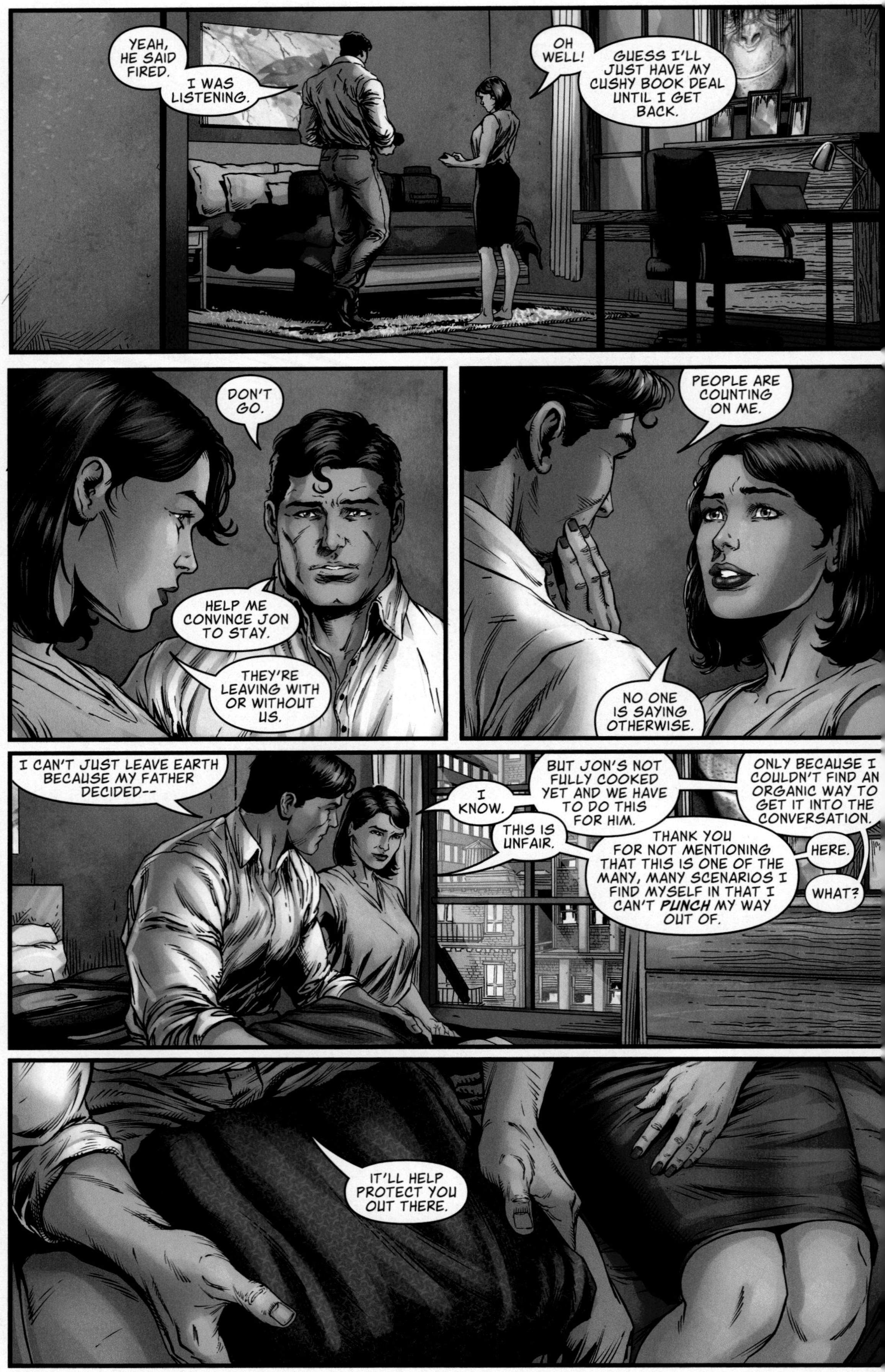
YEAH, HE SAID FIRED.
I WAS LISTENING.
OH WELL!
GUESS I'LL JUST HAVE MY CUSHY BOOK DEAL UNTIL I GET BACK.
DON'T GO.
HELP ME CONVINCE JON TO STAY.
THEY'RE LEAVING WITH OR WITHOUT US.
PEOPLE ARE COUNTING ON ME.
NO ONE IS SAYING OTHERWISE.
I CAN'T JUST LEAVE EARTH BECAUSE MY FATHER DECIDED--
I KNOW.
BUT JON'S NOT FULLY COOKED YET AND WE HAVE TO DO THIS FOR HIM.
THIS IS UNFAIR.
THANK YOU FOR NOT MENTIONING THAT THIS IS ONE OF THE MANY, MANY SCENARIOS I FIND MYSELF IN THAT I CAN'T PUNCH MY WAY OUT OF.
ONLY BECAUSE I COULDN'T FIND AN ORGANIC WAY TO GET IT INTO THE CONVERSATION.
HERE.
WHAT?
IT'LL HELP PROTECT YOU OUT THERE.

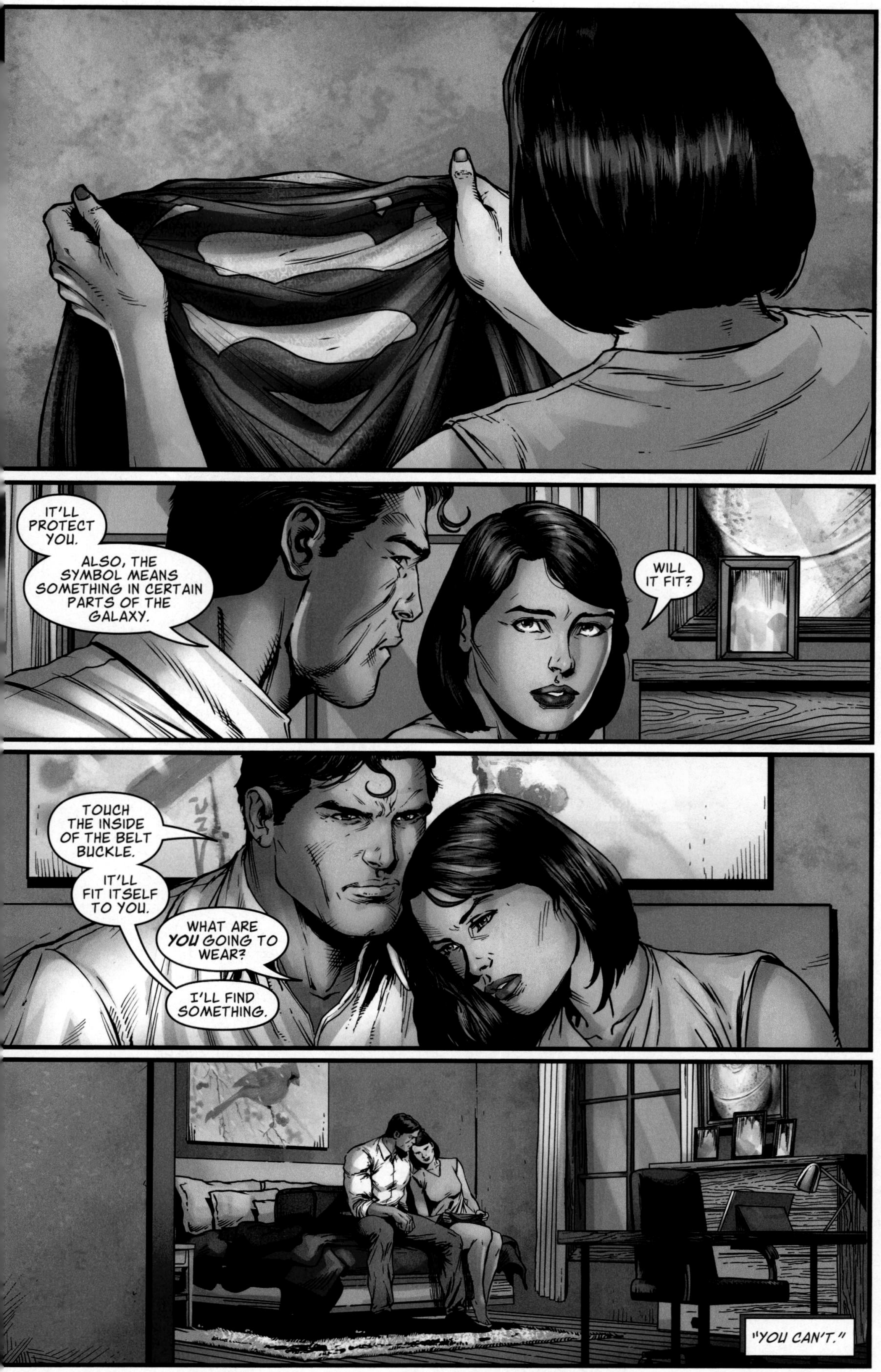
IT'LL PROTECT YOU.
ALSO, THE SYMBOL MEANS SOMETHING IN CERTAIN PARTS OF THE GALAXY.
WILL IT FIT?
TOUCH THE INSIDE OF THE BELT BUCKLE.
IT'LL FIT ITSELF TO YOU.
WHAT ARE YOU GOING TO WEAR?
I'LL FIND SOMETHING.
"YOU CAN'T."

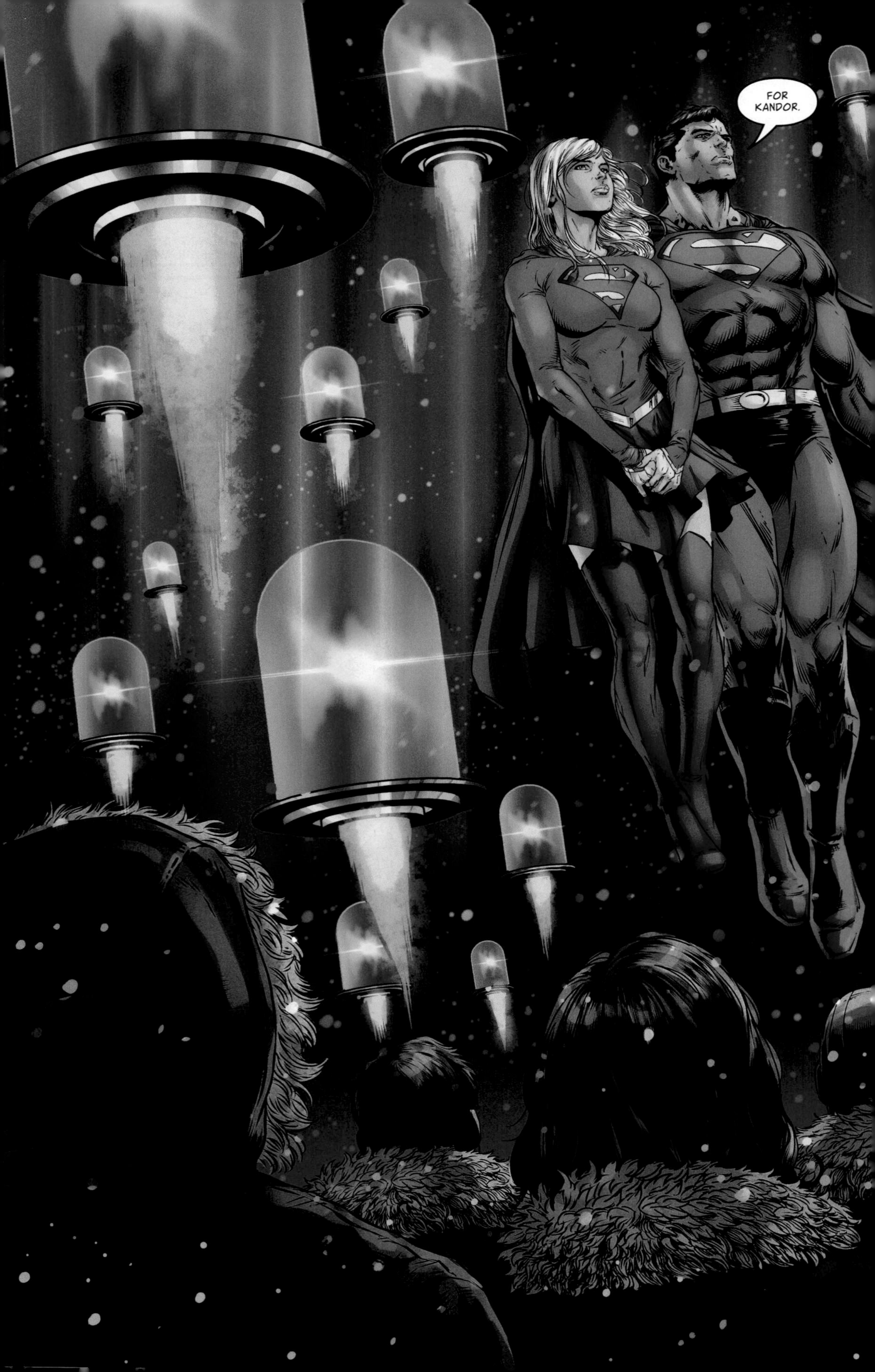
FOR KANDOR.

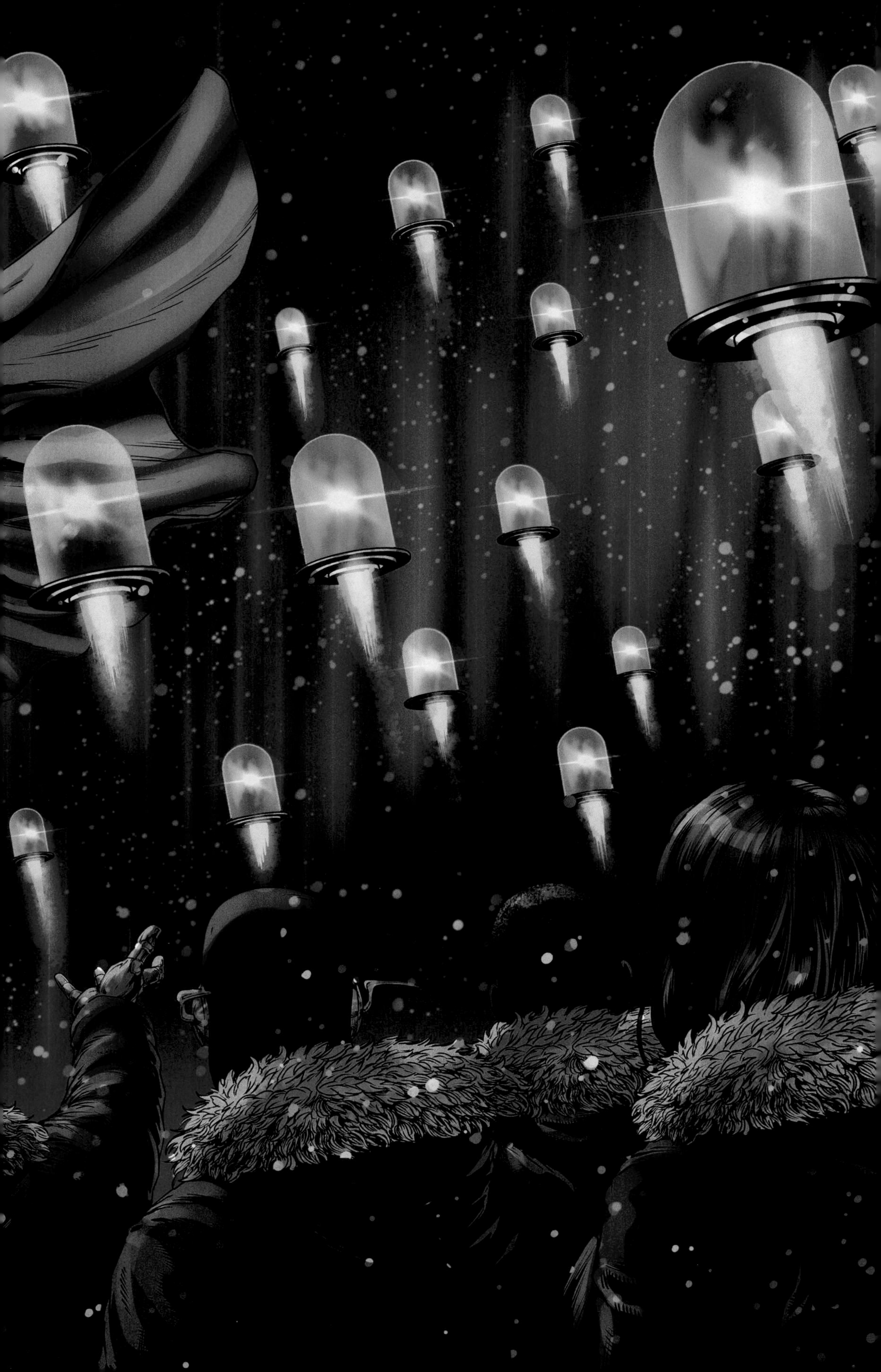

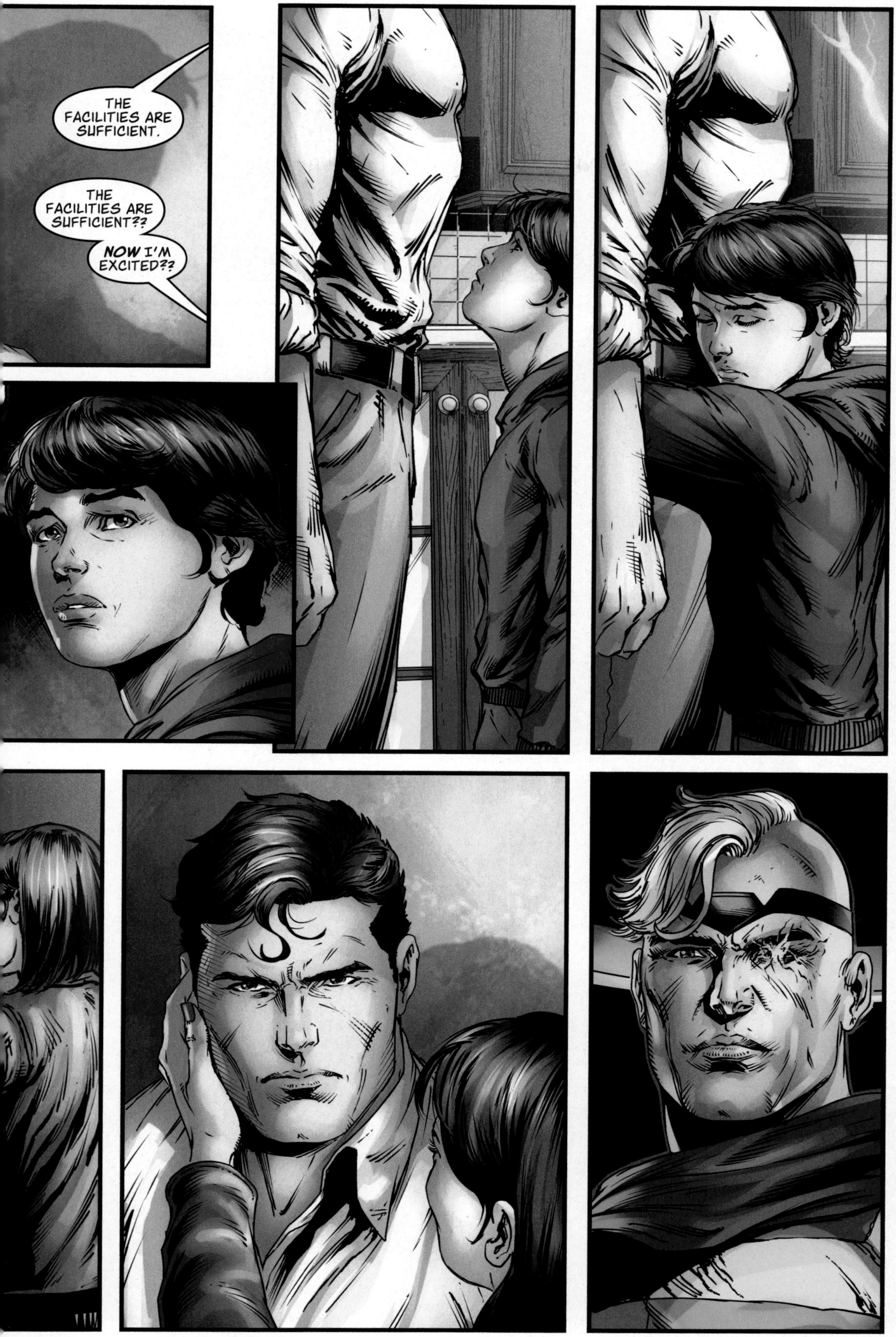
THE FACILITIES ARE SUFFICIENT.
THE FACILITIES ARE SUFFICIENT??
NOW I'M EXCITED??

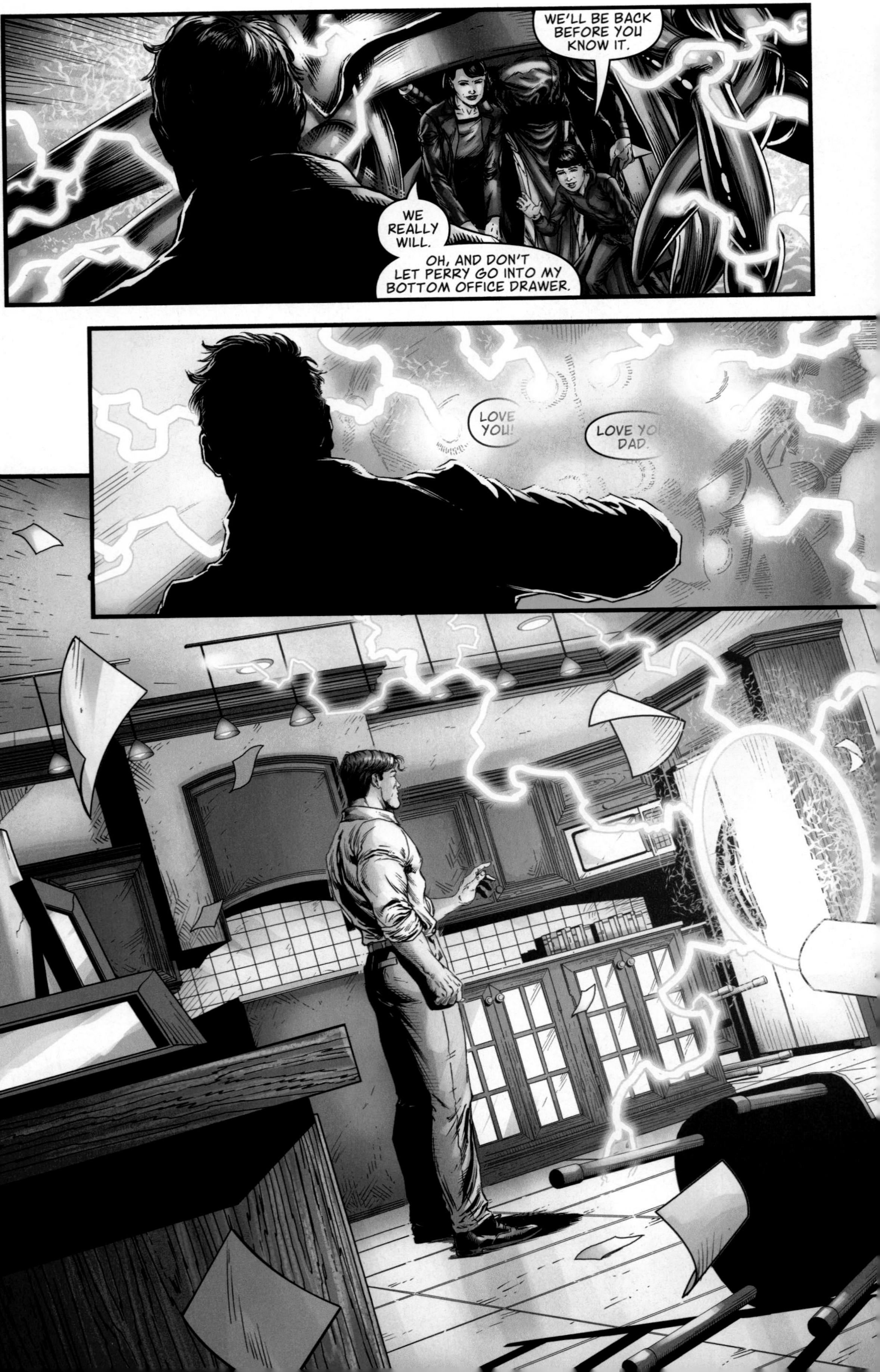
WE'LL BE BACK BEFORE YOU KNOW IT.
WE REALLY WILL.
OH, AND DON'T LET PERRY GO INTO MY BOTTOM OFFICE DRAWER.
LOVE YOU!
LOVE YO DAD.

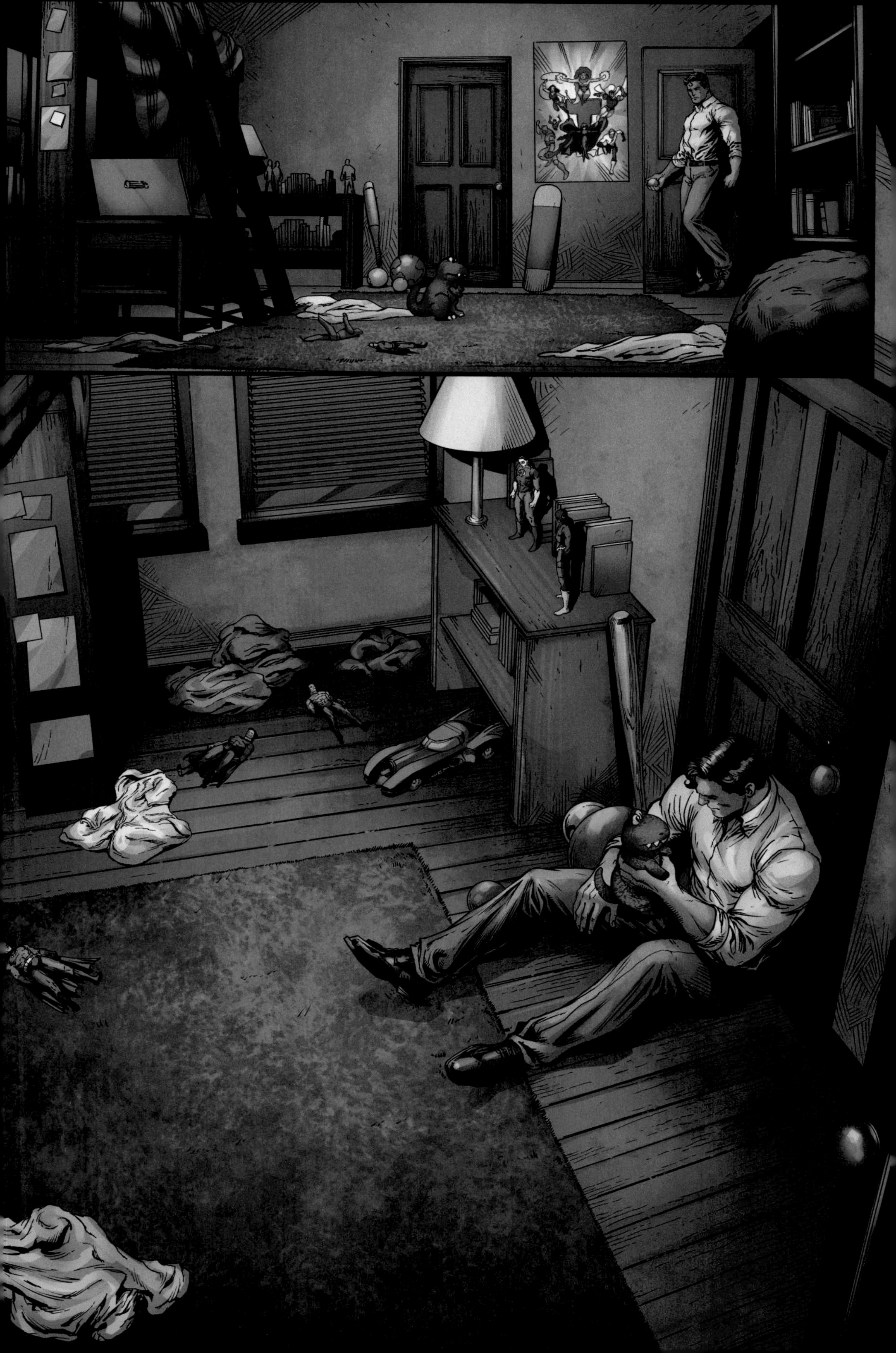

EXCUSE ME?

YOU CAN'T BE BACK HERE, KID.

DO YOU KNOW WHO I TALK TO ABOUT WHO'S BEEN STARTING THE FIRES?

I SAW ON TV THEY SAID THEY DON'T KNOW.

YEAH, KID, THAT'S RIGHT.

THEY DON'T KNOW.

WELL, I SAW.

I SAW WHO DID IT.

IT WAS SUPERMAN.

I SAW HIM.

I DON'T KNOW WHY HE DID IT.

I THOUGHT HE WAS DOING IT FOR A GOOD REASON, BUT ON TV THEY SAID NO.

I SAW HIM.

HALF OF FACE/
ARM SCARRED -
ROTTING ...

MUSCLE
& BONE
VISIBLE

... WOUNDS WHICH WOULD HAVE
KILLED ANY MORTAL BUT HIS
HATRED AND HUNGER FOR
VENGEANCE KEEPS HIM 'ALIVE'

HIS 'CAPE' IS A BATTLE WORN FLAG - THE
SOLE REMAINING ARTIFACT &
SYMBOL OF HIS HOMEWORLD.
THE INSIDE IS BLACK
WITH A THOUSAND STARS —
EACH REPRESENTING A
CONQUERED WORLD?

3-EYED SKULL ON BELT IS AN
ORACLE - SPEAKS TO HIM OR ALLOWS HIM VISIONS?

Rogol-zaar

CYBERNETIC
EYE?

SMALLER
FLAT
EAR

DAMAGED
SIDE

'EYEBROW'
HAIR RUNS
AROUND & UNDER
EYE

THIS SIDE BURNT/SCARRED
BATTLE DAMAGED. NOSE IS
LIKE SWAMP THING.

EAR
SCARRED
'CAULI-
FLOWER
EAR'

WITH SHROUD
OVER FACE

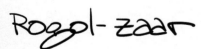
Rogol-zaar

AS ARMOR GAPS,
STRIATED CORDS OF GLOWING
ARMOR UNDERNEATH.
BRIGHTEST GLOW
AT TORSO - DARKER
AS YOU MOVE LOWER
AND OUT.

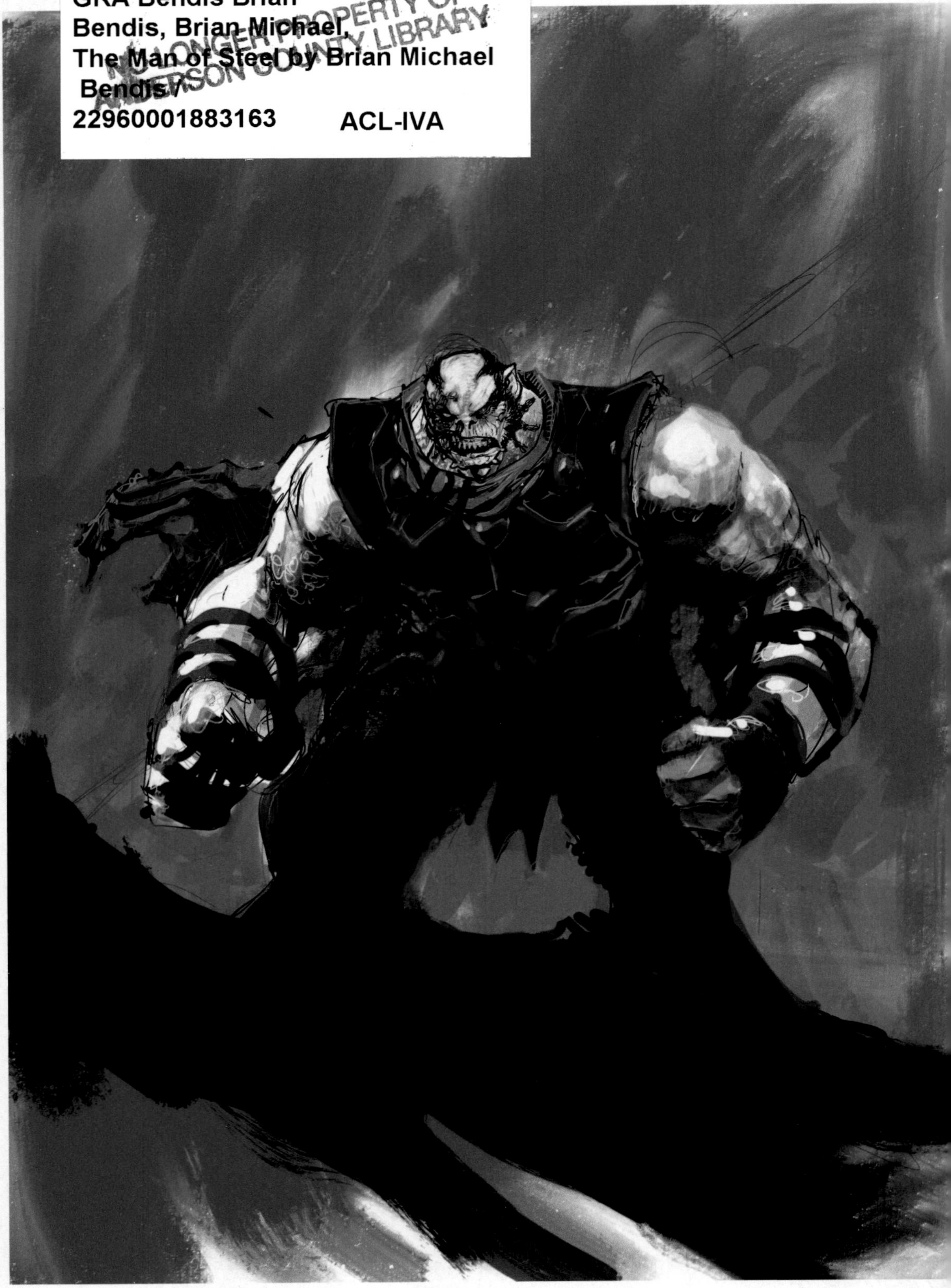